A Metaphysics of Elementary Mathematics

by Jeffrey Sicha

The University of Massachusetts Press Amherst

Library of Congress Catalog
Card Number 73-79504
ISBN Number 0-87023-149-9
Printed in the United States of America

Contents

Preface

Very few of the remarks I could make about this book would be helpful to those who have not yet read the book. Thus, out of the possible prefatory remarks, I confine myself to ones which are important because of a special feature of my book: though it is neither a book on logic nor a book on the philosophy of mathematics, it does treat some issues which are commonly thought to be within the province of logicians and philosophers of mathematics. Moreover, some technical topics are in the book because, according to some substantial body of current opinion, my views would not be plausible without some discussion of these topics. As a consequence, the book does contain a fair bit of technical machinery. For those who wish to avoid contemplating the crank-turning that is a consequence of this machinery, I provide a guide for a small tour of the book.

The itinerary of the small tour is: chapter 1 (section 1E contains a prospectus of the remainder of the book); chapter 2; sections 3A(i), 3A(ii) to the first paragraph of p. 80 and from the first paragraph of p. 85 to the end of the section, 3A(iii), 3B(i), any of 3B(ii), 3B(iii), and 3B(iv) that strike the reader's fancy, and 3C; sections 4A, 4B(i), 4B(ii), 4B(iii), 4C(i), 4C(ii), 4C(iv), and 4C(v); sections 5A, 5B, 5C(i) to the bottom of p. 290, and 5D; sections 6A and 6B(i).

The itinerary of the small tour, I must warn the reader, does not exclude all technical passages; but those it does include are generally of a milder sort and are not more, I hope, than are needed to convince the reader that the technical machinery does indeed work when the crank is turned.

Support for my work on this book came primarily from an Andrew Mellon Postdoctoral Fellowship at the University of Pittsburgh during the academic year 1967-68. Subsequently, money to defray secretarial costs came from Ford Foundation funds.

I owe the staff of the University of Massachusetts Press sincere thanks for their patience with me and their excellent work on this book. In particular, I thank the editor, Janis Bolster, and the typist, Nonny Burack. The reviewers of the book also deserve thanks for their helpful and penetrating comments.

Professor William Kneale gave me much help on the parts of the material of the book which appeared in earlier form in my doctoral dissertation. Bruce Aune and Jacqueline Thomason read through several late drafts of the book and provided detailed comments which led to what I believe are great improvements. In addition, I owe Bruce Aune, my friend and former teacher, much more for his help and our philosophical talks over the years. To Wilfrid Sellars I have a debt manifest throughout the book; so great is this debt that only the whole book, rather than any brief words I might write here, can express it.

Chapter 1: Introduction

A. Introduction

The appearance, roughly seventy years ago, of paradoxes in the foundations of mathematics produced three main philosophical responses: formalism, logicism, and intuitionism. Each of these philosophies of mathematics has, it is claimed, run against criticisms that have necessitated abandoning them as they were originally conceived. For example, it has been said that Gödel's proofs have written an end to the original program of formalism, that Brouwer's formulation of intuitionism is founded on a nearly unintelligible neo-Kantianism containing unpurged elements of psychologism, and that logicism has a variety of inadequacies ranging from problems with such principles as the axioms of reducibility and infinity to unacceptable platonism and obscurity on the nature and extent of logic. This much of the recent history of the philosophy of mathematics is familiar to most philosophers. But, it seems to me, the present situation in the philosophy of mathematics is far from clear to the philosopher dealing with general philosophical problems.

There are, perhaps, several different reasons for this unclarity. First, while Russell and Frege, Brouwer, and to a lesser extent Hilbert discussed their philosophies of mathematics at length and framed their positions in the philosophy of mathematics in light of views they held in more general philosophical areas such as epistemology and metaphysics, many of the discussions of logicism, intuitionism, and formalism which have followed theirs have dealt primarily with technical matters in logic and mathematics and with the *philosophy* of mathematics little or not at all. Moreover, many later writers who do have philosophies of mathematics have not discussed relevant general philosophical problems at sufficient length; for example, few have expounded their position on the general problem of abstract entities in enough detail that one could determine how their views on this problem relate to their views on the nature of numbers. Second, the post-World War II philosophical climate has not been congenial to systematic philosophy. And, of course, a writer must have some inclination toward systematic philosophy even to attempt an investigation of the relationship of his philosophy of mathematics to his general philosophical views.

In part, this book is an attempt to rectify the situation just explained; in part, it is not. It does not contain a survey of logicism, formalism, and intuitionism, nor does it try to elaborate these views and to sort and evaluate the criticisms laid against them. But it is meant to be an example of the derivation of views in the philosophy of mathematics from more general philosophical views. Of course, the book does not discuss everything that, in the long run, needs to be discussed; it does not even try to present a complete philosophy of mathematics. The treatment of both general philosophy and the philosophy of mathematics is limited to logical and metaphysical issues; epistemology is almost completely ignored. Further, of the philosophy of mathematics, that part which might be called the philosophy of elementary mathematics is discussed at length; of the philosophy of the real numbers and of other matters only glimpses are present.

B. Nominalism

To set the stage for the views I shall present in later chapters, I shall now undertake a brief investigation of an issue that arises in the context of a contemporary philosophy of mathematics which is akin to traditional formalism and which has the merit of being firmly rooted in general philosophy.

Its basic tenets can be succinctly set forth: Certain sentences of mathematics are to be regarded "merely as strings of marks without meaning"; our understanding of these mathematical sentences is given solely by the "syntactical or metamathematical rules governing these marks."[1] The sentences that are to be so regarded contain variables "calling for abstract entities as values" and cannot be "translated into nominalistic language."[2] These sentences comprise the part of mathematics which is "platonistic"; by regarding them solely as strings of marks one avoids any "question of truth" while leaving oneself with a syntactical account of their usefulness as "convenient computational aids."[3]

One of the familiar notes struck by this view is the notion of a computational aid or device. Mathematics is likened to an apparatus such as the abacus which, by virtue of its material structure and composition, can help us make computations. Similar remarks have been made about scientific theories. Thus there have been philosophers of science who termed their position "instrumentalism" and maintained that the primary function of scientific theories is to systematize and manipulate meaningful empirical statements about what is observable. To this end scientific theories have a describable structure provided in part by ordinary syntax and logic and in part by mathematical syntax and contain "strings of marks" which stand in various syntactical relationships to other strings of marks. Certain marks of this vast meaningless apparatus of theory are connected with observation language expressions which are meaningful. By moving from the observation language to the theory, utilizing the syntactical and mathematical relationships in the theory, and finally returning to the observation language, we use the theory as an instrument. The parallel thesis for mathematics is that the language of mathematics aids us in systematizing and manipulating statements about quantities and measures in the material world.

While this comparison between the instrumentalist position and the philosophy of mathematics indicated in the quotations may do a great deal to make us feel at home philosophically, it also raises several questions: Are there statements which stand to the apparatus of platonistic mathematics as statements about the observable stand to a scientific theory? How are these statements to be delimited? And can this be done without recourse to mathematical notions?

The answer to the first question is affirmative. Some mathematical formulae are nominalistically meaningful; this is attested by the fact that they can be "translated into nominalistic language" where a nominalistic language is one whose mechanisms of reference permit reference only to concrete objects.[4] Such formulae would provide the liaison between the mathematical apparatus and other nonmathematical statements about concrete objects in the most direct manner: namely, by being at once about concrete objects and yet in the apparatus of mathematics and hence connected by syntactical rules and logic to nominalistically uninterpretable formulae.

The most obvious candidates for statements which are in some sense mathematical and which can nevertheless be translated into nominalistic language are what I shall call "numerical quantifier statements"; the simplest numerical quantifier statements are of the following forms:

(1) there is one K,
there are two Ks,
there are three Ks,

and so on. Each of these statements is equivalent to a statement containing only ordinary quantifiers, connectives, variables, and identity. Thus

there are two Ks

is equivalent to

(2) (Ey)(Ex)(Kx and Ky and not(x = y) and (z)(if Kz, then x = z or y = z)).

Provided that 'Kx' is true of concrete objects, (2) is acceptable in a nominalistic language.

This success suggests further nominalistic translations.[5] Consider

(3) 5 + 3 = 8.

Among the various interpretations of (3), there is one which is nominalistic and which has the advantage of using numerical quantifiers. Thus (3) becomes, roughly,

(4) there are five things of a sort and there are three other things of the same or another sort if and only if there are eight things of some sort or other.

Let us, for the present, accept (4) as the basis of a nominalistic interpretation of (3) and thus ignore certain obvious questions (such as the precise logical form of (4)). What has been done for (3) can also be done for

(5) 4 x 3 = 12.

Thus a roughly formulated nominalistic interpretation of (5) is

(6) there are four things of a sort for each of which there are three things of the same or another sort if and only if there are twelve things of the latter sort.

Once again let us ignore any deficiencies and press on in our comparison of the instrumentalist view of scientific theories and the nominalist philosophy of mathematics.

Having come this far, the nominalist philosopher is in a position to make a bold stroke which has the dual effects of supplying a familiar sort of epistemology for his view of mathematics and completing the analogy with instrumentalism. He claims that statements such as (4) and (6) formulate truths about correct counting.[6] For example, if one counts that there are five entities of one sort and that there are three other entities of the same or different sort, then from (4) one knows that correctly counting all the entities would lead to the result that there are eight. Further, he points out that statements of the forms illustrated in (1) formulate the results of counting. Hence, these basic types of nominalistically interpretable mathematical statements are intimately connected with an activity that, in fundamental cases, enables us to gain knowledge about concrete objects. As observing and observation reports provide the epistemological foundation for scientific theories, so counting and statements of the types illustrated above anchor that great nominalistically uninterpretable part of mathematics in discourse about concrete objects and provide the link that allows the uninterpreted mathematical formulae to perform their function as instruments.

Of course, this move would fail if counting in some way involves numbers in a sense of the word 'number' in which numbers are abstract entities. This failure would be analogous to the failure that the instrumentalist view of scientific theories would suffer if it should prove that the epistemological viability of observation concepts depends on their being part of a total system of concepts which necessarily includes theoretical concepts. But such a failure in the present case seems unlikely, since there is a popular view of counting which fits the nominalist's needs exactly.

This view of counting, suggested by the remarks of contemporary philosophers,[7] can be roughly stated as follows: counting is the activity of putting initial segments of serially ordered strings of entities in 1-1 correspondence with the entities of some collection. In the most familiar sorts of cases, counting is no more than tokening (e.g., uttering) a string of numerals or numerical words while, say, pointing at the entities in some collection (e.g., books on a table). There are good reasons to think that such an activity need not be understood as in any way involving numbers as abstract entities. First, according to this view of counting, it is not even true that one must count with numerals or numerical words though in fact this is commonly the case. One could use any string of serially ordered expressions. Thus taking advantage of the historically produced serial order of the letters of the alphabet from 'a' to 'j' inclusive, we could count with the following serially ordered collection of expressions

(7) b, c, d, e, f, g, h, i, j, ba, bb, bc, bd, ..., ca, ..., da, ..., ..., ..., baa, bab, bac, ..., bba, bbb, bbc, ..., bca, ..., bda, ..., ..., ..., caa,....

Learning such a serially ordered collection as (7) can be accomplished by the sort of repetitive training that children do in fact undergo in learning our common numerical words. Clearly, the nominalist says, such training in no way involves or presupposes numbers as abstract entities; or else how could children who are obviously without mathematical concepts learn to count? Second, the notion of 1-1 correspondence which appears in the characterization of counting can be defined in purely logical terms and hence need not involve anything which might be taken to be mathematical abstract entities.

Thus the nominalist's account of methematics comes to rest heavily on an apparently plausible view of counting. Counting, as he presents it, is the activity which provides the epistemological foundation of those mathematical statements like "there are three cows (in the field)" which can be interpreted nominalistically and yet which are part of the mathematical apparatus. On the other hand, counting is not a mathematical activity in any sense of the word 'mathematical' which would provide solace to platonistic philosophers.

C. A Platonistic Objection

The nominalist's view of mathematics is, of course, not acceptable to philosophers with so-called platonistic turns of mind, and it is not difficult to locate a point at which the platonist might strike. Let us consider the following, perhaps not entirely clear, yet forceful, line of thought.

The most obvious weakness, the platonist claims, is in the nominalistic treatment of counting which has covertly assumed in the characterization of counting a mathematical fact which is _not_ translatable into a nominalistically acceptable fact about concrete objects. We must remember, the platonist insists, that for the nominalist counting is an activity in the material world; part of this activity is the actual production of concrete objects (e.g., sounds) which are put in 1-1 correspondence with other concrete objects. It is true of natural numbers, as working mathematicians commonly understand them, that if one correlates 1-1 the objects of some collection with the natural numbers less than or equal to 5, then there are five objects in the collection that is being counted (note that the natural numbers are assumed to begin with 1). However, this truth rests on a mathematical fact:

> for any natural number n the number of natural numbers less than or equal to n is n.

But, the platonist contends, there is <u>no analogous truth about concrete objects</u> (e.g., sounds). For example, from the fact that someone has produced, say, a token of the numerical word 'five' it does not follow that he has produced five tokens altogether, each of which is a token of one and only one of the numerical words which precede the numerical word 'five' in the conventional sequence of numerical words. Therefore, the platonist concludes, a correct characterization of counting must, whatever else it contains, speak of the 1-1 correlation of objects with initial segments of the natural numbers where the natural numbers cannot be concrete objects, like sounds, which might or might not be produced correctly.

While there is something to be said for the platonist's objection, his argument does not warrant the conclusion he draws. We can agree that linguistic objects and other concrete objects are not similar, in an important way, to the natural numbers. That is, simply from the fact that someone has produced a token of the numerical word 'five' it does not even follow that four other tokens have been produced, much less that the four other tokens are tokens of different numerical words, those numerical words which precede 'five' in the conventional serial order. Such considerations do indeed show that the nominalistic view of counting is inadequate in the form in which I have presented it. What the nominalist's view of counting explains in its present form is a method by which we can find out, if we proceed correctly, that there are as many entities in one group as there are in another. In order to be able to draw any conclusion of the form "there is(are) ___ Ks," we must have an additional statement telling how many entities one of the groups contains. Obviously what we must have is a statement saying how many tokens have been produced by the person who is counting. Of course, it follows that we cannot require that our knowledge of such facts about the production of tokens always be obtained by counting. Such a requirement would lead to a regress. However, knowledge that, for example, Jones has produced, while counting, one and only one token of each numerical word beginning with the numerical word 'one' and ending with the numerical word 'five' can rest on facts about the previous linguistic training of Jones, the present absence of factors which might disrupt the abilities he acquired through training, and so on.

From this vantage point, we can reconsider the platonist's view of counting and note that it too is inadequate and for much the same reason. The platonist suggests that counting is the activity of producing 1-1 correspondences between entities of some group and an initial segment of the natural numbers understood as abstract entities. But in many cases of counting the entities to be counted are concrete (e.g., ordinary physical objects). Establishing a 1-1 correspondence between concrete entities and the natural numbers which are, according to the platonist, not concrete can only be done by the mediation of yet other concrete objects. Tokens of numerals and number words are the obvious candidates. They are concrete and nevertheless stand in a special 1-1 relation to natural numbers that other concrete objects do not: namely, they are, according to the platonist, the names of natural numbers. Thus the 1-1 correspondence between the objects to be counted and the natural numbers is a product of two 1-1 correspondences, one between the numerals or number words and these objects and one between the numerals or number words and the natural numbers. But this scheme also leaves a question to be answered: Has the person who is counting produced the names of an initial segment of the natural numbers? He could, for instance, have omitted one. Thus even on the platonist's view of counting we must, in order to gain knowledge of "how many" by counting, know such facts as, for example, that there were five tokens of names of natural numbers which were produced by someone who was counting, and each of them was different from all the others, and they were tokens of names of natural numbers in an initial segment of the natural numbers.

Given this criticism of the platonistic view, the nominalist is in a position to claim that he need not forsake his nominalism, but simply amend his view of counting by recognizing the importance of numerical quantifier statements about linquistic entities. Though these numerical quantifier statements are essential to the activity of counting in a way in which he had not previously envisaged, he is not, he claims, driven to any form of platonism since, like all numerical quantifier statements about concrete objects, those about linguistic entities are nominalistically interpretable. With this amendment the nominalist appears to be entitled to claim that he has shored up his original view without changing it significantly.

D. Numerical Quantifiers and Counting

One of the original strengths of the nominalist's philosophy of mathematics as here presented is that the whole of mathematics appears to rest on counting, an activity which in no way involves abstract entities. Counting, the nominalist maintains, is an activity which requires the production of natural objects (usually linguistic) and which, though it presupposes a great deal of "know-how," no more utilizes natural numbers in any platonistic sense than other natural activities requiring "know-how" (e.g., swimming). And although a reflective understanding of counting necessitates understanding the notion of 1-1 correspondence, this notion is definable in purely logical terms. Thus the nominalist seems to be able to assure us that the fundamental epistemological means by which mathematics comes in contact with the empirical world is nominalistically unexceptionable.

It is no coincidence that philosophers who have nominalistic inclinations and whose remarks suggest they subscribe to the nominalist view of counting are tempted to think that any serially ordered sequence of entities whatsoever could be called natural numbers if, indeed, any entities whatever need be called natural numbers.[8] After all, these philosophers have thought, all that is required for counting is a serially ordered string of entities. Since these serially ordered strings of entities are the only entities figuring essentially in the activity of counting and since counting is the fundamental activity producing nominalistically interpretable mathematical knowledge about concrete objects, we are on solid ground in suggesting that these strings of serially ordered entities are the natural numbers.

However, as my reply to the platonistic objection demonstrates, matters are not so simple. My reply concedes to the platonist that for a person who is counting to arrive at an answer to a "how many" question by counting, he must not only bring about a 1-1 correspondence, but he must also know a numerical quantifier statement about the entities he is putting in 1-1 correspondence with the objects he is counting. It is not just that no one who literally does not understand numerical quantifiers can ever obtain answers (true or false) to "how many" questions by counting, since this point also follows from the fact that the results of counting are expressed by numerical quantifier statements. The point is rather that "know-how" with serially ordered strings of entities is not all that is <u>essential</u> to the activity of counting (as distinct from the statement of results). And this fact must surely raise a doubt about the line of thought that leads to the suggestion that any serially ordered string of entities would do as the natural numbers. This line of thought seems plausible because it presents the <u>serial</u> <u>orderedness</u> of strings of entities such as numerals as the sole feature essential to counting. Now, however, we know that the very activity of counting requires an understanding of numerical quantifiers.

At this juncture it would be well to remember a point that the nominalist cites in demonstrating the freedom of counting from a platonistic tinge: any string of serially ordered entities and not only the familiar one, such as the numerals and numerical words, can be used in counting. Thus even (7), the string of serially ordered letters of the alphabet, can be used in counting, though these letters seem to have hardly any connection with existence and difference, the two features which are essential to "numerousness." Reflecting on this point in conjunction with the remarks of the last paragraph and noting that, because of their definitions, numerical quantifiers are essentially connected with "numerousness," one might suggest that if anything were to be called natural numbers, it should be numerical quantifiers and not just any string of serially ordered entities.[9]

Certainly many philosophers would agree that numerical quantifiers are essential to counting and even that it is numerical quantifiers, rather than just any serially ordered entities, which capture the basic features of "numerousness" (i.e., existence and difference). Such agreement notwithstanding, these same philosophers would be little inclined to accept what must appear to them a very odd suggestion: viz., that numerical quantifiers are natural numbers. Moreover, for some, such a suggestion would seem far too restrictive and without the faintest hope of providing an account of the commonly accepted features of the system of natural numbers. Others, fearing the spectre of platonism, will wonder whether a treatment of the identity of numerical quantifiers (a treatment that surely must be provided) will not smuggle in platonism by having to appeal, in the long run, to a traditional account of synonymy. Yet others, having a deep-rooted distrust of logicism, will note that it is too important to be a coincidence that the expressions offered as candidates for natural numbers are definable solely in terms of the usual quantifiers, connectives, and identity.

Certainly, even more substantial philosophical doubts could be formulated. Despite all this, this suggestion about numerical quantifiers is the one I propose to elaborate. In the course of developing this suggestion, I shall take up matters which bear on the philosophical themes of this chapter. The road will be long, not simply because the problems are difficult, but also because the avowed aim of this book is to set forth a piece of systematic philosophy which, as far as it is possible, derives a philosophy of elementary mathematics from more general philosophical theses. For this reason, I spend the next section describing the strategy and topics of the remaining chapters and the goal of the book.

E. Prospectus

The main aim of this book, as the title suggests, is to provide a metaphysics of elementary mathematics. Thus the book has vey little to say about epistemology. It also has little to say about what branches of ordinary, intuitive mathematics should be counted as "elementary." I do not know that it is even possible to find an explanation of 'elementary' which would be satisfied by all and only those branches of mathematics which fit some intuitive conception of what elementary mathematics is. But, it seems to me, such botanizing would, if possible, be almost without interest. So, for the purposes of this book, elementary mathematics is taken to be the arithmetic of the natural numbers, integers, and rationals, and that part of the theory of classes which eschews the more exotic principles of that subject and which treats of the basic principles of the existence and identity of classes and the operations on classes. What exactly must be accomplished in the discussion of each of these pieces of mathematics will be explained when they are taken up.

A secondary aim of the book, as I have already said, is that it should be a piece of "systematic" philosophy. There are, of course, a variety of senses of the word 'systematic' in which the book is not systematic. For example, a book could be said to be systematic if the topics and problems treated in the book are characterized at the outset in such a way that one is able to determine the contents of the book from this characterization (plus, perhaps, a few collateral premises about the nature and practice of philosophy). This book does not even attempt to be systematic in this sense.

There are two systematic features of this book. First, the philosophy of elementary mathematics presented is, for the most part, derived from much more general philosophical views. The main example of this in the book is the derivation of my account of the natural numbers from a more general account of abstract entities.

Second, I attempt to forestall a number of possible objections by discussing certain topics not immediately related to those topics which must be discussed to accomplish the main aim of the book. My criterion for including a topic of this sort is the likelihood of a substantial group of philosophers thinking (rightly or wrongly) that my position on the central topics of the book would, in whole or in part, be vitiated if this subsidiary topic were not discussed. Of course, there is no _one_ group of philosophers to whom all the subsidiary topics would seem important. Not all of these subsidiary topics can be considered in the detail they deserve. But I hope that on any subsidiary topic I have said enough to make my whole enterprise credible to a reader who thinks that subsidiary topic crucial. A few subsidiary topics, those which seem to me most likely to cause confusion about the central topics of the book, are given considerable space.

Since the purpose of this introductory chapter is both to introduce numerical quantifiers with an example of their importance and to illustrate a case in which my view avoids both a nominalistic doctrine and a platonistic objection, I wish, before turning to a short description of the highlights of the coming chapters, to return to the points of this chapter by making some very general remarks about my account of elementary mathematics. This account, and the more general account of abstract entities from which it is derived, I prefer to describe as a "mild" nominalism. My choice of the word 'mild' will become clearer as the book progresses. But what can be said now, at the stage at which the reader knows almost nothing about the view, is that my account takes the language of elementary mathematics as a full-fledged part of language and does not try to relegate it to second-class standing as an "instrument." Nor do I worry about any strict standard of nominalistic acceptability such as the one described in section B. More than that, I accept that the statements of elementary mathematics are about numbers; according to the view I propose, it is, properly understood, true to say that natural numbers exist.

However, these admissions must be tempered by the observation that, on the view I propose, the language of mathematics is a very special sort of discourse and talk about numbers is very special talk. On this point nothing much can be said in advance of actually presenting the view. But the general strategy followed in the remainder of the book is adherence to a course between strong nominalisms which hold that mathematical statements either must be construed as ordinary statements about concrete, material objects or else must be classified as something less than ordinary meaningful discourse and those views which have been called "platonistic" and which maintain that mathematical statements are perfectly good parts of discourse that speak of those very special nonlinguistic, nonnatural objects, abstract entities.

Of course, the preceding sections have given only one illustration of the nominalist-platonist controversy and have not characterized nominalism or platonism. So, it is open to any reader, if he wishes, to characterize these two opposing positions in such a way that there is no course to steer between them or to locate them in philosophical waters different from those where I locate them. I do not wish to argue about what to call my view; as I said, I _prefer_ "mild" nominalism. If the reader understands the view and how it differs from other views on the subject, I will be content to let him call it what he likes.

The structure of the book is built according to the strategy I have described. Chapter 2 discusses a philosophy of language which eventually leads to an account of abstract entities. The source of the doctrines in this chapter is the writings of Professor Wilfrid Sellars. The most important issues in part A of chapter 3 are those surrounding variables and quantification. These issues cannot be avoided because of the now very common philosophical inclination to connect ontological commitment with the employment of the mechanism of quantification. To philosophers with this inclination the view of abstract entities sketched in chapter 2 could not be what it claimed to be. Part B of chapter 3 gradually moves into the topic (only partially discussed there) of identity and the entities involved in the account of chapter 2. This topic is taken up again later and the discussion of part B, chapter 3, provides the basis for an account of identity and natural numbers.

Chapter 4 derives from the material of chapter 2 an account of the natural numbers. After chapter 4, a variety of obvious questions remains to be answered: Can the account of chapter 4 be extended, in some consistent manner, to encompass the integers and the rationals and the elementary parts of the theory of classes which have commonly been used in class-theoretic accounts of the natural numbers? Is the account of chapter 4 a form of logicism? Is a formalist account of theorem and proof suitable to the account of chapter 4? What view of counting is available to my view? All these questions and other that arise because of special features of the material of chapter 4 are taken up in chapters 5 and 6.

A final warning, before I turn to the business of chapter 2, is in order. This book does not attempt to introduce mathematical or logical novelties. There are no contributions in it to mathematics or to mathematical logic as such. Those who look for such things will be disappointed. What novelties there are, if there are any, are philosophical, though they are directed toward matters which involve mathematics and logic.

Chapter 2: Language, General Terms, and Abstract Entities

A. Introduction

Recent philosophy has made much of an analogy between games and language. This analogy has not, I think, always been carefully drawn nor have the grounds for thinking that there is an analogy of an appropriate sort been well argued. Therefore, since I intend to make extensive use of the example of chess, I shall try to forestall any misunderstanding by setting out in the next section that analogy between games and language which is important for the work of this chapter. Essential to the analogy is a thesis I shall assume without argument: in specifiable respects, both language and games are activities governed by rules.[1] Hence, before I can indicate the extent of the analogy between games and language, I must discuss which rules I have in mind when I say "rules of language" and the respects in which language is so governed.

The topic of rules is vast and difficult and I shall do no more than present a few basic distinctions. My treatment follows very closely that of Professor Wilfrid Sellars, to whose works the reader can turn for a more extensive discussion.[2]

I shall say that a rule is something which permits, obliges, or forbids, not particular instances of repeatable activities, but the repeatable activities themselves. Thus rules are general. There are a variety of rules which govern linguistic activity. Some of them govern actions in the proper sense of this word, the sense which, following Professor Sellars, I shall call the "conduct" sense. Thus there are rules pertaining to promising.[3] But there are other rules which treat of linguistic actions only in that weak sense of 'act' in which anything spoken of by a verb in the active voice is an action. Thus a rule of this second sort, roughly formulated, is

(1) in standard conditions, one may respond to red objects by tokening
this is red.

Another example, once again only roughly formulated, is

(2) one may respond to a tokening of
this is red
with a tokening of
this is extended.

Closely related to these rules are ones which do govern actions in the conduct sense of 'act'. Thus there is the rule

(3) one ought to bring it about that in standard conditions, language users are disposed to respond to red objects by tokening
this is red.

Similarly, there is the rule

(4) one ought to bring it about that language users are disposed to respond to tokenings of
this is red
with tokenings of
this is extended.

Such rules as (3) and (4) govern the actions of those sophisticated language users who teach the language to novices.

I shall not be much concerned with the perpetuation of language through teaching. Thus all the rules I shall formulate will be ones like (1) and (2) which, again following Professor Sellars, I shall call "rules of criticism" (as opposed to (3) and (4) which are "rules of conduct").[4] Further, concerning rules of criticism my main concern is with rules like (2). And, <u>as a first approximation</u> of what I shall require later, I shall write (2) and rules like (2) in the following fashion:

(5) one may infer tokens of 'this is extended' from tokens of 'this is red',

or (6) tokens of 'this is extended' may be inferred from tokens of 'this is red'.

Thus inference in the sense in which it is introduced in (5) and (6) is not an action in the conduct sense, though it is in the weak sense an act.

It is at this point that an investigation of the analogy between language and games furthers our understanding of rules of criticism and language. As the heart of this investigation, I answer the question: What are the moves, pieces, and positions of language? Through answering this question and related questions, we acquire the resources with which to pursue a deeper investigation of language and to provide an account of abstract entities.

B. Moves, Pieces, and Positions in Chess and Language

What sorts of linguistic resources are needed in order to be able to speak of moves, pieces, and positions in chess? The linguistic resources needed to be able to speak about the pieces of chess are those of ordinary language (e.g., English) plus the general terms 'pawn', 'bishop', etc. The moves in chess are those of moving the pieces, or counters, of the game and they can be spoken of by using exactly the same resources used in talking about the pieces. To talk of the positions we need the same resources plus such general terms as 'row', 'column', etc. With this vocabulary, we can not only make remarks about particular moves, pieces, and positions of chess, but we can also formulate the rules of chess. For instance, there is a rule that one may move a pawn only one square forward in a column in any move after the first except when capturing another piece. This rule governs a player's manipulation of any counter that is a pawn. Derivatively, we can speak of this rule as being about the pawn itself (with reference to the players suppressed, as in the rendering, "The pawn may be moved only one square. . . .").

Let us extend this game terminology to language by deciding what in language are analogous to moves, pieces, and positions. The most natural decision would seem to be that the analogs of moves are inferrings. However, the word 'infer' was introduced above so that inferrings are responses to items of behavior with other items of behavior. Let us call these items of behavior "tokenings." Given the decision to say that inferrings are the moves of language, it seems that the tokenings ought to be the pieces. But while one can straightforwardly say that chess players move pieces, it is not very clear what would be meant by saying that language users move tokenings. The solution is that we have overlooked the fact that chess players move pieces "from position to position." Clearly it fits our intuitions to say that inferrings are moves from one position to another. Thus the tokenings _qua_ items of behavior having a place in the rule-governed structure of linguistic behavior mark the positions of language as the units of the chess players' board mark the positions of chess pieces; or, as we shall see, it is more accurate to say that a tokening marks a position in virtue of being of a certain type which marks a position in the rule-governed structure.

What is it, then, in language that moves? The answer is the language user. By inferring, the language user "moves from position to position." The tokening which is inferred marks the position which the language user has come to occupy.

His position is specified by the rule-governed structure in terms of the types of inferences he is permitted to make to and from a type he has tokened. My later discussion of types will help to clarify this way of drawing the analogy.

The terminology thus far established leaves several issues open. Consider the question: Does the language user occupy more than one position? Both answers to this question are, apparently, acceptable.

On the one hand, one could say yes. Presumably, then, the language user occupies all those positions which are marked by types which he is presently disposed to token. Further, in most inferences the language user moves from several position*s* to another position. In addition, by moving from a position or positions the language user does not necessarily "abandon" the positions he moves from (though, of course, he might abandon them). A person may still be, and usually is, disposed to token a type that he has used as a premise for an inference. Thus, in this respect, linguistic activity is unlike chess because the chess player does "abandon," in some sense of 'abandon', his position as he moves a piece.

On the other hand, the question could also be answered no. Then I should have to alter my earlier terminology a little to say that types do not mark positions, but rather mark "points" or "nodes" in a position. *The* position the language user occupies would be the total array of "points" which are marked by types the language user is disposed to token. This way of talking about linguistic activity is analogous to talking about the chess player as having *a* position or all his pieces being in *a* position. The position, in this way of talking, is understood to be the total array of the player's pieces on his board; all the pieces, at one time, are in the same position, though each is at a different "point" in the position. In the case of linguistic activity, all inferences are from one position, viz., <u>the</u> position the language user occupies at that time. In addition, each inference, in adding one new "point," insures that the language user "abandons" those "points" which are marked by the types which are the premises of his inference.

No doubt these issues, and many others, could be profitably discussed at length. But such discussions, gauged by the purposes of this chapter, would be a digression. Moreover, decisions on these issues have very little bearing on the subsequent discussion. But, for the sake of a fixed terminology, I shall adopt the first alternative.

The reader will no doubt have noticed that the language-chess analogy finds no place for two very important sorts of linguistic phenomena that one might be tempted to call "moves." One of these is illustrated by the case of a person who, while looking at a red object, tokens "that is red." Cases of this sort are indeed examples of a language user coming to occupy a position in language. However, the language user does not come to occupy this position by moving from another position in the language. He comes to occupy this position not as a matter of inference, but as a matter of the impact of nonlinguistic items on his senses. A case of the other sort of linguistic phenomenon is provided by the person who tokens "I shall raise my hand" and then does so. In this sort of case it is quite clear that the person is not moving from one position in the language to another. I shall call both of these sorts of linguistic phenomena <u>and inferences</u> "transitions."

As both sorts of examples illustrate, transitions which are not inferences are essentially involved with the natural connection of the linguistic and the nonlinguistic. Since the language-chess analogy provides an analog only for transitions from positions in the language to other positions in the language, it is clear why only these transitions and not the language-world ones are called moves. Hence, only rules like (2), and thus like (5) and (6), govern moves, while rules like (1) govern transitions which are not moves. I am convinced that there is good reason for treating only the language-language rather than the language-world transition as moves. Many of these reasons center around the issues of synonymy and intensionality. Though I do not have the space to argue at length about these matters, I shall return to them later to discuss how rules of inference help us to understand synonymy and intensionality (see 3B and 3C).

Before turning once again to the discussion of chess, it will be well to make a point that will be of some importance shortly. Tokenings come in many varieties (utterings, writings, typings, etc.), but it is obvious that each tokening, regardless of what variety it is, involves the production of a natural object. Thus, if the tokening is a writing, the natural object produced is a written inscription. If it is an uttering, the natural object is a sound pattern. I shall call the natural objects produced in tokenings "natural linguistic objects." Then we can say that, derivatively, the rules also regulate a person's production of natural linguistic objects.

In talking about chess we have at our disposal such terms as 'the pawn', 'pawn', 'the bishop', 'bishop', etc. These terms enable us to talk about such objects that play the role of pawns, etc. The first question to be settled is what it is to be a chess piece of a certain sort. Is, for example, being of such-and-such a shape what it is to be, say, a bishop? Though it is true that bishops usually have a characteristic shape, I think that this shape is, strictly speaking, not essential to being a bishop. Further, I think it can be shown that no combination of material properties of any piece that is a bishop constitutes what it is to be a bishop.[5]

An example will help demonstrate the irrelevance of the material properties of chess pieces to being the chess pieces they are. Suppose that Texans play a game called "tess." The counters in tess are automobiles: Volkswagens, a Cadillac, a Rolls Royce, and several other makes. The playing board is Texas and Texas counties are the squares. By observation of tess games and conversation with Texans we conclude that tess has rules that are very like chess rules: e.g., a Volkswagen may be moved only one county at a time except on its first move; a Cadillac may be moved only one county at a time, but in any direction; a Rolls Royce may be moved in any row, in any column, and in any diagonal any number of counties; etc. Yet while the rules of tess and chess are very similar, there is a difference. The difference accrues because of the following facts about chess and tess. Our usual conceptions of chess pieces (what I shall call our "pre-tess" conceptions of chess pieces) do involve, I think, the idea of their being, roughly, of the characteristic shapes we are all so familiar with. And a similar situation holds for tess and tess players: built right into the rules of tess and hence into the notion of tess pieces are the names of the various makes of automobiles; and the makes themselves are characterized by their shape and internal constitution which distinguish them from one another as kinds of automobiles.

However, there is nothing to prevent us from altering our common conception of chess pieces to bring it more in line with what we have learned about tess (and the same is true for tess players). The alteration is brought about by discarding the properties of shape, size, constitution, etc., that we formerly encompassed in these concepts. Our justification for discarding these properties is the similarity we notice between tess and chess. This similarity is between the structure of the two systems of rules. For example, we notice that both games have a rule which permits the moving of some piece in such-and-such a manner (we do not even need to specify the move in terms of "counties" or in terms of "squares on a board," but just in terms of "rows" and "columns"). To state these truths about the structure of the rules of tess and chess in no way requires that we refer to the natural properties of the pieces (though of course we know that they must have natural properties of some sort). Thus we can formulate one system of rules for both games in such a way that the only terms which are important to the game are the terms 'may', 'may not', or 'ought'; terms for moves and positions; and the terms for kinds of pieces (i.e., 'pawn', 'bishop', etc.). Once we have done this, the criteria for being a chess piece of a certain kind become purely prescriptive. Finally we (and tess players) come to see that tess and what I shall now call "conventional chess" are distinct <u>embodiments</u> of the same game, chess. Both the familiarly shaped pieces in chess, and Volkswagens, in tess, are pawns; a Cadillac, in tess, and a certain small piece of wood or some other material, in chess, are kings; and so on. Conventional chess players and tess players engage in different material embodiments of the same rule-governed activity.

Thus, from a penetrating point of view, the physical properties of the counters of chess are irrelevant to their being the chess pieces they are. What matters are the prescriptive properties: i.e., those properties which are derived from the rules which specify what may, may not, or ought to be done with the counters, regardless of what the material composition of the counters is. And indeed the counters may vary quite considerably in their material properties, for conventional chess counters and tess counters are not the only counters that could serve in embodiments of chess.

As Professor Bruce Aune has pointed out, one could play chess with squads of trained fleas. Of course the nature of the activities specified in the rules of any game tend to put general restrictions on the nature of the counters that can be used in embodiments of the activities of the game. Football requires certain activities that could hardly be satisfactorily performed by humans on, say, a brick instead of a football. But apart from these generic restrictions on the natural properties of counters, it is plain that what qualifies an object as an embodiment of a piece in a game is that it is suitably connected with human behavior which is governed by the rules of the game.

It is now time to rectify an oversimplification in the above account. I had claimed earlier that the rules of chess treated primarily of the moves of the players and only derivatively of the pieces of the game. Yet I have mainly discussed the nature of chess pieces and not the nature of the moves that are primarily spoken of in the rules. However, this lacuna can be easily rectified. Our pre-tess notion of chess moves involve descriptive properties just as our pre-tess notions of chess pieces do. For example, moving a pawn in (conventional) pre-tess chess is moving a such-and-such shaped piece on a certain sort of board. A similar situation obtains for tess players' pre-conventional chess notions of tess moves. Thus moving a pawn in tess is driving a Volkswagen from one Texas county to another. Yet by reasoning analogous to that used for the pieces of conventional chess and tess we can come to have new concepts of conventional chess and tess moves. This development in our concepts of the moves of conventional chess and tess is completely parallel to what was described for the pieces of conventional chess and tess. As the criteria for being a pawn become purely prescriptive (with the minor reservation made above), so the criteria for being a moving of a pawn become prescriptive and are formulated by our newly conceived rules (with minor reservations similar to those made for the pieces). Finally, then, the moves of conventional chess and tess can be understood as different embodiments of the moves of chess. And, of course, what has been done for the moves and pieces of conventional chess and tess can also be done for the positions.

What we need in order to connect this discussion of chess with language is some way of speaking of inferrings, tokenings, and the counters produced in tokenings. And we need not look far to find it. Though quotation is usually a device for forming a name of a particular expression (or sometimes a kind of expression), we do use it in at least one other way. For example, we sometimes say that there are four 'if's on a page. That is, we so use quotes that they form, instead of a name, a predicate.

Taking a hint from this, I shall employ asterisk quotes,

___,

to form a predicate true of all the tokenings in our language which involve the production of a natural linguistic object of the kind illustrated between the quotes.[6] (I ignore, temporarily, sounds, script, etc.) Thus we have as an example the predicate

triangular.

Primarily, this predicate is true of certain rule-governed human activities. But, secondarily, we can think of it as true of the characteristic natural linguistic objects that are produced by the activity.

Since tokenings are items of a rule-governed activity, viz., language, the properties necessary for being a *triangular* are in great part prescriptive. What is essential, as in the case of chess, is that the human behavior, i.e., *triangular*s, fit in as elements in a system of human behavior, i.e., inferring, which is regulated by the rules of the language. For example, one of the rules pertaining to *triangular*s is that from 'a is triangular' we may infer 'a is trilateral'. In general, we accept that a piece of behavior is, say, a *triangular* if we know that the speaker is one who has shown himself to be a competent, sophisticated speaker in other situations. But he can, by inferring something entirely unexpected and unrelated from 'a is triangular', cast doubt on whether some item of his linguistic behavior is actually a *triangular*. That is, his behavior can fail to be in conformity with the rules of inference pertaining to *triangular*s.

Because of the way in which asterisk quotes have been introduced in the paragraph before last, properties for being a *triangular* are not all prescriptive (like the properties for being a pawn before we discovered tess). Indeed being a *triangular* is being a piece of behavior which involves producing an object that has very definite physical design, the one illustrated between the asterisks. If we suppose the same quoting device introduced into German, we can form such predicates as

dreieckig.

And while it is true that 'a ist dreieckig' is the translation of 'a is triagular', nevertheless a *triangular* is not a *dreieckig*.

But our notion of the behavior that can play the linguistic role of a *triangular* is not so restricted as the last paragraph suggests. We accept things in English as *triangular*s that do not have much in common with the producing of the sort of physical <u>inscription</u> that is illustrated between the asterisks. The first example that comes to mind is the sound pattern that is produced in speaking. In addition there is the difference between script and printing and the wider difference between these and the Braille transcription of English, the electrical impulses of English in Morse code, and so on. So, we already accept an enlargement of the physical criteria for being a *triangular* from those limited properties that are associated with the producing of a printed inscription.

However, we can go on to make a much greater conceptual enlargement. We came, as you remember, to see conventional chess and tess as embodiments of the more abstract game of chess. We did this by noting similarities in the structure of the rules of the two games. Exactly the same thing can be done in the case of two natural languages. Indeed, according to the view I have been developing, the discovery of similarities between the rules of inference of two natural languages is essential to the process of translating one language into another. For example, in English, one may infer from 'a is triangular' to 'a is trilateral'. Thus if *dreieckig*s are to be the translation of *triangular*s, we should, and do, find that *dreieckig*s participate in a similar inference. (The method of discovering such similarities is very complex, but at very least one must have information about a considerable number of inferential connections in each language.) Therefore, insofar as we know that some language, e.g., German, is translatable into English and vice versa, there is no reason why we cannot extend our conception of these languages and come to understand them as two different embodiments of the same rule-governed activity (which I shall call "Human Language"). In order to accomplish this project, I introduce a new quoting device which forms metalinguistic predicates, called "Sellarsian general terms" (SGTs), which are prescriptive terms.[7] For this device I shall use colon quotes, called

"Sellarsian quotes"; thus, for example,

:triangular: and :dreieckig:.

By the use of Sellarsian general terms, we can formulate the rules of Human Language. For, though the general term ':triangular:' is constructed according to a general term-forming practice that involves the illustration of an expression of our language, nonetheless the properties for being a :triangular: are prescriptive and hence not tied to any one natural language. Thus both *triangular*s and *dreieckig*s are :triangular:s (and, of course, :dreieckig:s). There is, naturally, a very general descriptive component to being a :triangular:. But this is only what is required of any prescriptive kind (type) in Human Language: i.e., that its embodiments (tokenings) be recognizably different from the embodiments (tokenings) of other prescriptive kinds (types).

In summary, what I have in effect argued is that by applying a line of thought illustrated first for the case of chess moves, positions, and pieces to the moves and positions of language, we can come to see that the primary criteria for being a linguistic move of a certain kind, e.g., being an inferring of an :a is trilateral: from an :a is triangular:, are prescriptive. This truth about inferrings is guaranteed by the way in which we characterize tokenings, e.g., :a is triangular:s. The general term ':a is triangular:', like the term 'pawn', is characterized solely by prescriptive properties derived from the rules that speak of :a is triangular:s. Thus the notion of moving from one position to another in Human Language does not involve any natural properties. Though any particular inferring, i.e., any embodiment of a type of inferring, has to have natural properties, these natural properties are in no way essential to the inferring's being the inferring it is.

What we have done for the tokenings which are items of behavior, we can also do for natural linguistic objects which are produced in tokenings. As we can take '*a ist dreieckig*' to be derivatively true of natural linguistic objects, so we can take the predicate ':a is triangular:' to be derivatively true of the natural linguistic objects that are produced in tokenings which are :a is triangular:s. Being a linguistic object that is an :a is triangular:, like being an object which is a pawn, is not a matter of having certain material properties, but rather a matter of being connected with human behavior that is divided into kinds by prescriptive properties.

A careful review of the terminology I have been using will help fix the distinctions of this section. A <u>tokening</u> is an item of human linguistic behavior which is part of a system of behavior governed by rules of inference. Tokenings are divided into "prescriptive kinds" which I call "types." All tokenings are of some type; and a type is expressed by a Sellarsian general term in that all tokenings fall under some Sellarsian general term. As I have just characterized tokenings, not only are :a is triangular:s tokenings, but so are :triangular:s and :and:s and :Socrates:s and so on. After all, a :triangular: is as much an item of behavior caught up in a rule-governed system as is an :a is triangular:. What is needed is a term for those tokenings by which a language user comes to occupy a position in language, i.e., those tokenings such as :Socrates is a man:s which mark positions in the language in virtue of being of types which are the termini of inferences. Adopting a common philosophical term, I shall call these tokenings "statements." All these terms form part of the prescriptive terminology of language, the "game" terminology of language. Besides this terminology, there are the terms which apply to linguistic behavior as natural events and to the natural objects produced by this behavior. These natural objects I have called "natural linguistic objects." Natural linguistic objects also come in kinds, but the kinds are natural kinds, not prescriptive kinds. To these terms, I shall now add another prescriptive term. I shall say that natural linguistic objects qua produced in tokenings, i.e., qua produced in human behavior which is governed by rules of inference, are "tokens." Given what has been said about tokenings and types, it follows that, derivatively, tokens also fall into types.

If I introduce yet one more variety of quotes, a crucial distinction can be handily illustrated. I introduce dash quotes '--___--' to form general terms which are true of natural linguistic objects of the natural kind illustrated between the dashes. The properties for being an --a is triangular-- are natural properties: namely, the properties that characterize the physical design of the natural linguistic object between the dashes. Ignoring, for the sake of simplicity, that English has embodiments involving materials other than inscribings (e.g., vocalizings), we can make the following points. As a matter of high statistical regularity in English, the English embodiments of :a is triangular:s, i.e., *a is triangular*s, are items of behavior which involve the production of --a is triangular--s. That is, in English, as a matter of purely empirical regularity, tokenings which are :a is triangular:s involve the production of --a is triangular--s. Also in English as a matter of statistical regularity, inferrings of :a is trilateral:s from :a is triangular:s involve the production of --a is trilateral--s and --a is triangular--s. Hence, natural languages are marked off from one another, in part, by the different kinds of natural objects that are characteristically produced in embodyings of of the types of Human Language.

Let me compare the linguistic situation to that of chess.

The chess situation also allows a threefold distinction. First, there are the terms 'pawn', 'bishop', etc., which appear in the rules of chess. Second, consider the various embodiments of chess such as tess and conventional chess. In the rules of an embodiment of chess, the terms 'pawn', 'bishop', etc., have a descriptive component which is determined by the important natural properties of the natural objects which are manipulated in games of the embodiment. These natural objects are the materials of the embodiment. Thus, third, there are such terms as 'such-and-such shaped piece of wood', 'Volkswagen', etc.

Chess corresponds to Human Language; tess and conventional chess, to natural languages like English and German (and, indeed, to ones that are "contrived," like Esperanto); such-and-such shaped pieces of wood and automobiles, to natural linguistic objects like --a is triangular--s. Or, put another way, 'pawn' in chess corresponds to terms like ':a is triangular:' in English and ':a ist dreieckig:' in German; 'pawn' in conventional chess, to terms like '*a is triangular*' in English and '*a ist dreieckig*' in German; 'such-and-such shaped piece of wood', to terms like '--a is triangular--' and '--a ist dreieckig--'.

Finally, it is important to understand certain aspects of the process of contriving new embodiments of chess or Human Language by providing the materials and explaining the connection of these materials with the rules of chess or Human Language. The materials themselves are not the embodiment, though some materials or other must at least be <u>described</u> (<u>not</u> necessarily produced) in order for there to be an embodiment. Suppose someone explains that embodiment of chess, mentioned above, which is played with squads of trained fleas. Among other things, he says: "In this embodiment of chess (call it 'fess'), squads of fleas with such-and-such properties are pawns" (where the term 'pawn' is from the vocabulary of chess). What this person has done is to tell us what some of the materials for this embodiment are. What he has <u>not</u> done is to say anything, in general, about pawns as they are characterized by the rules of chess. All his remark amounts to is: <u>in fess</u>, nothing is a pawn and not a squad of fleas with such-and-such properties, and nothing is a squad of fleas with such-and-such properties and not a pawn. This remark does tell us that certain squads of fleas will be involved in certain moves that are specified in the rules of chess. It also tells us what descriptive component must be added to the term 'pawn' as it appears in the chess vocabulary in order to characterize the term 'pawn' as it appears in the rules of fess.

A similar situation obtains in the case of contrived embodiments of Human Language. To say that <u>in Logishese</u>, --&--s are :and:s is to say that <u>in Logishese</u> nothing is an --&-- and not an :and: and nothing is an :and: and not an --&--. Such statements tell a great deal about the regularities pertaining to the production of --&--s by correct users of Logishese. And from this statement we can determine the descriptive component of terms like '*&*' in Logishese. But such remarks neither alter nor change what :and:s are nor tell us anything, in general, about :and:s, any more than does our discovering, for example, that --und--s are regularly produced in :and: tokenings in German.

These points bear, to various degrees, on the discussion of the next two sections; they are particularly important to section D.

C. Abstract Entities, Abstract Singular Terms, and Sellarsian General Terms

Even a sketchily constructed road to an account of abstract entities is long. But if one is ever to discuss natural numbers and properties of natural numbers intelligibly, the general problem of abstract entities has to be treated. And in an informal way we have already introduced one of the main travellers on our road. This is the term 'the pawn' or, in general, 'the K'.[8] The word 'the pawn' appears in examples of chess rules I have cited and I have discussed some of the features of the related general term 'pawn'. The first question concerns the connection between the pawn and pawns. In some sense the pawn is a one and pawns are a many. A second question, then, is how this instance of the problem of the one and the many is related to the problem of universals, which is another part of the controversy over the one and the many.

First, note that the device we are using to form the singular term 'the pawn' is one that is also applied to predicates for natural kinds. In addition to

the pawn may be moved in such and such a way

we have

the whale is a mammal
the elm is deciduous

and the human being (man) is rational.

What is referred to by these singular terms is not a class nor a universal; on the contrary, neither mankind (a class) nor humanity (a concept) is rational, just as the class of pawns and the concept of a pawn are not what may be moved in certain ways.

But how are we to understand the role of the 'the' which appears in these examples? Actually we do not have to search far for a schema which satisfies our needs. The clue for the schema is that what can be said about the pawn can also be said about pawns; the same is true about the whale, the elm, and man.

The schema is

(5) 'the K is F' is equivalent to 'all Ks are F'!

where the exclamation mark at the end of (5) indicates, for reasons which will become clearer, that not all statements which might be said to have the form 'all Ks are F' may have (5) applied to them. In common cases (e.g., biological ones), the general statement gives a defining property of the items in question or a property of the items which they can be shown to have, by means of some principles (e.g., biological laws), as a consequence of their defining properties. In traditional terminology, one could say that the only statements of the form 'all Ks are F' to which (5) applies are those which state a property "essential" to the kind of item in question. A closer scrutiny of (5) will be undertaken in chapter 4 where a more thorough account becomes necessary.

I shall call individuals like the pawn, the whale, and so on "distributive individuals," and I shall call terms like 'the pawn', 'the whale', and so on "distributive singular terms" (DSTs). I shall call the sort of 'the' which appears in a DST an "institutional" 'the'.[9] A small warning should help to avoid confusion: not every singular term tokening which involves the production of an English --the-- with a kind term is a DST. The only singular terms which are DSTs are those which "distribute" in accordance with (5). I shall not attempt to give criteria which would, once and for all, separate the occurrences of English --the--s which are produced in tokenings of the institutional 'the' from all other occurrences of English --the--s. It is sufficient for my purposes that there are clear cases of DSTs and that they satisfy the schema I have laid out.

The first move in the account of abstract entities is the suggestion that abstract singular terms like 'triangularity' play roles which are such that they can be reconstructed in those roles as metalinguistic DSTs. I do not intend to try to specify, generally, the contexts in which English --triangularity--s have these roles. I shall handle several important cases to illustrate the strategy of my account while admitting that there are many other cases to deal with, some of which require different, rather special treatment.

Two cases with which I shall commence my account are:

(6) triangularity is a universal (in particular, a concept)

and (7) triangularity is an (abstract) individual.

I shall return to (7) later. My immediate concern is with triangularity as that which is spoken of by (6).

As a first approximation of the reconstruction of (6), it becomes a statement in which the metalinguistic DST, 'the :triangular:', appears. Thus (6) becomes a statement commencing

the :triangular: is a. . . .

But the question is: Is a what? From (5) we know that the statement which reconstructs (6) must be equivalent to a statement about all :triangular:s. And this statement is:

(6.2) all :triangular:s are predicates.

And thus the statement which reconstructs (6) must be:

(6.1) the :triangular: is a predicate.

That is, the :triangular: is one kind of distributive individual.

What has been done for concepts must be done for propositions. Indeed propositions play a more crucial role than other abstract entities, since traditionally it is propositions that are said to be true or false. Moreover, in the long run, some sort of account of concepts in terms of propositions must be given, for even if, in some way, the notion of a concept helps us to understand better the nature of propositions, nonetheless, on the view I am developing, concepts are reconstructed as predicates, and predicates do not mark positions in the game. Their appearance in rule-governed linguistic activity is dependent on statements. This point will come out more clearly as the discussion progresses, particularly in section D.

My account of propositions is much like the account of concepts. The first sense of 'proposition' handled is the one in which many philosophers have spoken of a plurality of tokenings "expressing" the same proposition. This talk about propositions is the analog of talk about concepts in which it is said that the same concept is "expressed" by many different predicate tokenings. This sort of talk is not to be confused with the talk of concepts having many instances or of the classes associated with the concepts having many members. The instances of humanity are men and the members of mankind are men, but the items that "express" the concept humanity are :man:s.

The reconstruction of the proposition that a is triangular is

the :a is triangular:

and hence

(8) that a is triangular is a universal (in particular, a proposition)

proceeds through the following metamorphosis:

(8.1) the :a is triangular: is a tokening (in particular, a statement),

i.e., (8.2) all :a is triangular:s are tokenings (in particular, statements).

The next step in the account of abstract entities is one that will provide a reconstruction of the statement

(7) <u>triangularity</u> is an (abstract) individual

and its counterpart in the case of propositions

(9) <u>that a is triangular</u> is an (abstract) individual.

I might add that the contrast between triangularity as a universal and <u>triangularity</u> as an individual is parallelled by the contrast subject-attribute and the Fregean contrast object-concept.[10]

A hint to the correct way to proceed in the case of (7) and (9) is provided by the metalinguistic therapy I have performed on the term 'concept'. Roughly speaking, the term 'concept' is reconstructed as the term 'predicate'. Thus we had

(6.2) all :triangular:s are predicates

and hence by schema (5)

(6.1) the :triangular: is a predicate.

To continue the same pattern, I must reconstruct 'individual' as 'individual constant' (or, if you prefer, 'singular term', as I do not distinguish individual constants and singular terms). If we consider

(10) a is an individual,

we must eventually arrive at

(10.2) :a:s are individual constants.

By schema (5) we must therefore begin with

(10.1) the :a: is an individual constant.

Applying this to (7), we begin by substituting the reconstruction of triangularity and obtain

(7.1) <u>the :triangular:</u> is an (abstract) individual.

But we know that this must be reconstructed in accordance with (10.1) as

(7.2) the :the :triangular:: is a (metalinguistic) individual constant,

that is, as

(7.3) all :the :triangular::s are (metalinguistic) individual constants.

Similarly, we have for (9)

(9.1) <u>the :a is triangular:</u> is an (abstract) individual,

and thus

(9.2) the :the :a is triangular:: is a (metalinguistic) individual constant,

and finally

(9.3) all :the :a is triangular::s are (metalinguistic) individual constants.

It will be convenient at this point to take care of some rather minor matters. The first point concerns the word 'metalinguistic'. In one sense, any statement which is about linguistic items as elements of language is metalinguistic. The metalanguage is, then, just that sublanguage of language as a whole by means of which we speak about language. It is important to remember that, on the Sellarsian view, discourse <u>about language</u> is, strictly speaking, always <u>prescriptive</u>. Such discourse, to invoke the analogy of games, utilizes a "game" terminology. So, for example, to talk about natural linguistic objects as natural objects is <u>not</u> to speak metalinguistically. Discourse about natural objects as natural objects is no more metalinguistic than discourse about the natural properties of certain pieces of wood or certain automobiles is "game" discourse about chess.

However, in other cases, one wishes to distinguish, within the metalinguistic as I have just characterized it, the metalanguage from the metametalanguage and these from the metametametalanguage and so on. Any statement which is about language, but only about language which is not itself about language, is metalinguistic in this second sense. The metametalanguage is that sublanguage in which we speak about the metalanguage; or, to put it another way, it is that discourse in which we speak about that discourse in which we speak about discourse in which we do not speak about language. I shall employ the word 'ML' in this second sense of 'metalinguistic' and 'metalanguage'; in the same vein I shall employ 'MML', 'MMML', and so on.

The second point concerns a few additions to our ML and MML terminology. While (7.3) and (9.3) are true, there are considerable differences between :the :triangular::s and :the :a is triangular::s which are not indicated in (7.3) and (9.3). Suitable machinery can be introduced by noting what level of language is being spoken of and of which sorts of linguistic items certain SGTs are true. Thus, first,

> :Socrates:s are object-language(OL) individual constants

while

(7.4) :the :triangular::s are ML individual constants

and (9.4) :the :a is triangular::s are ML individual constants.

Just as clearly it is true that

:the :the :a is triangular:::s are MML individual constants.

Second, note that ':triangular:' is true of predicates and ':a is triangular:' is true of statements. Further, the individual constants in which these general terms appear are distributive singular terms (DSTs). Thus, we have

(7.5) :the :triangular::s are ML !predicate! DSTs

and (9.5) :the :a is triangular::s are ML !statement! DSTs.

The exclamation marks indicate that an SGT of a certain sort (e.g., one true of predicates) is enclosed within a brace of Sellarsian quotes. Yet another brace of quotes would require another pair of exclamation marks; I shall discuss this notation again when we have convenient examples in chapter 4.

The third matter concerns (5). Schema (5) is adequate for reductions in, I should think, all the common cases of statements containing distributive singular terms. However, I shall make use of DSTs in quite unusual and new contexts, thus extending the conceptual framework of DSTs. Consequently, I should offer reduction schemas in addition to (5). But I will not do this as yet. Instead I shall say that in this introductory discussion the reader is to understand that each new reduction not covered by (5) is backed by a new schema that is not explicitly formulated. Moreover, it is a relatively trivial matter to set out a reduction in any given case in such a way that it is clear what the schema for it would be.

It is hardly worth discussing what the present reconstruction amounts to in plain philosophical terms, since we shall shortly discover good reason to complicate it appreciably. These reasons will become apparent in the next section, where I discuss the role of predicates in statements. Such a discussion is forced on us if we are serious about reconstructing abstract entities. For, according to some philosophers, succeeding in a reconstruction of abstract singular terms is not sufficient for even a "mild" nominalism, since all primitive predicates and primitive relation terms name abstract entities (either universals or classes). And hence, even granting the reconstruction of abstract singular terms, abstract entities still exist as primitive, i.e., not constructed, objects which have not been shown to be amenable to the linguistic therapy practiced in this section.

D. The Perspicuous Language, SL

According to some philosophers, who are usually called "platonists," if the predicate 'F' in 'Fa' is undefined, then it stands for, or names, a universal (or, a class). Similarly, if the relation term 'R' in 'aRb' is undefined, then it too stands for, or names, a universal (or, a class). If there were no alternative to this view, the whole enterprise of the last section would appear to be brought into doubt. Whether such a view actually does make the account of the last section untenable I shall not attempt to say, since the discussion prompted by this objection aids me in the project of this chapter and thus is helpful in its own right.

But, first, I wish to dispel the impression that such a view of predicate and relation terms could arise only through traditional metaphysical confusion. So, I shall take a moment to remind the reader of a very familiar, modern doctrine which I shall call "semantic formalism" and which, if it is pushed in a very plausible direction, is in an important respect indistinguishable from the more traditional view just described.

Everyone who has read a good modern logic book[11] is familiar with semantic formalism; so I shall explain just those tenets of the doctrine which are germane to my present purpose. According to this doctrine, a language has two parts or aspects. The first is a system of items (usually a selection of ordinary natural linguistic objects with a few special additions) called a "syntactical system." Such a system is highly structured and its items and sequences of items, such as "well-formed formulas," can be distinguished effectively. The second is a class of relations, in fact, functions, whose main purpose is to make it possible to divide the class of well-formed formulas into ones that are true and ones that are not. These functions which I shall call "assignment" fuctions assign entities to various kinds of syntactical items which appear in well-formed formulas. Thus consider the simple example of an atomic well-formed formula, 'Pa'. If 'P' is assigned a class or a property and 'a' is assigned an individual, then 'Pa' for that assignment says that the individual is a member of the class or has the property.

Though the above account is neither complete nor wholly unambiguous, the crucial feature of this doctrine is clear: one has a language, properly speaking, only when one has a syntactical system and a class of assignment functions. These assignment functions assign some object to any predicate and relation constants in the syntactical system. The most favored objects are classes, but properties and relations are also used.

Suppose someone is really convinced that the semantic

formalist account of language is the only intelligible one. Then, unless he is willing to give up the claim that natural languages are, in any proper sense, languages, he must maintain that natural languages can be seen, after a cleaning up, to be syntactical systems with a class of admissable assignment functions and that at any given time, one of these functions provides the assignments for the syntactical system. For my purposes the important thing to note is that semantic formalism _as a general doctrine of language_ has the consequence that the predicate and relation terms of a language stand in a relation to some objects or other (e.g., classes or properties and relations). One must remember that these relations lack none of the logical features of relations. They are not like 'thinks of' in

Jones thinks of the fountain of youth

where from this statement it does not follow that there is a fountain of youth. The assignment function is understood to have the feature that if the property, humanity, is assigned to the predicate 'man', then there is such a property to which 'man' stands in a relation. The term 'man' is an item of language, as opposed to an item of a syntactical system, only because it does stand in a relation to this property. Thus, in this respect, semantic formalism as a general account of language is one form of the view mentioned in the first paragraph of this section.

In order to construct an alternative view, I begin by considering the atomic relational statement 'aRb'. Let us ask what other function the 'R' might have than naming, or standing in a relation to, a relation. The answer is supplied by a certain reading of a passage in the _Tractatus_:

> 3.1432 We must not say: "The complex sign 'aRb' says 'a stands in the relation R to b'";

> but we must say, "That 'a' stands in a certain relation to 'b' says that aRb."[12]

A first statement of my reading of this passage is that the 'R' in 'aRb' insures that the 'a' and the 'b' are dyadically related in a determinate way (in this case the relation is that of having an 'R' between them). In general, the role of all relation tokenings is to insure that the name tokenings in atomic relational statements are related.[13] But before I can go into this any further, I must extend this account to atomic predicate statements. (Henceforth, I shall take it as understood that, unless otherwise specified, I am speaking of only atomic statements.)

The extension is accomplished through reflection on the natural linguistic objects that are produced in tokenings which are relational statements. For example, tokenings of :a is lighter than b:s in English produce natural linguistic objects other than those natural linguistic objects which are produced in tokening the names in these statements. Consider the typed natural linguistic objects that would be produced in tokenings of :a is lighter than b:s in these pages. These natural linguistic objects are --a is lighter than b--s and contain --is lighter than--s as separate items. However, if one considers what I have just said about the role of relation tokens, it is clear that the appearance of separate natural linguistic objects like --is lighter than--s could be misleading. It could be misleading because one might easily decide that all tokens whose embodiments involve separate natural linguistic objects name, or stand for, objects. A less misleading embodiment of relational statements would not involve these separate natural linguistic objects.

It is not hard to provide the materials for an embodiment of relational statements that does not involve the production of separate natural linguistic objects like --is lighter than--s (see the end of 2B on materials and embodiments). Thus I type :a is lighter than b:s in a Sellarsian language, called "SL" as follows:

a .
 b

Thus we have written a dyadically related *a* (in SL) and *b* (in SL). It would follow in the case of predicates that the natural linguistic object produced in the tokening of an *a* (in SL) would appear monadically related or configured. And this can be nothing else than its appearing in a special way, i.e., configured determinately.

For example, we can, in SL, type an :a is triangular: statement as a boldface *a* (in SL). (Due to the way in which this book is produced, I indicate that a letter is in boldface by overlining and in extraboldface by double overlining.) Thus

$\overline{a}$

is an :a is triangular: statement in SL.

A more comprehensive list of examples of typed tokens of SL, with paired English tokens, follows:

English	SL
Object-language individual constants:	
a, b, c, . . .	the same tokens in a neutral style (in this case, the ordinary type font)
Statements (monadic atomic):	
triangular a, trilateral a, . . .	$\overline{a}$, $\overline{\overline{a}}$, . . . (a boldface *a* and an extraboldface *a*)
Statement matrices:	

Predicate constant, individual variable:
triangular x, trilateral x, $\bar{x}$, $\bar{\bar{x}}$, . . .
. . .

Predicate variable, individual constant:
Fa, Gb, Hc, . . . individual constants in neutral styles: a, b, c, . . .

Predicate variable, individual variable:
Fx, Gy, Hz, . . . individual variables in neutral styles: x, y, z, . . .

The same sort of list can be constructed for relational statements by configuring names variously. For simplicity the following discussion treats explicitly only of predicates.

There are a few peculiarities in SL. For example, while it is a commonplace that the most general form of a predicate in PMese (i.e., any language in which atomic statements are written in the manner of *Principia Mathematica*) is really 'Fx' rather than simply 'F', it is not often said that the most general form of a name in PMese is 'Fa' rather than simply 'a'. In SL, the natural linguistic objects that play the role of names are the same as those that play the role of one sort of statement matrix. Though this may seem a bit unusual at first, it is really quite consonant with my previous claims. Indeed it is probably the only position that manifests the truth of the claim that statements are the primary parts of language. By treating both names and predicates as statement matrices, we are aided in explaining the roles of names and predicates as derivative from that of the role of statements. Thus names and predicates will be, as Professor Gilbert Ryle so nicely put it, abstractables rather than extractables.[14]

A further discussion of SL requires one or two preliminary remarks. First, in setting up SL I have relied, and will continue to rely, on a metalanguage for SL that is not its own metalanguage, but one constructed from the resources of English. Thus in order to avoid confusion in the use of asterisk-quote general terms, I have been careful to write 'an *a* (in SL)' to indicate that I am speaking of SL, not English.

Second, I have sketched the language SL by giving instances of natural linguistic objects which would be produced in typed tokenings of SL statements. This procedure could lead to misunderstanding if it is forgotten that the typed signs are only one sort of possible materials for SL. Materials for SL, sufficient for my purposes, could be given in sound. Differences in pitch could replace different styles of type font.

Third, it should be remembered that in speaking of a natural language, I mean primarily a system of tokenings, i.e., items of behavior which are embodiments of the types of Human Language. And as I pointed out earlier, the Sellarsian general terms developed in this chapter are true primarily of tokenings. But the most easily recognizable and isolatable feature of a tokening is that it is a production of a natural linguistic object, a counter which is usually either an inscription or a sound. Thus we can treat a natural language, secondarily, as a system of tokens, i.e., as the system of natural linguistic objects _qua_ role players, i.e., _qua_ produced in tokenings. And correspondingly, the metalinguistic general terms can be thought of as being true of these tokens. We discern which natural language, i.e., which embodiment of Human Language, some person is speaking (or writing, etc.) by noting what kinds of natural linguistic objects he characteristically produces, just as we would tell what embodiment of chess a person is playing by noting what kinds of natural objects he is moving. But these truths should not be allowed to obscure the fact that the properties necessary to being a token of a type are those that pertain to playing a linguistic role which is specified by the rules of language.

However, I would never wish to deny that a person comes to have understanding and knowledge of the roles of Human Language by learning to play one or another of the embodiments of Human Language. In learning a natural language, one is coming to know and understand both the rules that govern tokenings and inferrings and also which natural linguistic objects are characteristically produced in tokenings in his language. Once again chess provides a good parallel: coming to be a player of chess can be accomplished by learning to play that embodiment of chess that I have called "conventional chess." And what a conventional chess player comes to know is both the rules of chess in a form restricted to conventional chess and which natural counters are characteristically found in that embodiment of the rules of chess. It is this double aspect of language using that is captured by asterisk quotes. Thus a speaker of SL, call him "Jones," must, since SL is constructed as one more embodiment of Human Language, come to know the rules of Human Language in a form restricted to SL; and since SL is an embodiment of Human Language different from, say, English, Jones also learns that, e.g., in SL, being of a thick type font is, characteristically, what indicates that a tokening of an *a* (in SL) is an :a is triangular: tokening. Similarly, an English speaker must learn that, characteristically, an English tokening of a typed *a* concatenated with a --triangular-- is an :a is triangular: tokening. Of course, this understanding of the different determinate configurations characteristically relevant to our recognition that a tokening in some natural language is the type of statement it is is not arrived at piecemeal. It is part of the total progressive learning of a natural language and is acquired, more or less, as a whole. Moreover, the evidence provided by the recognition of the natural properties of the tokenings in a language is only one piece of evidence among many.

To conclude these reflections on SL, I return to a consideration of the purpose for which SL was constructed. SL, I have emphasized, is in one sense a natural language. It is not a natural language in the sense that anyone regularly produces the natural linguistic objects characteristic of it (that is also true now of linear B) or in the sense that it developed over a long period of time. But SL is a natural language in that it is one embodiment of Human Language. Kinds of natural linguistic objects, the objects produced in typed tokenings of SL, have been illustrated. But SL is a very special embodiment of Human Language: the natural properties of its tokens are supposed to show, in a nonmisleading way, the role of these tokens. That is, the tokens of SL are supposed to embody <u>perspicuously</u> statements, names, and especially predicates. In English, unfortunately and unperspicuously, predicates and relations are embodied by tokens that are actually separate parts of statement tokens. And thus it has been easy to claim that predicate tokens and relation tokens are names. I deny this claim about predicate and relation tokens. SL's presentation of materials for a perspicuous embodiment of predicates and relation tokens helps to clarify this denial and the alternative view I adopt.

SL illustrates how a statement tokening, and, derivatively, the statement token, can be logically articulated and yet in another way unitary. In broad terms, this is accomplished by distinguishing two elements of any atomic statement and showing how these elements embody in different ways the complexity and structure of the type. One is the name, or names.

The other is that "abstractable" which is the configuration of the name or names. The configuration contributes to the statement by being the material indication that the statement tokening participates as premise or conclusion in certain inferences which belong to some predicate or relation role. These inferences are ones in which the name, or names, remain the same.

Let me make these points in a different way. In SL, atomic monadic predicate statements involve the production of an object configured nonrelationally. In English and similar languages, such statements involve the production of an object configured relationally. In English, objects like --triangular--s make these relational configurations possible (e.g., being concatenated with a --triangular--). What SL illustrates is that it is the name configured determinately, and, derivatively, the determinate configuration which is important and not such objects as --triangular--s. Thus from the more penetrating view of this section, we see that terms like ':triangular:' and ':lighter than:' are true of a name or names as determinately configured and conceived in "game" terms.[15] Just as chess pieces as determinately configured and, derivatively, chess piece configurations can be spoken of in the game terminology of chess without any descriptive commitment, so names as determinately configured and, derivatively, name configurations can be similarly spoken of by the prescriptive terms of the rules of Human Language. By comparison, notice that though the English term '*triangular*' is also true of a name as configured and, derivatively, name configurations, its descriptive component insures that the configuration is relational; characteristically, it is being concatenated with a --triangular-- (once again ignoring, inter alia, other materials than typed inscriptions).

Though there is much more of the language SL that could

be sketched, nonetheless I think that the point the language illustrates is fairly clear. Now what is needed is an account of the relation of the reconstruction of abstract singular terms to the perspicuous rendering of the role of predicate and relation tokens in SL. The total strategy thus far has been to explain the workings of abstract singular terms in terms of predicates and then to give the rudiments of an account of predicates which disavows the idea that the role of predicate tokens is to name, or stand for, abstract entities (either universals or classes). But now, if the total maneuver is to succeed, some elucidation of the connection between these two pieces of the strategy must be given.

E. Sellarsian Quotes and SL

Harmonization of the two pieces of strategy hinges on the perspicuous representation of DSTs in SL. But even a casual glance would convince anyone that it is not going to be easy to find a place for 'the :triangular:' in SL's own perspicuous metalanguage. In part, the problem is that of constructing terms like ':triangular:' in SL: a feat which cannot be entirely straightforward, since SL does not contain separate objects such as those which are produced in the tokenings of English *triangular*s. Since SGTs like ':triangular:' are built on the principle of illustration, they apparently cannot be constructed in SL. In any case, SGTs are predicates and thus their tokening in SL cannot involve the production of separate natural linguistic objects like --:triangular:--s. These problems can be dealt with only after further work on the reconstructions of section C.

Since triangularity as a universal was reconstructed in section C, roughly speaking, as a predicate, the reconstruction is in need of a revision which will bring it more in line with what has been said about predicates in section D.[16] The main theme to be taken into account is that to say that a statement contains a certain predicate is to say that a name is configured determinately. What is necessary, then, are ML terms which reflect the dependence of predicates on names and, thus, on statements. Remembering that the most general form of a predicate (typed in PMese style) is something like 'Fx', we might try *as a first approximation*:

triangular x.

Notice that general terms of this sort can be constructed using SL tokens in an English metalanguage for SL. Since the translation of

triangular x

into SL is

$\overline{x}$,

we can construct the general term

$\overline{x}$.

And also in this same metalanguage we can construct the terms ':$\overline{x}$:' and 'the :$\overline{x}$:'.

Returning to our original reconstructions, some simple alterations are in order. The reconstruction of triangularity as a universal (now in PMese style) becomes

the :triangular x:.

Thus we reconstruct

(6) triangularity is a universal

as (6.3) the :triangular x: is statement matrix,

i.e., as

(6.4) all :triangular x:s are statement matrices.

Statements (6.3) and (6.4) make a very important point: the *x*s within the quotes are not, strictly speaking, variables. The SGT ':triangular x:' is composed of two SGTs, viz., ':triangular:' and ':x:'. The latter of these SGTs is true of variables, but it is not itself a variable. Hence what ':triangular x:' is true of is statement matrices like

triangular x, dreieckig x and $\overline{x}$

and not statements.

This point takes on greater significance in the explanation of why (6.3) is not satisfactory. It is not far off, but as it stands it will not suffice. The key to improving (6.3) lies in coming to grips with the fact that Sellarsian quotes work on a principle of illustration. The natural linguistic object illustrated between the quotes in an SGT is one that is characteristically produced in <u>our</u> language (or in some other language we understand) in tokenings of which the SGT is true.

We shall be able to understand the problem of the illustrating nature of SGTs and to advance the reconstruction of (6) beyond (6.3) if we start from scratch with a reconstruction of

(11) triangularity entails trilaterality.

A reconstruction of (11) with ':triangular x:' and ':trilateral x:' would have to be:

the :trilateral x: may be inferred from the :triangular x:

which would reduce to

:trilateral x:s may be inferred from :triangular x:s.

There are several difficulties. First, as I just pointed out, a :trilateral x: is not a statement, but rather a statement matrix, and thus does not mark a position in language. Though we can arrange it so that we may infer to and from such tokens as :triangular x:s, we do so only derivatively. Primarily, we infer to and from such statements as :trilateral a:s, and they are not :trilateral x:s. In short, we are dealing with the wrong Sellarsian general term.

Second, since the *x*s in ':trilateral x:' and ':triangular x:' are between quotes, they are not variables and hence cannot be "bound" together. That they should be bound is suggested by a more informal rendering of (11) as

> that anything is triangular entails that it is trilateral.

The 'it' and the 'anything' are obviously meant to be "connected."

The solution rests in introducing <u>nonillustrating</u> SGTs. For example, I shall write 'PREDCON' and 'INDCON' where the first SGT is true of predicates and the second is true of individual constants. As nonillustrating SGTs for, as it were, species under these two genuses, I write

> PREDCONA, PREDCONB, PREDCONC, PREDCOND, PREDCONE, etc.

and INDCONA, INDCONB, INDCONC, INDCOND, INDCONE, etc.

Thus suppose that :a:s are INDCONAs and :b:s are INDCONBs and that :triangular:s are PREDCONAs. Then corresponding to

> x is a :triangular a:

and x is a :triangular b:,

we have respectively,

> x is a (PREDCONA INDCONA)

and x is a (PREDCONA INDCONB).

There is no reason to confine ourselves to pure combinations of all illustrating or all nonillustrating SGTs. It is possible to form mixed combinations such as

(12) (:triangular: INDCON)

which is true of any statement in which the predicate is a :triangular: and in which there is one individual constant. From (12) we obtain the DST

(13) the (:triangular: INDCON).

Similarly, there is the mixed term

(14) (PREDCON :a:)

which is true of any statement in which the individual constant is an :a: and in which there is a predicate. From (14) we obtain the DST

(15) the (PREDCON :a:).

The easiest approach to the remaining steps in the reconstruction of

(11) triangularity entails trilaterality

is via its paraphrase:

(16) that anything is triangular entails that it is trilateral.

Let us try as the reconstruction:

(17) the (:trilateral: INDCON) may be inferred from the (:triangular: INDCON)

which becomes

(18) (:trilateral: INDCON)s may be inferred from (:triangular: INDCON)s.

The difficulty which remains with (18) is that it obscures its own double generality. 'INDCON' was introduced as the predicate for a genus and 'INDCONA', 'INDCONB', etc., were predicates for species of the genus. From this it follows that (18) entails any statement made by replacing 'INDCON' by 'INDCONA' or 'INDCONB' and so on, or by any illustrating SGT like ':a:' or ':b:', much as a statement about primates entails any statement with the term 'primate' replaced by the term 'man' or 'ape' and so on. This generality is better brought out by construing 'INDCON' as an <u>ML variable</u> and understanding both illustrating and nonillustrating ML SGTs which are true of individual constants as substituends for the variable (see 3A about variables and quantification). Further, changing from the genus-species relationship to the variable-substituend relationship also insures that the reconstruction can correctly mirror the connection between the 'anything' and the 'it' in (16).

With 'INDCON' as a variable, (18) is no longer a statement. This point must be thoroughly understood. The term 'INDCON' is now an ML variable and hence the ML term

(:triangular: INDCON)

is <u>not an SGT, but rather a matrix for SGTs</u>. The ML term ':triangular: INDCON' is like the OL term 'white F' which is a matrix for such OL general terms as 'white horse'. Consequently, (18) must be universally quantified; it becomes

(18.1) (INDCON)((:trilateral: INDCON)s may be inferred from (:triangular: INDCON)s)

where the double generality is indicated by the quantifier and plurals. Using (18.1), we find that (17) has become

(17.1) (INDCON)(the (:trilateral: INDCON) may be inferred from the (:triangular: INDCON)).

Let us return to the task of reconstructing (6) and ask what the reconstruction of (11) shows about the reconstruction of triangularity as a universal. The major point should be obvious from what has been said. Statement (6) must undergo yet another and more penetrating reconstruction; it becomes

(6.5) (INDCON)(the (:triangular: INDCON) is a statement),

i.e., (6.6) (INDCON)((:triangular: INDCON)s are statements).

That (6.5) and (6.6) contain the appropriate predicate can be seen by noting that, given that :a:s are individual constants, (6.6) entails

(:triangular: (:a:))s are statements,

i.e., :triangular a:s are statements.

This last statement is clarly true as are all similar instances.

Obvious alterations must be made in the reconstruction of _triangularity_ as an individual and hence in the reconstruction of (7). The essential new ingredient is that the term

the :the :triangular::

no longer fits in with the new reconstruction of triangularity as a universal. For the above DST contains the DST 'the :triangular:' which was in the beginning used in the reconstruction of (6). However, since 'the (:triangular: INDCON)' is now used in reconstructing statements about triangularity as a universal, the term needed at the MML level to handle statements about _triangularity_ must contain

the :the (:triangular: INDCON):.

But as I added the variable 'INDCON' to ':triangular:', so I must add a variable (in this case, an MML variable for ML SGTs true of predicates) to 'the :the (:triangular: INDCON):' and the result is

the (PREDCON :the (:triangular: INDCON):)

where the fact the 'PREDCON' is an MML variable is indicated by the underlining. At the moment, though, I wish to go no further in discussing abstract entities as individuals. The points I shall make about SGTs in the remainder of this chapter and in the next chapter are, with little change, applicable to both ML and MML SGTs. The present discussion of abstract entities as individuals will be resumed in chapter 4. The questions that arise over the exact construction of such metalinguistic complex terms as '(:triangular: INDCON)' and the use of quantification with SGTs must be delayed till chapter 3.

I now return to the topic of how the metalinguistic account of triangularity can be carried on in SL itself. It is this project, not yet done for SL, which led to new reconstructions of (6) and (11). The direction of the technical work on this project is dictated by the fact than an SL metalanguage must, like the SL object language, represent its atomic statements as names configured.

Consequently, I shall assume that an SL metalanguage contains names for linguistic items *qua* linguistic, i.e., *qua* items in a rule-governed linguistic structure. Something similar in the case of chess is having names for chess pieces *qua* game items. These metalinguistic names configured determinately are metalinguistic atomic statements. I shall not concern myself with illustrating materials for an SL embodiment of metalinguistic statements. Though matters are a little more complicated, the principle is no different from that which was applied in the case of the SL object language. So I shall assume that an SL metalanguage has the means to handle metalinguistic atomic statements. Further, I shall assume that the SL metalanguage has an equivalent of the phrase 'may be inferred from'.

Now comes the crucial part. Remember that ':triangular a:' is true of any statement in which there is one :a: and which, in addition, is such that, in any embodiment of Human Language whatever, this :a: has that which is :triangular:.[17] That is embodied, in a PMese version of English, in materials which have the relational property of being concatenated with a --triangular--. But, in my example, the corresponding property of SL materials is that of being in boldface (if we ignore other than typed materials). Further, in a PMese English metalanguage, --triangular--s appear within the term ':triangular a:', thereby indicating which statements this SGT is true of. SL has no such separate pieces, but it can follow a principle analogous to the one just described. SL can write an ML name in boldface. Writing a name in boldface in the SL metalanguage is the analog of writing a --triangular-- within Sellarsian quotes in the term ':triangular a:'. Thus, in SL, that the tokenings of an ML name of a statement involve the production of a natural linguistic object in boldface characteristically indicates that the name is the name of a statement which, as we would say in an English metalanguage, has a :triangular: monadic configuration.[18]

Now I introduce ML variables for these names. These variables come in sorts. For example, one sort of variable is such that its tokenings in SL characteristically involve the production of a natural linguistic object in boldface. The substituends of this sort of variable are those ML statement names whose tokenings in SL characteristically involve the production of a natural linguistic object in boldface. Thus, as illustration, there is in the SL metalanguage,

$\overline{\text{STAT}}$

and $\overline{\overline{\text{STAT}}}$.

(See the list of typed materials in section D for the significance of overlining.) Notice two things: 'STAT' in SL's own metalanguage, unlike 'INDCON' in SL's English metalanguage, is an individual variable; nothing about the individual constant which appears in a statement named by a substituend of the ML variables 'STAT', 'STATA', and so on is indicated by the variables themselves.

As a start on the reconstruction of (6) in SL, we have:

($\overline{\text{STAT}}$)($\overline{\overline{\text{STAT}}}$ is a statement).

A small catch occurs if we approach (11) in the same simple way. Because, as I just pointed out, the ML individual variables indicate nothing about the individual constant in a statement named by a substituend of one of these variables, the following will not do as a beginning of an SL reconstruction of (11):

($\overline{\text{STAT}}$)($\overline{\overline{\text{STAT}}}$)($\overline{\overline{\text{STAT}}}$ may be inferred from $\overline{\text{STAT}}$).

Since it would be too great a digression to investigate SL further, I must settle for the following as the starting point of an SL reconstruction of (11):

($\overline{\text{STAT}}$)($\overline{\overline{\text{STAT}}}$)(if $\overline{\text{STAT}}$ and $\overline{\overline{\text{STAT}}}$ have the same individual constant, then $\overline{\overline{\text{STAT}}}$ may be inferred from $\overline{\text{STAT}}$).

From this point the project requires such things as a defense of my recent assumptions about the SL metalanguage, accounts of quantification and DSTs in SL, and one or two other things. These additions provide many technical complications but no impossibilities though, of course, further delving into SL raises new questions which would have to be answered in a more complete account.

In summary, I have in this section shown how, in a PMese English metalanguage, abstract singular terms are reconstructed in a way which harmonizes with the principles illustrated by the representation of predicates in SL, and I have sketched a part of the work of reconstructing (6) and (11) in SL itself. Therefore I think that I have succeeded in showing that the mild nominalism I espouse is a viable alternative to varieties of semantic realism or platonism which rest on the claim that primitive predicate and relation tokens are names (or, stand in a "semantic" relation to some object). On the view I have been developing there are no primitive names for universals (or, as shown in 6C, for classes). Abstract singular terms are, in one sense, names, but they are not primitive. They stand for constructed entities: the statements in which they occur are, in the final analysis, reduced to statements without such singular terms. And predicate and relation tokens are just not names at all.

F. Summary of the Main Stages of the Reconstruction

I begin by reviewing the reconstructions of

(6) triangularity is a concept

and (8) that a is triangular is a proposition.

In section C, the following reconstructions were offered:

(6.1) the :triangular: is a predicate,

i.e., (6.2) all :triangular:s are predicates

and (8.1) the :a is triangular: is a statement,

i.e., (8.2) all :a is triangular:s are statements.

Thus it appeared in section C that triangularity is the distributive individual, the :triangular:. But since statements about the :triangular: are reducible to ones that speak of all :triangular:s, in the final analysis it seemed that talking about triangularity is to be understood as talking about all the tokenings of a certain type, a type of tokening which, in English printing, characteristically involves the production of a natural linguistic object of the natural kind illustrated between the Sellarsian quotes in the term ':triangular:'. Indeed we found in section E that this account is not too far wrong. What it lacks is real insight into the general role of predicates. Filling this conceptual hiatus in section E led to the reconstruction of triangularity by the new term:

the (:triangular: INDCON).

And the reconstruction of (6) became

(6.5) (INDCON)(the (:triangular: INDCON) is a statement),

i.e., (6.6) (INDCON)(all (:triangular: INDCON)s are statements).

Statements (6.5) and (6.6) emphasize the point that triangularity as a universal is part of what is expressed by all statements that are logically articulated in a certain manner. This logical articulation is characteristically represented, in English PMese, by concatenating an individual constant with a --triangular-- while, in SL, it is represented by producing an individual constant in boldface. In general, triangularity is that which is contributed to any statement that is articulated in a manner which, in the embodiment of Human Language in which the statement appears, is produced by human behavior governed by rules of inference of which one example is (18.1).[19]

The reconstruction of propositions did not have to be changed in section E for the simple reason that, in the case of propositions, we do not need to ask what the tokenings that express propositions contribute to statements. These tokenings are statements. Talk of propositions thus reduces to talk of all the statements of a given type, i.e., all the tokenings (and, derivatively, tokens) that play a conceptual role which is encapsulated in a Sellarsian general term true of statements.

The case of abstract entities as abstract individuals is slightly more complicated to set out but does not involve anything in principle new. Since I will not completely finish the reconstruction of <u>triangularity</u> as an individual till chapter 4, I will say what I can conveniently say now by commenting on the reconstruction of propositions as individuals. Thus consider

(9) <u>that a is triangular</u> is an abstract individual.

Statement (9) becomes in the end

(9.5) all :the :a is triangular::s are ML !statement! DSTs.

That is, to speak of abstract entities as abstract individuals is to speak of complex eliminable metalinguistic singular terms, viz., those ML DSTs that appear in the reconstruction of abstract entities as universals. Thus <u>that a is triangular</u> is still connected with :a is triangular:s, though only in a tenuous way that is reflected in the fact that the DSTs which are used in reconstructing that a is triangular (a universal) contain the SGT ':a is triangular:'. In general, the reconstruction of abstract entities as individuals is concerned with the fact that, at the first level of reconstruction, the abstract singular terms which stand for abstract entities as universals must be reconstructed as singular terms, albeit eliminable ones, i.e., DSTs, which are themselves constructed from SGTs. There will be ample opportunity to study this difference in levels in chapter 4, for there I shall be discussing abstract singular terms for which it is worthwhile to explain both levels in more detail.

Chapter 3: Quantification, Entailment, and Identity

A. Quantification

(i) The Rejection of Extended Semantic Formalism

According to a well-known doctrine of ontological commitment which is closely associated with a widely accepted interpretation of quantification, my practice in chapter 2 of using quantification with predicate variables commits me to abstract entities--in particular, to properties and relations (or, classes). If I cannot defend myself against this charge, my attempt at a mild nominalism may yet fail. The object of this section is to give an account of quantification that derives from the view of language in chapter 2 and to show that, on this account, my practice in chapter 2 does not commit me to unwanted abstract objects.[1]

In order to understand clearly this objection against my views, one must understand the view of quantification which it assumes. This view is commonly called the "objectual interpretation." In contemporary philosophical literature, this interpretation is associated with the general view that I called, in 2D, "semantic formalism."

According to semantic formalism, a syntactical system with quantifiers is interpreted, or "given a semantics," by assignment functions that assign to various syntactical items entities from a domain. Once assignments have been made to the syntactical items which are supposed to have something assigned to them, the quantified sentences speak about the entities in the domain. In most formal languages, quantification utilizes variables and the variables are said to "range over" or "have as values" the entities of the domain. If formulas with free variables are to be evaluated for truth-value under a given assignment, then the assignment functions must assign to each free variable some entity from the domain the variables "range over."[2]

The objectual interpretation is usually taken to lead to a particular doctrine of ontological commitment. This doctrine may be held in a number of forms, of which the following are typical. The simplest is that one is committed to the existence of those entities in the domain the variables "range over."[3] Second, one is committed to the existence of those entities which are required to be in the domain in order that the quantified sentences one accepts come out true.[4] Third, one is committed to the existence of those kinds of entities which are such that at least one entity of the kind must be in the domain in order that the quantified sentences one accepts come out true.[5] The objection to my view that is prompted by the objectual interpretation does not depend on which form of the doctrine of ontological commitment is chosen. I formulate and accept statements involving predicate variable quantification, and this, according to any of the forms of the doctrine, commits me to the existence of abstract entities as the "values" over which my predicate variable "range."

In 2D, I distinguished semantic formalism as a doctrine of formal languages that subscribes to their characterization and investigation by mathematical means from semantic formalism _as a general doctrine of languages formal or otherwise_. Let us call the first "semantic formalism" and the second, "extended semantic formalism." The extended semantic formalist is convinced that the semantic formalist account of formal languages is the _only_ intelligible account of _language_ and is committed to the view that anything which is _properly speaking_ a language is understandable, perhaps despite its outward appearance, by means of the semantic formalist notions used in the characterization and investigation of formal languages.

3A(i)

As I have indicated, the objectual interpretation is a characteristic part of semantic formalism. But in order for the objection against my mild nominalism to succeed, it must assume extended semantic formalism so that the objectual interpretation is not simply part of a mathematical account of the workings of certain operators (called "quantifiers") in a certain mathematical structure (called a "formal language"). Only the assumption of extended semantic formalism makes the objectual interpretation a general account of quantification in language.

No doubt extended semantic formalism seems, to many writers, obviously correct, so much so that they do not distinguish between the philosophical claims of extended semantic formalism and the mathematical doctrines of semantic formalism. Not only does this book distinguish the two, it is part of the basic message of the book that extended semantic formalism should not be accepted. I do not offer a direct attack on extended semantic formalism. I attack it only indirectly by working out the Sellarsian doctrine of language which is a competitor of extended semantic formalism (though not, of course, of semantic formalism). The power and advantages of my alternative are displayed throughout the book.

To say, simply, that I reject extended semantic formalism does not answer an important question: What that is essential to the objectual interpretation does the Sellarsian doctrine reject in not accepting extended semantic formalism? Inter alia, it rejects the mechanism of "assignment functions" and indeed the whole notion of "giving a semantics" for a language by means of establishing "semantic relations" to a domain of entities. That the Sellarsian account does not involve such things as the extended semantic formalist understands them is clear from chapter 2 and will be further evidenced in the next subsection.

The rejection of extended semantic formalism, by undercutting the objectual interpretation as a philosophical account of quantification, leaves the objection to my mild nominalism without an essential premise. In subsection (ii), the provision of my account of quantification and the demonstration that this account leads me to no difficulties about ontological commitment complete my reply to the objection.

The only generally recognized alternative to the objectual interpretation is the so-called substitution interpretation. Since the view I am defending rejects the former interpretation as part of its rejection of extended semantic formalism, it might be thought that my view is committed to the latter interpretation.[6] This opinion is reinforced by the fact that defenders of the substitution interpretation support it by emphasizing that it avoids precisely those difficulties about ontological commitment that I have been discussing. The Sellarsian view, however, does not accept the substitution interpretation.

The key to the substitution interpretation is the syntactical notion of substitution for variables. Consider any universally quantified formula in which the universal quantifier binds at least one occurrence of a variable within the subformula on which the quantifier operates. This subformula has at least one free variable and has as substitution instances those formulas that result from making an appropriate substitution for the free variable(s) in the subformula. On the substitution interpretation, the truth of the universally quantified formula is explained in terms of the truth of these substitution instances: the universally quantified formula is true if and only if all these substitution instances are true. One might also say that the universally quantified formula says no more and no less than all the substitution instances say.

3A(i)

The reason that my account of language cannot incorporate as its view of quantification the substitution interpretation comes back to extended semantic formalism. The substitution interpretation employs a notion of substitution which is defined for the syntactical system of a formal language. The only ground for speaking of substitution and substitution instances, in the semantic formalist's sense of 'substitution', in language in general is the extended semantic formalist's assumption that all language must be understood by means of the mathematical devices developed for the study of formal languages. Once this assumption is made, one can speak about the substitution interpretation as a view of quantification _simpliciter_, rather than as just a view of the mathematical workings, in a special sort of mathematical system, of operators called "quantifiers."

Since I have rejected extended semantic formalism, the substitution interpretation is clearly not my view of quantification. There is, however, a question analogous to one asked earlier: What that is essential to the substitution interpretation does the Sellarsian doctrine of language reject in not accepting extended semantic formalism?

The distinctive feature of semantic formalist notions like substitution is that there is an effective procedure for their application. Thus in a formal language, one can determine effectively that one formula results from another by substitution. These effective procedures depend on, among other things, effective procedures for deciding the syntactical classification of the basic signs belonging to the syntactical system of the formal language. There must be effective procedures for determining whether a sign is an individual variable, whether it is a predicate constant, whether it is a logical constant, and so on. The usual method for insuring that there are such effective procedures is through a list which is described by giving a sign (or signs) and the means of generating the remainder of the list. For example, the list of individual variables might be an 'x' and all the other signs that can be produced by suffixing a stroke, '/', repeatedly to it. Such lists depend on the natural features, the "designs," of the signs.

The Sellarsian view of language includes neither effective procedures for deciding the classification of linguistic tokens nor lists of predicates, logical constants, and so on. As chapter 2 and subsection (ii) of this section make abundantly clear, linguistic items are categorized and determinately classified by role. In short, the Sellarsian view of quantification cannot be the substitution interpretation because the Sellarsian view does not, among other things, include what is essential to the semantic formalist's notion of substitution.

This position on syntactical systems and syntactical notions does not commit me to the view that the system of natural linguistic objects of a natural language at a given time cannot be regimented so that it becomes a syntactical system. But even if we assume that this regimentation is possible, it does not follow that, on the Sellarsian account of language, the properties and structure of this now regimented system are appropriate for elucidating quantification. My account does recognize the existence and importance of systems of natural linguistic objects. But my characterizations of items of language are metalinguistic in Sellars's sense of 'metalinguistic' and thus are prescriptive and make no mention of lists of natural linguistic objects or the features and structure of even a regimented system of natural linguistic objects. It is, of course, important to my view, as is clear from 2D, that the natural features and structure of such a regimented system can "reflect" important aspects of the prescriptive structure of language.

In summary, the Sellarsian account of language rejects both the objectual and the substitution interpretations of quantification as a consequence of its rejection of extended semantic formalism.

Further, there is no question, on Sellars's view, of choosing one account of quantification in one context and another account in other contexts. There is an account of quantification that develops from the Sellarsian view of language. This account is _the_ Sellarsian account of quantification.

I now present this account in a way chosen because it clearly displays which topics this account takes to be connected and which separate.

(ii) The Sellarsian Account of Quantification

I begin by explaining what corresponds in my view to what logicians usually call "first-order quantification." This point must be remembered since my terminology is the one best suited to my account and is not the terminology of logicians.

My account centers on statements which contain a predicate token combined with a quantifier. (For the present discussion, I contrast predicate tokens with relation tokens.) I call these statements "quantified predicate statements." I attend only to such statements which are universally quantified.

In addition to a predicate, universally quantified predicate statements contain a token of a type which is such that

[i] a token of that type combined with a predicate is a statement

and [ii] from these statements may be inferred any statement which is a token of that predicate combined with any singular term and [iii] these statements may be inferred from all the statements which are a token of that predicate combined with any singular term.

The type of linguistic item just characterized is, of course, the universal quantifier. This characterization incorporates the two rules:

(1) from a universally quantified predicate statement may be inferred any statement which is a token of that predicate combined with any singular term.

and (2) a universally quantified predicate statement may be inferred from all the statements which are a token of that predicate combined with any singular term.

Notice that (2), and correspondingly [iii], must be understood analogously to the rule

> a statement may be inferred from another statement and a conditional statement which has as its antecedent a token of the same type as the latter statement and as its consequent a token of the same type as the former statement.

It does not follow from this rule, by a rule for conjunction, that

> a statement may be inferred from another statement.

Thus (2) is not to be understood as

(2.1) a universally quantified predicate statement may be inferred from every (or, each) statement which is a token of that predicate combined with any singular term.

It <u>does</u> follow from (2.1), <u>but</u> <u>not</u> <u>from</u> (2), that

> a universally quantified predicate statement may be inferred from this statement which is a token of that predicate combined with a singular term.

Moreover, given certain rules of negation and the above consequence of (2.1),

> (2.2) from the negation of a universally quantified predicate statement may be inferred every statement which is the negation of a statement which is a token of that predicate combined with a singular term

follows from (2.1) and vice versa. But with these rules of negation, (2.2) may <u>not</u> be inferred from (2), and (2) may <u>not</u> be inferred from (2.2). Given the rules of negation, what may be inferred from (2), and vice versa, is

> (2.3) from the negation of a universally quantified predicate statement may be inferred some statement which is the negation of a statement which is a token of that predicate combined with a singular term.

Given that a permissible inference is one which, in some sense, guarantees that the conclusion of the inference is true if the premise(s) is(are) true, then the following principles about the truth of universally quantified predicate statements are a consequence of the above characterization of these statements:

> if a universally quantified predicate statement is true, then all the statements which are a token of that predicate combined with any singular term are true

and if all the statements which are a token of a predicate combined with a singular term are true, then the universally quantified predicate statement which is that predicate universally quantified is true.

Notice that the above account of universally quantified predicate statements does not appeal to any syntactical system and its properties or even to the properties of an unregimented system of natural linguistic objects.

The account also lacks any indication of what sorts of differences there might be among predicates. There is nothing said about complex predicates and how they are connected with simpler predicates. Though, in the long run, a great deal would have to be said about this matter, I shall confine myself to those observations which enable me to extend my account of quantification.

One means by which complex predicates are obtained from simpler ones involves statement connectives. Statement connectives are also characterized, in the Sellarsian account, by rules of inference. Statement conjunction forms a statement from a statement and a statement (perhaps the same statement); the statement so formed (called a "conjunction") is such that either of its statements may be inferred from it and it may be inferred from the statements. Analogous accounts can be given for the other statement connectives.

With conjunction, we may easily characterize conjunctive predicates. Given a predicate and a predicate (perhaps the same predicate), the "associated conjunction" is a conjunction of which one statement is one of these predicates combined with a singular term and the other statement is the other of these predicates combined with another token of the same singular term. These predicates are a conjunctive predicate if and only if any statement which is a singular term combined with these predicates may be inferred from the associated conjunction and from any such statement the associated conjunction may be inferred. Many other sorts of complex predicates can be handled in a similar fashion.

Notice, once again, that the foregoing remarks do not appeal to any collection of natural linguistic objects or to the natural characteristics of natural linguistic objects. Further, nothing has been said about how one might best or most easily provide an embodiment of conjunction, conjunctions, or conjunctive predicates. Finally, no claims about natural or contrived embodiments follow from what I have said: that --and--s are produced by English speakers in tokening conjunctions is a claim that is not a consequence of my account of conjunctions. What I have said about conjunction is necessary for determining the truth of such claims about languages, but these claims are not included in any way in my remarks on conjunction.

The complex predicates thus far dealt with are only a fraction of all complex predicates. Of the remaining complex predicates I shall discuss only those formed with the help of relation tokens. For simplicity's sake, I shall confine my remarks to two-place relation tokens. I shall also continue to treat explicitly only of the universal quantifier and reserve my remarks on the E-quantifier for later (though much of what I shall say applies without alteration to the E-quantifier).

The strategy of the following paragraphs is to characterize statements with complex predicates by means of their inferential connection with statements that contain complex predicates which have already been characterized. This was the point of the example of conjunctive predicates. As this job goes forward, we come to have ever more kinds of complex predicates whose universal quantification can be handled by rules (1) and (2) until, in the end, we have taken in even multiply quantified relational statements.

Consider a dyadic relational statement which has a singular term token in each of its two places. Associated with such a statement are two relational predicates. One of the relational predicates is the relation token with one of the singular terms in its place; the other is the relation token with the other singular term in its place. I shall call such relational predicates "singular term relational predicates." To these relational predicates my previous remarks on the universal quantifier and rules (1) and (2) apply without change.

The next sort of relational predicate arises through quantification. If a relation token is quantified in one place, the quantified relation token is a predicate which I shall call a "quantified relational predicate." Given that a quantified dyadic relational predicate combined with a singular term is a dyadic relation token quantified in one place combined with a singular term, the following is a characterization of statements which contain such quantified dyadic relational predicates. A statement is a dyadic relation token quantified in one place combined with a singular term if and only if this statement and a statement which is a quantified dyadic singular term relational predicate in which

[i] a relation token of the same type is quantified in the same place

and [ii] a token of the same singular term occupies the other place

are mutually inferrable (i.e., may be inferred from each other). The statements with quantified dyadic singular term relational predicates are one sort of quantified predicate statement. If the quantification is universal, these quantified predicate statements come under (1) and (2), and thus the universal quantification in the statements which are quantified dyadic relational predicates combined with a singular term can be handled through their connection with the quantified predicate statements. (The same would be true of E-quantification.)

A new consideration is that since relation tokens have two places to quantify, it must somehow be indicated which of the two places is quantified. I shall call this new function "quantifier place-indicating." I shall assume that this function is performed even in those cases, already discussed, in which it is not necessary.

There are several features of quantifier place-indicating worthy of remark. Quantifier place-indicating <u>need not</u> involve tokens which have other functions as well. Of course, many common embodiments of quantification do make use of just such tokens, which the authors of logic books usually call "variables." In most cases, variables do have other functions besides their function in quantifier place-indicating. Ordinary English, to the extent that it utilizes quantifier place-indications, makes use of pronouns which, like variables, have other functions than the one they have as quantifier place-indicators. However, it is clearly not difficult to think of embodiments in which the quantifier place-indicators have that function alone. Moreover, there are ways of insuring adequate quantifier place-indicating without any special tokens over and above those tokens which are the embodiments of the quantifiers.

The conceptual function of quantifier place-indications is reflected in inference, but in a complicated way. I shall illustrate the function of quantifier place-indications with the sort of quantified relational statements I have already discussed; in light of the above discussion, my remarks can be transferred to statements with quantified relational predicates.

Consider two universally quantified dyadic relational

statements with relation tokens of the same type. One statement has one place quantified; the other statement has the other place quantified. Both statements have singular term tokens of the same type in the remaining place. Roughly speaking, the "inferential contribution" of a universal quantifier to a universally quantified statement insures that the premises from which that statement may be inferred are all statements of a certain sort and that all these statements may be inferred from the quantified statement. In the case of the two universally quantified statements we have envisaged, the statements from which they may be inferred and which may be inferred from them are not the same for both quantified statements. For the one quantified statement, the statements in question differ among themselves (as types) in having different singular terms in one place; for the other quantified statement, the different singular terms are in the other place. Thus we have an example of the role (or, function) of quantifier place-indications. Of course, all quantifier place-indications have the same generic function; but, as the example shows, they can be distinguished in specific contexts by the determinate functions which are reflected, as illustrated above, in inference. Another such example appears in the case of multiply quantified relational statements.

Once we have come this far, the treatment of multiply quantified relational statements requires little additional machinery. Using dyadic relation tokens again, I note that multiply quantified relational statements are statements which have both places quantifier place-indicated. The only new consideration is that of what I shall call "quantifier-ordering." Thus of the two quantifiers, one is the "first" and the other is the "second." The order of the quantifiers is determined by which of the two is the quantifier of a quantified relational predicate; this quantifier is the "first" quantifier.

Different embodiments may employ vastly different ways of indicating quantifier-order. For example, one way would be to require that no multiply quantified dyadic relational statement is tokened without also tokening a different quantified relational statement. This second quantified relational statement has [i] one of the two quantifiers, [ii] a relation token of the same type as the relation token of the multiply quantified relational statement, and [iii] any singular term whatever in the place which is not quantified. The quantifier which appears only in the tokening of the multiply quantified relational statement is the "first" quantifier; the quantifier which appears in both is the "second." (Notice that there is no problem in generalizing this account to more than dyadic relational statements.) Such sequences of tokenings would, as it were, give the "ancestors" of the multiply quantified relational statement. A more usual device is to arrange for some ordering of the quantifier tokens themselves.

Differences in quantifier-orderings, given appropriate quantifier place-indications, are manifested by which statements may be inferred solely by the quantifier rules from a multiply quantified statement and by which statements a multiply quantified statement may be inferred from solely by the quantifier rules. For example, consider a dyadic relational statement whose first quantifier is a universal quantifier; as first quantifier, this quantifier quantifies a quantified relational predicate. The statements which may be inferred "immediately," i.e., solely by the universal quantifier rule, from this multiply quantified statement are statements which have

[i] a singular term in the place to which the universal quantifier is place-indicated in the

multiply quantified statement

and [ii] a quantified relational predicate which has

[a] a relation token of the same type as the multiply quantified statement and

[b] a quantifier of the same type as the second quantifier in the multiply quantified statement and

[c] this quantifier place-indicated to the same place as the second quantifier of the multiply quantified statement.

These statements are also the ones from which the multiply quantified statement may be immediately inferred. By contrast, the statements from which the statements with the quantified relational predicates may be immediately inferred and vice versa (if I may so put it for the sake of brevity) are simply relational statements with no quantifiers. So, to put my point of the beginning of this paragraph in a slightly different way, the determinate conceptual significance of a quantifier-ordered, place-indicated quantifier in a multiply quantified statement is in exactly which statements are immediately inferrible from the multiply quantified statement (and vice versa). (This explanation of the function of quantifier-ordering with place-indication is, without hitch, extendable beyond the dyadic case.)

Some paragraphs back I noted that though place-indications all had the same generic function, i.e., place-indicating, the total function of a place-indication is determined by the specific context. Thus in a given statement, one place-indication may be distinguished by its total function from another. The same is true of quantifiers. All universal quantifiers have the same generic function which is formulated by rules (1) and (2) (or, if you prefer, by (1) and (2) and their extensions, which are implicit in the preceding discussion). But as the above example has, in effect, demonstrated, a quantifier-ordered, place-indicated universal quantifier can be distinguished from any other by the logical features of the statements which these quantifiers bring into immediate inferential connection with the statements the quantifiers are in. Thus both quantifiers and place-indications are, through their total "inferential powers" in specific statements, distinguishable.

At this point I have covered many of the basics of what corresponds in my view to what logicians commonly call "first-order quantification." Since I have been, and will be, emphasizing the differences between my view and the more familiar views of quantification, I do not wish to employ the phrase 'first-order quantification'. Moreover, it will soon be clear that the notion of an "order" of quantification finds no interesting place in my view. So, I shall call the quantification I have been discussing "singular term quantification."

I now turn my attention to three topics closely related to the previous discussion. First, there is the topic of what I shall call "predicate quantification" which appears in statements which I call "quantified singular term statements" because they have, in the simplest cases, a singular term combined with a quantifier. (Here and in what follows I include relation-tokens under the heading of predicates.) Predicate quantification corresponds in my view to what most logicians would call "second-order quantification."

Predicate quantification introduces nothing which has not already been introduced in the discussion of singular term quantification. In fact, given that I employ a Sellarsian characterization of predicates, what I have said about quantifier place-indicating and quantifier-ordering in the case of singular term quantification applies, with little change, to predicate quantification. The main difference is that a slightly more general account of quantifier place-indicating is necessary.

Quantification of yet other kinds could be developed along similar lines. Though an example is to be found in section 6B, I shall not bother to pursue this issue at the moment.

The second topic to which I briefly address myself is E-quantification. Plainly nothing in the account of quantifier place-indicating and quantifier-ordering needs alteration in order to handle E-quantification. Further, as the simplest of several alternatives, I explain E-quantification by universal quantification and negation. Thus any E-quantified statement, i.e., any statement whose first quantifier is an E-quantifier, is the negation of a universally quantified statement. This universally quantified statement is, to put it loosely, the same as the E-quantified statement except, of course, for the universal quantifier and except for yet another negation. Given the structure of my treatment of universal quantification, an account of the negation which appears in the universally quantified statement would be handled by taking up each of the cases discussed for the universal quantifier. Although this is a tedious task, it is possible.

But, even when all this is said and done, it will still not be clear what rules of inference govern E-quantification. This difficulty arises partly because I have not discussed negation but also because the relationship of the rules of E-quantification and the rules of universal quantification would be explicated only by a discussion of practical discourse. For obvious reasons, then, no extended investigation of the rules of E-quantification can be undertaken here.

Nevertheless, something can be said about the principles of truth for E-quantified statements.

It would appear from a perusal of the principles of truth for universally quantified statements that the analogous principles for the E-quantifier should be: if an E-quantified statement is true, then some other statement (of a sort which can be described) is true and if some such statement is true, then the E-quantified statement is true. For the purposes of this book, I shall assume that the principles of truth for E-quantifiers are, in essentials, as I have just stated them. These principles of truth figure interestingly in a line of thought to which I now turn.

One of the main questions about E-quantified statements is whether, solely in virtue of being E-quantified, they are, in some sense, existence statements. A related question is whether accepting an E-quantified statement commits one, solely in virtue of the E-quantification, to the existence of anything. The importance of these questions is easily made clear. My treatment of quantification was begun, in part, in response to an objection based on a doctrine of ontological commitment which is closely linked with the objectual interpretation of quantification. I trust it is clear that whatever difficulties my account of quantification may have, one of them is <u>not</u> the problem about ontological commitment sketched by the objection. Quantification, on my view, whether it is singular term quantification or predicate quantification, has no special or privileged connection with ontological commitment. Quantification may appear in various ways in any account of ontological commitment that I might present, but the acceptance of quantified statements does not, by virtue of their being quantified, bring commitment to the existence of anything. But E-quantified statements might be though to require special attention. Thus someone might (rightly or wrongly) believe that E-quantification is sufficiently distinctive that the questions at the beginning of this paragraph must be answered in their own right apart from the general problem of quantification and commitment.

My answer to these questions is that a statement, solely in virtue of being an E-quantified statement, is not, in any sense, an existence statement, and accepting such statements does not commit one to the existence of anything. But someone may object that, though my account of quantification allows me to avoid ontological commitment to abstract entities while nonetheless allowing me predicate quantification, it does so only at the expense, contrary to what I just claimed, of making all E-quantified statements existence statements. The existence which follows from E-quantified statements is the existence of linguistic items. Certainly it is not satisfactory, the objection concludes, that every E-quantified statement, even one not concerning language, entails the existence of items of language.

There are, it seems to me, at least two different mistaken claims which together would lead someone to think that my account of E-quantification has the consequences alleged by the objection. The first is the claim that the metalinguistic characterizations of the roles of the quantifiers entail the existence of linguistic items; the second, that quantified statements entail whatever the metalinguistic characterizations of their quantifiers entail.

Both these claims are rejected by the view I am defending. I can find no grounds for the first claim save ones which suppose that the quantifiers in the metalanguage are given a different account from those in the object-language. But there is no possibility of this on the Sellarsian view which contains, as I said earlier, one account of all quantification. The second claim I also reject. The statements in the metalinguistic characterizations of the quantifiers do not "say," or "assert," the same thing as the quantified statements of which they speak. The characterizations of the roles of quantifiers do not provide definitions for quantified statements. Thus these characterizations do not turn all quantified statements into metalinguistic statements or even into strong equivalents of metalinguistic statements (any more than the characterizations of statement connectives do this).

The application of these points to the principles of truth for E-quantified statements is instructive. It would appear that, unlike the metalinguistic characterizations of the roles of quantifiers, the principles of truth do involve statements which are "equivalent" to quantified statements. Thus the statement that a certain quantified statement is true is "equivalent" to that quantified statement. Further, it does seem apparent that a statement which refers to another statement and says of it that it is true does entail the existence of the statement said to be true. Therefore, an E-quantified statement must entail the existence of a linguistic item, i.e., a statement.

But, of course, the conclusion does not, on my view, follow. The reason for this is a special case of my rejection, in the preceding paragraph, of the second claim. I deny that there is any "equivalence" between the quantified statement and the statement that this quantified statement is true stronger than agreement in truth-value. That is, the quantified statement is true if and only if the statement that it is true is true. Since all true statements agree in truth-value and all false ones agree in truth-value, I, for one, do not wish to allow that such "equivalence" is sufficient to insure that "equivalent" statements have the same entailments. (Section A of chapter 4 contains more about truth and statements of truth.) Consequently, even though I would agree that the acceptance of certain (but not all) statements asserting the truth of (an)other statement(s) commits one to the existence of linguistic items, this admission does not force me to abandon the claim that E-quantified statements are not, in virtue of being E-quantified, existence statements.

Upon reflection it will be clear that the above objection was of more general application than my statement of it made it appear. The argument of the objection, if it worked, would work not only for E-quantified statements, but for all statements quantified or not. Thus, it does not, strictly speaking, make a case for treating E-quantification as a special issue. However, there is one more line of thought that might appear to do this and also to provide an argument for the claim that, on my view, E-quantified statements are existence statements.

This line of thought begins with the observation that the principles of truth for E-quantifiers utilize E-quantification. Indeed, this is correct. Moreover, a similar claim is surely correct for the rules of inference for E-quantifiers. No doubt these rules, whichever they turn out to be, utilize E-quantification in some manner similar to that in which rules (1) and (2) for the universal quantifier utilize universal quantification. Without even considering the further development of this line of thought, I can explain my reply. My reply just invokes remarks I made in rejecting the first claim of several paragraphs back: viz., the E-quantifications which appear in the principles of truth and in the rules of inference for E-quantifiers are E-quantifiers as I have characterized them. Thus if the principles of truth and the rules of inference do require the existence of linguistic items, they do not do so solely in virtue of containing E-quantification. (This point is of particular importance in connection with the rules of inference discussed in section 5B.)

The third topic concerns what are usually called "variables." One of the features of my account of quantification is that in the entirety of the preceding discussion, I have not introduced what correspond in my view to what are usually called variables. Of course, variables can be, and could have been, introduced. After their introduction, they could have been offered as the items which, whatever else they did, were also quantifier place-indicators. But it is part of the point of my account of quantification that quantifier place-indicating need not be done by those items which correspond in my view to what are usually called variables. Indeed variables do not even have to be mentioned in order to treat quantification.

For the sake of simplicity, I deal, at first, only with what correspond in my view to "individual variables." Correspondents of other sorts of variables I explain along the same lines developed in the restricted case. I shall not talk in the following discussion about variables. Since I wish to emphasize the differences between my view and the one commonly found in logic books, I see no reason to use the term 'variable'.

What I shall be considering is a variety of linguistic items which I shall call "representatives" of other linguistic items. I shall not attempt to provide a general account of representation in the sense in which it is relevant to the present discussion, though the major themes will be apparent. Among the various kinds of representatives are those I shall call "proxies." Proxies represent whole categories of linguistic items. In accordance with my above decision, I restrict my attention to singular term proxies (STPs), though what I say about them can without difficulty be extended to other proxies.

A necessary condition of representation and, in particular, of being a proxy is similarity of role, or function. The similarity of role that is relevant to my account is similarity that is due to some of the same things being true of proxies with respect to their role as are true of singular terms with respect to their roles. As I understand representation in this discussion, the above kind of similarity insures that proxies represent each and every item of a linguistic category. If the role of STPs is shared by STPs and all singular terms, then the requirement of similarity of role is satisfied. In order for the role of STPs to be shared by STPs and all singular terms, each singular term must share part of its role with every other. Therefore, the following discussion, though it is billed as introducing STPs, is also an investigation of what each singular term has in common with respect to its role with all other singular terms with respect to their roles. To put it another way, the role played by STPs is a role each singular term plays in playing its own determinate role.

First, then, STPs are configured by predicates (in which I am still including relation tokens) as singular terms are. If I may borrow a way of speaking, I would say that STPs have the same basic "syntax" as singular terms. STPs combined with predicates are linguistic items which I call "statement representatives." For example, a linguistic item which is an STP configured with a :man: is a representative of any statement which is a singular term configured with a :man:. Since it is STPs which appear in these statement representatives, I shall call such a statement representative an "STP statement representative." (There are, of course, those statement representatives which are statement proxies, but they are not important here.)

Suppose that any statement which is a token of any singular term configured with an :animal: may be inferred from a statement with a token of the same singular term configured with a :man:. This inference does not depend on any one singular term or on the singular terms in any group of singular terms. It does depend on which singular term appears in the statements which are the premise and the conclusion, in that two tokens of the same singular term, one in the premise and one in the conclusion, must appear in the inference. But no singular term, regardless of its determinate role, is barred from appearing in both the premise and the conclusion. (I leave aside the question of "category mistakes," i.e., in this case, the question of whether any singular term can properly be configured with a :man:; if it is decided that there are categories of singular terms and that certain predicates may configure only singular terms of a specific category, it would change my discussion only to the extent that I should have to allow STPs to be "sorted.")

Given such inferences which are, in the sense described, independent of the singular terms appearing in them, we can extend the notion of inferring to encompass the move from (a) statement representative(s) to a statement representative. For example, there is an inference from the statement representative which is token of an STP configured with a :man: to the statement representative which is a token of the same STP configured with an :animal:. (There is a sense in which these inferences involving statement representatives "represent" inferences involving only statements; but it is not necessary to go into this here.) I shall call those inferences involving statement representatives "SR-inferences"; inferences involving only statements I shall call simply "inferences."

The permissibility of SR-inferences is judged by the permissibility of inferences. Which inferences are relevant to this decision for a given SR-inference is determined by which statements the statement representatives in the SR-inference represent. This brings up a new consideration concerning representation.

But, first, notice that the above paragraphs characterize a further part of the role of STPs. Both STPs and singular terms share the same "syntax" and appear in certain cases of a practical activity, i.e., inferring, in the same way. Thus far, then, the role of STPs, properly described, is a role which all singular terms play in playing their determinate roles.

The new consideration concerning representation leads to issues not unlike those already found in the case of quantifier place-indicating and quantifiers. The main point is that in judging the permissibility of SR-inferences, the statement representatives cannot, in general, be allowed to represent "independently." To use the same example, if one statement represented by one STP statement representative is picked out and the statement is a :man Socrates:, then the choice of a statement represented by the other STP statement representative is determined; it must be an :animal Socrates:. There are numerous ways of indicating nonindependence of representation. Once that is accomplished it can be employed to give an account of when, in the context of an SR-inference, two STPs are different: two STPs are different in that context if they appear in STP statement representatives which represent independently. Since this is so, the easiest way to perform the function of indicating nonindependence of representation is to distinguish the embodiments of STPs in some manner and then to state that STP statement representatives with tokens of the same STP do not represent independently. Each embodiment, of course, settles for itself which natural features of its materials characteristically indicate that one is dealing with the same STP. The most common natural characteristics chosen are the styles of the STPs (e.g., --x--s are of one style; --y--s, of another).

Without going through all the details, I note that through the function of indicating nonindependence of representation, STPs have, in specific SR-inferences, determinate roles which distinguish them from each other. (Similar remarks could be made about other contexts such as "conjunctions" of STP statement representatives.) The present situation is much like that found in the case of quantifier place-indications and quantifiers. The important point is that when I speak of _the_ role shared by STPs and singular terms, I am not speaking of the more determinate roles made possible by the function of indicating nonindependence of representation but only of the _generic_ role of _all_ _STPs_.

I turn now to another case of inferences in which singular terms appear, but appear less trivially than in the inferences just discussed. Consider a universally quantified predicate statement. One rule for universal quantification tells us that we may infer, from this statement, any statement which is any singular term combined with a token of that predicate. Since any singular term may appear in the conclusion, we can allow an inference from the universally quantified predicate statement to a statement representative which is token of that predicate combined with an STP. The generality which is brought into the rule of inference by the phrase 'any singular term' is "shown" in the SR-inference by the appearance of an STP in a statement representative which, with respect to the SR-inference itself, has no restriction on its representation. In fact, in this case, no restriction need be added because of any other STPs which may appear in other premises of a larger argument to which the SR-inference may belong.

I continue to use the example of a universally quantified predicate statement. Another rule for universal quantification says that this statement may be inferred from all the statements which are a token of that predicate combined with a singular term. The handling of this case is complicated. But the central point is clear: the inference to the universally quantified predicate statement is assured if, given our premises, we reach a statement which is a singular term combined with a token of the predicate of the universally quantified predicate statement by employing rules of inference for which the appearance of that singular term is not at all a condition for the correct application of the rule. In such circumstances, the inferences could be reproduced with any other singular term. The analogous point for the case involving an STP is that the STP statement representative in which this STP appears must not have its representation restricted by this STP in the context of the argument. The simplest condition which fulfills this requirement depends for its phrasing on the fact that dependence of representation is tied to sameness of STP. The condition is that if the STP statement representative is inferred from statements which do not contain a token of the STP which appears in the statement representative, then the universally quantified statement may be inferred from these statements. While my discussion of this point is necessarily incomplete, it should be clear that no impediment stands in the path of elaborating these matters along lines which are analogous to familiar ones.

In summary, the point of this exposition has been to illustrate how the role of STPs is played by all singular terms. The role of STPs is part of that which marks off singular terms from predicates, statements, and so on. This is not to deny that certain singular terms may be distinguishable from other singular terms by a role which the former singular terms all play and which the others do not. All that is required in my claim about the role of STPs is that all singular terms play this role, a generic role, in playing their own determinate roles.

Reflecting upon the cases that appeared in the discussion of the role of STPs, I might put my point by saying that the role STPs play is the "formal" role which all singular terms play in virtue of being singular terms. If I may revert to the *Tractatus* again, I can point out what I take to be a similarity between the view I have explained and the view of individual variables in the *Tractatus*. Remember that, roughly speaking, I have reconstructed 'individual', or 'object', in one kind of case at least, as 'individual constant', or 'singular term'. If we also reflect on what I have been saying about the "formal" role common to all singular terms, the role which is, in general, *the* role of singular term proxies, then it should not seem strange that I, too, would be willing to say:

> 4.1271 Every variable is the sign for a formal concept.
>
> For every variable represents a constant form that all its values possess, and this can

be regarded as a formal property of those values[7] (where, of course, I understand 'formal' as explained above and 'values' as 'linguistic items for which the variables, i.e., the proxies, are proxies').

All these remarks do not preclude the possibility that STPs should be given other functions which not only are not common to all singular terms but are not had by any singular term whatever. Thus there is nothing to prevent our employing STPs, in some manner or other, in quantifier place-indicating. Such a move would extend the role of STPs. What I have said about STPs and singular terms is, of course, not true of STPs in any such extended role, but only in the unextended role.

I shall, as I already have in this book, give STPs (and other proxies as well) a function in quantifier place-indicating. Further, quantifier place-indicating will be handled, with respect to the distinctive natural linguistic objects which are the materials for the embodiments of STPs, in the usual way. Thus differences of place, of quantifier place-indicator, and of singular term proxy (of other proxies as well) will be indicate, in my materials, by differences in the style of proxy. Further, for ease and familiarity of expression, I shall revert to speaking of variables, statement matrices, and instances of statement matrices, though the reader is to understand that this manner of speech does not commit me to anything but what has been explained in this chapter.

I do wish to observe that the usual notation for quantification does force on one certain distinctive devices which I have not discussed. First, there are parentheses. Second, quantifiers combine with statement matrices, instead of predicates. This arrangement has the advantage of making possible a direct physical resemblance between quantified statements and statement matrices. I shall utilize both these devices.

Finally, I note that the employment of individual variables, i.e., STPs, in quantifier place-indicating has the consequence that an instance of one of the kinds of natural linguistic objects which are produced in the tokening of STPs accompanies the natural linguistic object which is produced in the tokening of quantifiers. Which kind of natural linguistic object, of course, depends on the natural linguistic object(s) which is(are) produced in the tokening(s) of the proxy (proxies) which is(are) in the place(s) to which the quantifier is quantifier place-indicated. The crucial point, on my view, is that the tokening which produces the natural linguistic object (e.g., an --x--) that accompanies the natural linguistic object produced by the tokening of a quantifier is _not_ a tokening of an STP. An STP has the "syntax" of a singular term and, on my view, nothing of that syntax belongs with a quantifier. This point is brought up again in the next subsection.

What has been done for individual variables can also be done for predicate variables (i.e., predicate proxies). I shall not, however, go through the account for predicate variables, as it is, with obvious changes, the same as that given for individual variables.

(iii) _More About What the Sellarsian Account is Not_

In this subsection, I point out further differences between the account of subsection (ii) and the more usual accounts of variables and quantifiers.

The place to begin is with two sorts of points that have regularly been associated with the objectual interpretation of quantification. The first sort of point concerns the nature of variables; the second sort, the so-called readings of the statement matrices

(3) (Ex)Fx

and (4) (x)Fx

as (5) there is an object x such that Fx

and (6) every object x is such that Fx[8]

respectively, or as

(7) something is an object x such that Fx

and (8) everything is an object x such that Fx[9]

respectively.

I begin with the points about variables. First, variables have been said to be like pronouns.[10] On my account variables are not pronouns and not even like pronouns, save in one respect. The respect in which they are similar is that both can function in quantifier place-indicating. But one must remember that on my account variables need not be given any function in quantifier place-indicating; nor need pronouns be given any such function.

The role of pronouns is well illustrated in such statements as:

Jones stood up. Then he walked over to the table.

Speaking roughly, I would say that the main function of the word 'he' in the above statements is to insure that the second statement refers to the person that is referred to by the statement containing the word 'Jones'. This would be so regardless of which person is referred to in the first statement (given appropriate changes for gender). This example illustrates the fact that a pronoun can refer to whatever entity is required by the context. However, such reference is not involved in quantifier place-indicating. The fact that pronouns are involved in reference in one of their functions does not show that reference is involved when those natural linguistic objects which are produced in tokening pronouns are also produced in tokening quantifier place-indicators. It simply shows that the ways of achieving quantifier place-indication are quite varied. The natural linguistic objects which are materials for variables can be employed in quantifier place-indicating though variables do not refer; on the other hand, the natural linguistic objects which are the materials for pronouns can also be employed in quantifier place-indicating though pronouns are involved in reference.

Second, variables have been called "ambiguous names."[11] On my account, variables are not names, not "indefinite" names nor "ambiguous" names, not any kind of name at all.[12] They are proxies whose role is shared by all the items for which they are proxies. But playing _just this role_, while it is a necessary condition for being in a category of linguistic item (i.e., for being a singular term) and is part of what distinguishes this category of linguistic item from other categories of linguistic items, is not a sufficient condition for being in that category.

Along with the idea that variables are ambiguous names goes the idea that associated with interpreted variables is a collection of entities which the variables "range over," or which are the "range of values" of the variables, or, simply, the "values" of the variables.[13] These two ideas have an obvious affinity: if variables are ambiguous names, then there had better be some entities for them to name ambiguously. The problem of ontological commitment is now easily approached from these remarks. If a variable is an ambiguous name, or the like, and it has values, then it seems reasonable that "to be the value of a variable is to be." Or, perhaps more accurately, by claiming that there are variables with a certain range of values, we are committed to the claim that the entities in the range of values exist.[14] Of course, given what I have said about variables, I need not accept this criterion of ontological commitment or similar ones of the sort described in subsection (i).

But another argument to show that variables and quantification bequeath ontological commitment originates in reflection on the "readings" of the contrived notation for quantifiers. If (3) and (4) are to be "read" as either (5) and (6) or (7) and (8), respectively, then, so the argument goes, quantifying over a kind of entity certainly commits us to the claim that such entities exist. After all, the argument continues, the phrases before the 'Fx' in (5), (6), (7), and (8) are "specially selected, unequivocally referential idioms of ordinary language."[15] Further, in order to "read" quantification of any sort, we must, given the "readings" (5), (6), (7), and (8), introduce a category word. Thus, for example, if (3) is "read" as (5) or (7), then

(9) (EF)Fa

must by parity be "read"

(10) there is a property F such that Fa

or (11) something is a property F such that Fa.

And what could be a better indication of commitment to properties than the appearance of the term 'property' in the "readings" of (9)?

Needless to say, I am not inclined to concur with these "readings." In fact, the whole talk of "readings" is not to be found in my account. The question, on the Sellarsian account of language, is: Which English tokens are quantified statements and which are quantifiers? Before answering this question, I note that the characterizations of quantified statements are, in a respect yet unmentioned, incomplete: nothing at all has been said about the relevance or irrelevance of tense. On my view, this situation is not, in the long run, satisfactory. But, for this chapter, I shall assume it to be sufficient to say that considerations of tense do not substantially affect the issues I am discussing. Furthermore, I shall, whenever, it is necessary or convenient, change from, for example, 'man Socrates' to 'Socrates is a man' without comment on possible complications because of tenses.

Which English statements are quantified? Which English tokens are E-quantifiers and universal quantifiers? Among others, English *something*s in statements which are instances of

(12) something is (a) F

are E-quantifiers and, among others, English *everything*s in statements which are instances of

(13) everything is (a) F

are universal quantifiers. It is essential to remember that such claims do <u>not</u> imply that the natural linguistic objects which are --something--s are always produced in the tokenings of E-quantifiers. Some are, but many may not be. And the same is true of --everything--s and universal quantifiers. Furthermore, many other natural linguistic objects are produced in English tokenings of quantifiers (e.g., --some--s, --any--s, --every--s, --all--s).

Consequently, it is (12) and (13) which I offer as the English tokens which correspond, insofar as we are considering only the inferential powers of the quantifiers, to (3) and (4) respectively. In (12) and (13) the word 'object' does not appear.

On my view, there are excellent reasons why 'object'

does not appear in the English correspondents of (3) and (4) though it does in (5), (6), (7), and (8). First, I point out a simple reason. Let me take as an example

(7) something is an object x such that Fx.

What corresponds to (7) written in the technical notation is

(7.1) (Ex)(object x and Fx),

not (3). Despite the fact that <u>on</u> <u>some</u> <u>accounts</u> of quantification

(Ex)(object x)

is true, (7.1) is not the correspondent of (12).

A more important reason, on my account, is that I do not allow 'object' (or 'individual') to remain uninvestigated. On the account I provided in chapter 2, 'object' (or 'individual') is reconstructed as, roughly speaking, 'singular term'. Thus on this account of 'object', <u>all</u> the instances of (5), (6), (7), and (8) are some sort of metalinguistic statements. But this need not be the case for some instances of (3) and (4).

Of course, it is possible that (7) is supposed to be no more than a peculiar way of writing (12), a way, as it were, of writing (12) baroquely. I am happy to allow anyone, even a philosopher, to indulge his aesthetic urges, but no philosophical capital can be made from such indulgence.

Even if (7) is a peculiar way of writing, not (12), but

(14) something, x, is such that Fx,

I am not dismayed. As an English correspondent of (3), (14) would be perfectly acceptable <u>provided</u> <u>that</u> we imagined English to have been provided with proxies, with that manner of performing quantifier place-indicating which utilizes these proxies, and with the mechanism of having quantifiers combine with statement matrices. Given the satisfaction of these conditions, (12) and (14) both correspond to (3). But note the crucial point: the term 'object' does not appear in (14).

The real bite of this philosophical barking is discovered when we turn to (9) and (11) (and (10)). On my account, the very same dilemma arises in this case and for the same reasons given above: either the word 'property' does appear in (11) and thus (11) does not correspond to (9) or (11) is some baroque manner of writing something which does not contain the word 'property'. Either way the thrust of the argument from the "readings" is lost.

What, then, on my view is the English correspondent of (9)? It is not necessary on my view that English have a correspondent of (9). English speakers may not have need of the statements which would be instances of a correspondent of (9), or they may have statements, which in the contexts dealt with by ordinary speakers, are in some loose way equivalent to the instances of a correspondent of (9). However, I have no hesitation, whether it be "common" English or not, to offer

(15) a is (a) something

as the correspondent of (9).[16] Notice that (15) trades on the characteristic significance of the left-to-right order of typed English natural linguistic objects. It is clearly not necessary for (15) to contain the word 'property' (indeed, how it would be fitted in is not obvious).

Before turning to a more substantial question, I wish to consider

(16) (F)Fa.

The English correspondent of (16), on my view, would not have the word 'property', and there would be no reason to add it. This correspondent for (16) would be contrived. Such contriving, built on the word 'everything' (or, 'every'), could certainly be accomplished, but it is not worth the effort. I am by no means committed to the idea that we must find, in presently available English tokens, correspondents for anything we are able to say after considerable reflection and reasoning.

This discussion and that of subsection (ii) lead to an obvious question: Which statements are existence statements? A complete answer to this question cannot be undertaken here. But I am prepared to give examples of statements which are, in some sense, existence statements. First, there are those statements I called in section 1D "numerical quantifier statements." Numerical quantifiers are those quantifiers which combine with general terms to form statements which say exactly how many of some sort there are. As we shall see in detail in chapter 4, these quantifiers have characterizations which involve the universal quantifier and the E-quantifier.

Why should numerical quantifier statements be, in some sense, existence statements while E-quantified statements are not? In part, the answer is that numerical quantifiers are characterized not only by the two ordinary quantifiers but also by identity (and difference) and that numerical quantifiers combine only with general terms, i.e., sortal predicates, and not with just any predicate. Thus numerical quantifiers are sufficiently unlike the two ordinary quantifiers that an attempt to argue that numerical quantifier statements are, in some sense, existence statements, though E-quantified statements are not, is not doomed to failure at the outset.

I shall not, however, attempt to make such a case for two reasons. First, that numerical quantifier statements are existence statements is not crucial for the reconstructions of chapter 4. Second, the sense in which numerical quantifier statements are existence statements is not, from the perspective of the philosophical debate over ontological commitment, very interesting. So that there should be no confusion about these two claims, I hasten to point out what they do not say.

The first does not claim that it is irrelevant to the doctrines of this book that numerical quantifier statements are, in some sense, existence statements. On the contrary, it is their being existence statements which is essential to their connection, mentioned in section 1D, with "numerousness" in its basic manifestations. This connection is the source of one of the intuitive considerations which lend support to the move of placing numerical quantifiers in a central position in the account of natural numbers. But, thought this is true, it does not figure in any way into the work done in chapter 4, and thus pursuing this connection would lead us too far astray.

The emphasis of the second reason must be on the phrase 'from the perspective of the philosophical debate on ontological commitment'. I shall state my position on this issue baldly: from a philosophical perspective, the only things one can be committed to the existence of are "simple," not "complex," entities. *Within the framework of a general philosophical view which has some claim to having done justice to the relevant issues*, the claim that certain sorts of entities are "complex" is the essential premise in the argument that one is not committed to the existence of these entities. Notice, first, that the "complexity" of these entities need not be understood in any one way (thus, for example, as solely a matter of "parts" and "wholes"). Second, according to the philosophical position I am defending, all talk of the "complexity" of entities is really talk about language. To show "complexity" is to show the eliminability of certain linguistic items (within, as I said, a general philosophical view which can defend itself tolerably well on the relevant issues). In the cases discussed in this book, the linguistic items are those singular terms and general terms found in discourse about abstract entities; and the argument for eliminability is lengthy, since it includes both theses about these linguistic items and theses about the statements involved in the reconstructions of these linguistic items.

The existence involved in numerical quantifier statements is, by contrast to that just discussed, a "common" or "garden-variety." Thus if we suppose that houses of cards are "complex" and cards are the "simples" with respect to which the "complexity" of houses of cards is to be understood, it may still be true to say, in a given situation, that there are ten cards on a table and there is one house of cards on the table. Numerical quantifier statements are not, as it were, sensitive to differences of "complexity" and "simplicity."

It will have been noted that in my selection of common or garden-variety existence statements, I have not included certain of the statements in whose English tokening --there is a(n)--s are produced. Some of these statements are existence statements in, I suspect, the same sense as numerical quantifier statements, for they, too, must contain sortal predicates and not just any predicates. But we must remember that --there is a(n)--s are also produced in the tokening of statements some of which are merely E-quantified, some of which are numerical quantifier statements, and some of which are involved with spatial location. I shall take it that the garden-variety existence statements which involve the production of --there is a(n)--s and which are not of any of the sorts just mentioned are those which are adequately rewritten in English with the phrase 'there is at least one'. More is said about this phrase and related ones in 4A and 5B.

Moreover, the recognition of this second species of garden variety existence statement does not confer, on my account, any new philosophical difficulties. It does, however, give me an additional reason, over and above those already given, for rejecting (5) as the English correspondent of (3). I do not agree with the sentiment that the E-quantifier is "modeled" after 'there is a(n)'.[17] The English phrase has a role which requires that it combine with sortal predicates. The E-quantifier combines with any predicate and, according to my view, even with singular terms in the case of predicate quantification. The role of :there is a(n):s is too restricted for statements with :there is a(n):s to be the correspondents of instances of (3). This way of putting it highlights the fact that, on my account, English contains (not completely worked out) several quantificational devices, only one of which, viz., the "something-everything" idioms, is "modeled" by quantificational logic.

The final topic of this subsection is a reply to an objection which arises because of certain similarities between the Sellarsian account of quantification and the substitution interpretation. The substitution interpretation, in some of its forms, is not without difficulties. For example, according to the substitution account of the universal quantifier given in subsection (i), the inference from

Fa, Fb, Fc, ...,

where this list includes <u>all</u> the substitution instances of 'Fx' available in the language, to

(x)Fx

ought to be valid. But any formal language has some precisely delimited stock of substituends for any variable. Thus in the case of the individual variable in our example any formal language has a precisely delimited stock of substituends for this variable. Let us call these substituends "singular terms." Now the criticism of the substitution interpretation can be stated as follows: from the fact that, under a given assignment of individuals to the singular terms and classes (or properties and relations) to predicates, all the instances of 'Fx' are true in some formal language, it does not follow that the formula '(x)Fx' is true in that language. After all, the domain of the semantics of the formal language may contain indivivuals which have been assigned no singular term in the language and which may <u>not</u> be in the class assigned to the letter 'F' (or may <u>not</u> have the property assigned to the letter 'F'). Crudely put, a formal language may not, under any given assignment from the class of admissible assignments, "name" all the individuals in the domain. Thus the above inference may lead from true premises to a false conclusion.

Within the most generally accepted tenets of semantic formalism it is possible to provide a response to this criticism, which is obviously a telling one against the simple form of the substitution interpretation I have sketched. This response is possible because of a maneuver which is usually attributed to Professor Leon Henkin. In simplest terms, the maneuver depends on being able to add another singular term to the singular terms of a given language. The result of adding this new singular term to the singular terms of a formal language is to produce a formal language which is an extension of the original language. A sequence of such extensions can be constructed by simply repeating the same maneuver with each new formal language. Since the criticism depends on the deficiencies of single formal languages, the response is to consider <u>all</u> these extensions of a formal language (where the language is understood to be one of its extensions). Then, roughly speaking, '(x)Fx' is true in L if and only if all the substitution instances of 'Fx' in all the extensions of L are true. That this response to the criticisms is mathematically satisfactory can be shown.[18] Whether it answers all the problems of the criticism is irrelevant to my present purpose. The point of this excursion into the debate on the substitution interpretation is that what I have thus far sketched is similar to an objection that might be thought to apply to the Sellarsian account of quantification.

That this sort of objection is not applicable to the Sellarsian account of quantification, despite its superficial resemblance to the substitution interpretation, follows directly from the Sellarsian account of language. The Sellarsian characterization of the universal quantifier does speak of _all_ statements of a certain kind. But on the Sellarsian account, to talk of all statement or all statements of a certain kind is not to talk about statements in some one natural or contrived language, i.e., in some one embodiment. Statements and statements of a certain kind (e.g., relational, predicate, conjunctive, etc.) are characterized by role, i.e., functionally. No reference to embodiments of role structures is made in these characterizations.

Thus the Sellarsian talk of "all statements" is not limited in the way in which the analogous talk of the defender of the substitution interpretation is. The lack of such a limitation is sufficient to prevent the objection from going through since there is no way to establish, on the Sellarsian view, the validity of the inference described above. That is, on the Sellarsian view, even if one set out conditions satisfied by denumerably many statements of a given kind, there would be no reason to believe that a denumerable list would contain all the statements of that kind. The exact reasons for this situation are complicated,[19] but it is a corollary to the fact that the embodiments which are our languages and the structure of roles our languages embody are in a variety of ways inadequate. Thus our claim in any such language to _list_, even denumerably, all the statements of a given kind cannot, in general, be supported. The inferences that are sanctioned by rule (2) are not, in general, such as begin with a list of the sort envisaged in the case of the formal language employed by the defender of the substitution interpretation. In summary, on the Sellarsian view, the functional characterizations of statements and other categories of linguistic item ensure that, in general, the "reach" of a universally quantified statement exceeds the resources of the language in which it is tokened.

B. Linguistic Rules, Entailments, and Necessary Statements

(i) Linguistic Rules Again

In section 2A, I commented briefly on linguistic rules. Now that I am approaching the end of my general discussion, I wish to comment again on linguistic rules and, in particular, on the general form of rules of inference.

Let us begin with an example of a rule of inference:

2E(18.1) (INDCON)((:trilateral: INDCON)s may be inferred from (:triangular: INDCON)s).

This rule was developed in the reconstruction of

2E(11) triangularity entails trilaterality.

With certain minor qualifications, 2E(18.1) can serve as a standard example of a rule of inference. The first qualification is that we cannot, in general, suppose that a rule of inference can be formulated as a completely unconditional rule, as 2E(18.1) is. Hence, in general, a rule of inference will begin with

given C,....

Second, in its complete form, a rule of inference will also include some specification of the group of persons to whom the rule applies. Thus we have, for example, given C, speakers of English may....

Third, rules which begin by specifying the speakers of some particular natural language, like English, may contain asterisk-quote general terms instead of colon-quote general terms. Correspondingly, the metalinguistic variables in such a rule must be understood as variables for asterisk-quote general terms.

In addition to rules of inference, we could have rules pertaining to unconditional tokening. Thus we could have

(17) (STAT)(speakers of Human Language may token (:if: STAT :then: STAT)s).

But any such rules can be derived from rules of inference. In the case of (17) the relevant rules of inference are those of statement logic. Later we shall have examples of unconditionally tokenable statements which depend on the rules of quantificational logic. But, for the most part, I shall treat only of rules of inference, while assuming that my remarks are transferable to rules of unconditional tokening.

There are, as well, other rules pertaining to inference, those which forbid tokenings either conditionally or unconditionally. These rules, though important, are not incorporated into either the previous reconstructions or those of chapter 4.

This subsection is also intended to remind the reader that entailment (which I take to be one kind of implication[20]) is reconstructed by permitted inference. This general feature of my strategy thus far is well illustrated in the example of 2E(11) and 2E(18.1).

No one would claim that the philosophical literature on entailment has been entirely unproblematic; the truth of the matter is nearly the opposite. But there are several properties characteristically attributed to entailments. And no matter how confused and benighted the philosophical practice involving this term, any reconstruction of 'entails' must supply some account of these alleged properties.

I shall, therefore, consider the following claims about entailments. First, according to many philosophers, entailments cannot be rendered in classical statement and quantificational logic and hence are not, in one sense, truth-functional. Second, entailments are held to be one variety of necessary statement and thus to have the properties ascribed to necessary statements. Examples of such properties are timelessness with respect to truth and falsity and epistemological worthiness (or, unworthiness) that is not based on the actual course of our world. Third, some philosophers have said, in part by way of accounting for the necessity of entailments, that the truth (or, falsity) of entailments, indeed all necessary statements, depends on the meanings of the terms which appear in them. I take up this view under the slogan "necessary truths are true *ex vi terminorum*."

In the following three subsections, I take up these topics and make what remarks I conveniently can make within a limited space. I do not, however, wish to suggest that these topics are unimportant to the later parts of this work. My treatment of elementary mathematics utilizes much the same notions and machinery as my reconstructions of entailments. Moreover, mathematical statements are often thought of as prime examples of necessary statements. What I say in these subsections must serve as a guide to what I would say about these topics as they appear in the context of the philosophy of mathematics.

(ii) Truth-functionality and Entailment

A view to which I myself subscribe is that entailments

cannot be adequately transcribed into classical extensional logic. My reconstruction accounts for this by turning them into rules of inference. This places the burden of the non-extensionality with respect to classical logic on the fact that these statements prove after investigation to be in the most general case, of the following sort:

(18) given C, speakers of Human Language may infer ... from ___

or, deleting the reference to the speakers as I usually do, of the sort:

(19) given C, ... may be inferred from ___.

Hence the fact that entailments cannot be adequately transcribed in classical extensional logic is due to their being instances of (19). Since (19) contains a modal word which is neither part of the primitive vocabulary of classical logic nor definable in that vocabulary, (19) cannot be reproduced in classical statement or quantificational logic.

It is important to note that my remarks in the above paragraph speak to but one of two separate and often confused strands in the debate over truth-functionality. These strands are summed up by the following two statements which do not, on my account, agree in truth-value:

(20) The notion of entailment cannot be rendered in the vocabulary of classical truth-functional logic.

(21) Entailment statements are instances of statements

[i] which are logically complex in that other statements occur within them

and yet

[ii] whose truth values are not a func-

tion of the truth values of the statements occurring within them.

I have claimed that (20) is true because entailment statements are reconstructed as statements which contain a logical constant which is not part of the vocabulary of classical truth-functional logic and which cannot be defined in terms of that vocabulary. On the other hand, on my view statement (21) is false. It is false because in the rules which are the reconstructions of entailments _no statements occur_, though, of course, general terms true of statements occur.

Some philosophers have thought that in entailment statements such as

that a is triangular entails that a is trilateral

other statements, an :a is triangular: and an :a is trilateral:, occur. Given my reconstruction of the above entailment statement, neither an :a is triangular: nor an :a is trilateral: nor any other statement occurs in it. What is true is that two natural linguistic objects, an --a is triangular-- and an --a is trilateral--, are parts of the natural linguistic object produced in the tokening of the entailment in English. Of course, it is also true that an --a is triangular-- appears in any English token of the Sellarsian general term ':a is triangular:'. But this demonstrates only that instances of a kind of natural linguistic object may be produced in tokenings of different types, as was clear from my discussion in chapter 2. Thus --a is triangular--s characteristically occur in English tokenings of both :a is triangular:s and ::a is triangular::s. But an :a is triangular: is not of the same type as an ::a is triangular::. An :a is triangular: is a statement; an ::a is triangular::, a general term.

Thus, unlike the views of many who have discussed entailments, my account of entailments is entirely consistent with the classical thesis of truth-functionality: namely, that the truth-value of any statement within which other statements do occur is determined by the truth-value of these latter statements.

(iii) Necessity and Entailment

This subsection takes up properties which entailments are alleged to have in virtue of being necessary statements. Two such properties were listed at the end of subsection (i): epistemological worthiness (or unworthiness) that is not based on the actual course of our world and timelessness with respect to truth and falsity. I begin with the topic of epistemological worthiness and give an account of this matter which captures what seems to me to be sensible and intelligible in the traditional talk about this topic.

Let us review several properties of the rules of inference that are the reconstruction of entailment statements like 2E(11). First, these rules are general in two respects. They involve, like

> 2E(18.1) (INDCON)((:trilateral: INDCON)s may be inferred from (:triangular: INDCON)s),

metalinguistic universal quantification with the variable 'INDCON' and plurals. Second, like 2E(18.1), they contain no token that refers to or requires the existence of some particular object, event, or circumstance, not even a linguistic object, event, or circumstance.

All this is not to say that there is no sense in which 2E(18.1) refers to or is about particular things, indeed concrete objects. Given that :a:s are individual constants, 2E(18.1) entails

> (22) (:trilateral:)(:a:)s may be inferred from (:triangular:)(:a:)s

and this becomes, by an application of the rules pertaining to the composition of SGTs,

(23) :trilateral a:s may be inferred from :triangular a:s.

Rule (23) governs such reasonings as

triangular a
hence, trilateral a.

The statements which figure in these reasonings are singular statements and are directly about an object, and their truth does require the existence of that object. Hence, since rule (23) governs reasonings with these singular statements, we can say that (23) is "indirectly about" what these singular statements are about. Then because (23) follows from 2E(18.1), 2E(18.1) can also be said to be "indirectly about" what (23) is indirectly about.

More importantly, all linguistic rules, like all general statements, are, in another sense, about things. What 2E(18.1) and (23) are about in this latter sense are linguistic items. Consider (23), which is the reconstruction of

(24) that triangular a entails that trilateral a.

In virtue of being a general statement a rule like (23) is about all statements of the types specified in the rule. Rule 2E(18.1) shares this feature with (23) and hence is about all the statements that (23) is about and is also about all the statements which differ from :triangular a:s and :trilateral a:s only in the singular terms they contain.

However, given my characterization of 'indirectly about', it does not follow from the statement that (23) is indirectly about triangular and trilateral things that

there exist triangular and trilateral things which

(23) is indirectly about.

Second, it no more follows from the statement that (23) is about :triangular a:s and about :trilateral a:s that

> there exist :triangular a:s and there exist :trilateral a:s which (23) is about

than it follows from

> the statement that all dodoes are birds is about dodoes

that

> there exist dodoes which the statement that all dodoes are birds is about.

Similar remarks obtain for 2E(18.1). Hence the fact that these rules of inference, and hence entailments, are, in several senses, about things does not show that these rules of inference require the existence of anything.

Thus, my first claim, given the points of the last paragraph and of the second paragraph of this subsection, is that from these rules of inference, and hence from entailments, it does not follow that anything exists.

A third feature of the rules of inference that reconstruct entailments is that they speak of what _may_ be inferred. They do not say anything about what _is_ or _is_ _not_ the case. Of course, it does not follow that what is or is not the case is not at all relevant to a rule of inference. But whatever the connection, it surely is not very direct.

We can easily give examples of the sort of statement which has very direct connections with what is or what is not the case. Consider a statement which is a :this horse is brown:. That this statement is in one way directly connected with what is or is not the case is trivially obvious; after all, it says of some horse that it is brown. But there is another way in which this statement is connected with what is or is not the case: it contains a demonstrative and a tense indication which tie it to some particular circumstances. And whether or not the statement is credible, i.e., worthy of our belief (or acceptance), depends on what circumstances the statement is tokened in.

My second claim is that rules are not connected with any particular circumstances in this direct way. A rule's being tokened in the circumstances in which it is tokened could not be what is required for these circumstances to be relevant to its credibility. That is, even if the particular circumstances in which a rule is tokened are relevant to its credibility, this will not be so <u>because</u> the rule is tokened in these circumstances. The relevance or irrelevance of the circumstances is independent of the question of which circumstances the rule was in fact tokened in. And this is just what is not so for statements which contain token reflexives or full-fledged tense indicators.

It seems to me that my two claims about these rules of inference, and hence about entailments, capture important parts of traditional claims about necessary statements. Thus, given my claims, entailment statements do not require the existence of the spatio-temporal items they are indirectly about or the existence of the linguistic items they are about, and their truth-value and credibility do not depend directly on their being tokened in any particular circumstance. Thus, in these two ways and in virtue of being reconstructed as statements about what is permitted, the epistemological worthiness (or unworthiness) of entailments is, on my reconstruction, independent of the course of our world.

The other property to be discussed in this subsection is that necessary truths are timelessly true. They are said to contain neither token reflexives nor tenses. Is this true of the rules which are the reconstructions of entailments? Though they contain no token reflexives, they are tensed and indeed in the present tense (with qualifications which will emerge in the ensuing discussion). Rules like 2E(18.1) speak of what is permitted, not what will be permitted at some future time nor what was permitted at some past time. This admission commits me to the position that at least some necessary truths are really not timeless nor atemporal, as they have often been held to be. And I do hold this to be true. However, that there is nothing very damaging about this admission can be seen from what follows. (The ensuing discussion is restricted to entailments between concepts, though it could be extended to other entailments and other necessary truths with little alteration.)

The difficulties over maintaining that entailments like 2E(11) are in the present tense center around the fact that it seems strange to say

(25) triangularity did entail trilaterality

or (26) triangularity will entail trilaterality.

Yet if 2E(11) is in the present tense, one would think that there should be nothing strange about (25) and (26) and that they might even be true.

The strangeness of (25) and (26) is heightened by the following argument. The appearance of full-fledged, ordinary past, present, and future tenses in (25), 2E(11), and (26), respectively, implies that it is possible that 2E(11) is false, i.e., that triangularity does not entail trilaterality. The point, put in general terms, is that the three basic tenses appear as their proper selves only in contexts in which it is possible that the statements in which they appear are false. Presumably then, the argument continues, anyone who wishes to maintain that 2E(11) is necessary must deny that it is possible that triangularity does not entail trilaterality and hence deny that full-fledged tenses appear in (25), 2E(11), and (26).

My reply to this line of thought is straightforward. First, the argument is not unambiguous about the terms 'possible' and 'necessary'. In one sense of 'possible', i.e., 'logically possible', it _is_ possible that triangularity does not entail trilaterality. That this fact is without dire consequences should have been obvious from the beginning, since no one should take 2E(11) as a truth of logic and the necessity of 2E(11) as logical necessity. However, if 'it is possible that 2E(11) is false' means that the falsity of 2E(11) is consistent with our rules of inference, both logical and nonlogical, then it _is not_ possible that 2E(11) is false, since 2E(18.1) is one of our rules. Second, the argument contains a premise the force of which, in light of the first point, is difficult to assess. It is just not clear in what sense of 'possible' it must be true that statements with full-fledged tenses are possibly false.

But rather than continue this line of exploration, I suggest that the peculiarity of (25) and (26) can be explained if we elaborate a point contained in my discussions in chapter 2. Let me approach this point by reminding the reader of a tenet of my view of conceptual meaning: having meaning is having a linguistic role, i.e., being caught up in a system of human behavior governed by rules among which are rules of inference. It follows that adopting a new rule of inference for predicates or discarding one literally alters linguistic roles. Let me say the same thing differently. The linguistic rules are literally constitutive of the meaning of the items of language. Thus (with minor qualifications made in the next section), changing the rules is changing the meaning of these items. For instance, in contemplating doing without rule 2E(18.1), which now pertains to :triangular:s, we are contemplating changing the role of the tokenings which are now :triangular:s. Indeed, we are contemplating doing without :triangular:s, since one of the present criteria for being a :triangular: is the prescriptive property derived directly from 2E(18.1). And hence we are envisaging a world which would not have the constructed, distributive individual triangularity. Though natural linguistic objects which are --triangularity--s might still appear in this world, these natural linguistic objects could not be produced in tokenings of a singular term which stands for the constructed object that the singular term 'triangularity' stands for in our world. (The same is, of course, true of 'trilaterality'.)

What then can be said about (25) and (26)? First, insofar as they lead us to envisage other worlds and different (though related) conceptual schemes, they suggest something that is irrelevant to any linguistic behavior involving our present concepts, whether this linguistic behavior occurs in the past, present, or future. This fact tends to distinguish the tenses in 2E(11), (25), and (26) from tenses in more ordinary contexts.

But this point is minor compared to another one drawn from the last paragraph: if the singular term tokens in 2E(11), (25), and (26) are all our :triangularity:s and hence all stand for the same distributive individual, then the truth of (25) and (26) follows from the truth of 2E(11). Put loosely, in order for (25) and (26) to talk about the same distributive individual as 2E(11), i.e., triangularity, they cannot, given that 2E(11) is true, be false. And this point, I take it, goes a long way toward demonstrating that entailments participate in inferences not available to more ordinary tensed statements.

On the other hand, this point does not demonstrate that entailments are tenseless or atemporal. It does, I hope, demonstrate that their involvement with temporality and tense is quite complicated. We cannot explicate this involvement without shifting the discussion from its present level to a more penetrating treatment of rules of inference. Such a shift, while necessary to prove that (25) and (26) really do say something completely intelligible, is not necessary to demonstrate that my qualified admission about the tense of 2E(11) does not lead to immediate, damaging consequences.

(iv) Truth *ex vi terminorum* and Entailment

One by-product of the discussion of entailment and tense is that the essentials for a treatment of 'true *ex vi terminorum*' are at hand. Little more need be said to show that I can provide an explication of the claim that entailments are, if true, true *ex vi terminorum*, i.e., true in virtue of the meanings of their terms. Entailment statements are unreconstructed forms of rules of inference. And rules of inference are constitutive of the role of tokenings which they govern. For example, there would be no :triangular:s and no :trilateral:s without rule 2E(18.1). The Sellarsian general terms ':triangular:' and ':trilateral:' would not, without 2E(18.1), have the same criteria. And we have seen in chapter 2 that 'triangularity' and 'trilaterality' require ':triangular:' and ':trilateral:', respectively, in their reconstructions. Hence without rule 2E(18.1), 'triangularity' and 'trilaterality' would not have the roles they do. Therefore, the truth of the entailment statement 2E(11) is a necessary condition of 'triangularity' and 'trilaterality' having the meanings they do. On the other hand, our acceptance of all the rules pertaining to :triangular:s and :trilateral:s is clearly a sufficient condition of 'triangularity' and 'trilaterality' having the meanings they do. Hence, the truth of entailments which speak of triangularity or trilaterality is a necessary and sufficient condition of 'triangularity' and 'trilaterality' having the meanings they do. Thus entailments are true _ex vi terminorum_.

An account of the necessity of entailments also follows from the fundamentals of my account of meaning, rules of inference, and entailment. The very same facts about an entailment which account for its being true ex vi terminorum, if true, also account for its necessity. The following remarks depend on the argument of the last paragraph and my comments in the previous subsection on tense and possibility.

A given entailment is true in each world of some collection of worlds and false in all the worlds not in that collection. But any specification of a world which is sufficient to distinguish it from all other worlds determines which entailments are true and which are false in that world. For example, if a world is specified by which objects it contains and which properties and relations they can exemplify, the entailments that are true in this world can be determined from the specifications of the objects, properties, and relations of this world. Suppose that in a given world an object can exemplify triangularity. Then, on my account, 2E(11) must be true in that world since it is reconstructed as the rule 2E(18.1) and either this rule or an equivalent rule must be referred to in the specification of triangularity as a property of that world.

An alleged property of necessary statements which has not been discussed is incorrigibility. My treatments of necessity and truth _ex vi terminorum_ and, before that, of entailments and tense lend little support to the notion that entailments, or for that matter necessary truths in general, are incorrigible. Of course, it is no idle nor minor matter to decide to abandon a rule of inference or to accept a new rule, for, to use traditional terminology, such rules determine the meanings of the terms in our language. Thus, roughly speaking, tampering with the rules is changing our conceptual scheme. Thus, though it is possible to abandon a rule or to accept a new one, we are not likely, and ought not to do such a thing without good reason.

These remarks raise the question of whether I am committed to any form of what has been called "conventionalism." The answer is, I think, that I am not committed to many claims typical of conventionalism as it has usually been adumbrated. First, I do not hold that we, or anyone else, literally made up all our linguistic rules nor that it is proper for us, or anyone else, to make up arbitrarily or to stipulate any of our linguistic rules. Of course, some rules were made up and then accepted by us or our ancestors and others have been abandoned by us or our ancestors. But this process is a rational one and requires a great deal of critical reasoning as a prelude to any such acceptance or rejection. Second, I do not think that rules are in any way "ultimate." They are certainly not epistemologically ultimate in the sense that citing a rule necessarily puts an end to disagreement. One is still faced with the task of showing that the linguistic rule is one we do accept and, even if one has done that, of supporting the claim that it is a reasonable rule, one that ought to be accepted.

I subscribe to only one tenet which is reminiscent of conventionalism: the claim that we might have other linguistic rules. But, of course, I understand this claim not as "We might have other linguistic rules if we wanted them," but rather as "We might have other linguistic rules if sufficiently weighty reasons were given for having them." In view, then, of my divergences from accepted expositions of conventionalism, I shall continue to use the phrase 'linguistic rule' or just 'rule' and not use the word 'convention', thereby saving myself from the unwanted implications of this term.

Finally, I must disavow any claim that coming to know linguistic rules or entailments and other implications involves anything mysterious, e.g., *a priori* intuition. On the contrary, many of these rules are learned, by and large, as a whole in coming to learn a natural language. The remainder are learned by further study in which the usual techniques appropriate to the discipline under study are employed.

C. Identity and Abstract Entities

Most philosophers, I take it, would agree that my treatment of abstract entities is not complete until I say something about the problem of the identity of abstract entities. This section takes up part of that problem; in chapter 5, I return to the problem as it appears in my reconstruction of elementary mathematics. The discussion of this section highlights only one sort of abstract entity, viz., concepts; the doctrines expounded for them are with appropriate alterations applicable to other sorts of abstract entities.

My remarks are restricted to reconstructions of concepts. Reconstructions have certain features which ordinary language embodiments of concepts generally lack. In a reconstruction, it is decided, as far as it is relevant to the reconstruction, which concepts are primitive and which defined and which rules of inference are primitive and which derived. My discussion includes no account of the sort of reflection on one's own language which goes into making such decisions.

The main question of this section is whether

(27) triangularity = trilaterality

is true. In order to get the necessary running start, I turn to a discussion of definition and to an even simpler example than that of triangularity and trilaterality. The reason for treating definition is that, in my preferred reconstruction of our geometric concepts, triangularity and trilaterality are defined.

The sort of definition which is germane to this section is what I shall call "explicit" definition. All explicit definitions are reconstructed as special rules of inference. Thus an explicit definition of a predicate permits the inference, from a truth of logic, of a universally quantified biconditional with the defined predicate as the sole predicate of one statement matrix of the biconditional and the defining predicate as the sole predicate of the other statement matrix of the biconditional. The truth of logic is a universally quantified biconditional with the defining predicate as the sole predicate of both statement matrices of the biconditional. Further, the defining predicate must have a complexity which is due to logical connectives or quantifiers or both and which is not present in the defined predicate.

Suppose, as it is usually put, that 'squed' is defined as 'square and red'. This definition permits us to infer the universally quantified biconditional

> (28) (x)(x is squed if and only if x is square and red)

from the truth of logic

> (29) (x)(x is square and red if and only if x is square and red).

<u>With (28)</u>, it follows that the inferential powers of :squed:s and :square and red:s are, <u>in one sense</u>, the same: namely,

> (INDCON)(any statement that may be inferred from a (:square and red: INDCON) may also be inferred from a (:squed: INDCON) and vice versa).

Further, by an obvious line of reasoning the following two

rules are derived rules of inference:

(30) (INDCON)((:square and red: INDCON)s may be inferred from (:squed: INDCON)s)

and (31) (INDCON)((:squed: INDCON)s may be inferred from (:square and red: INDCON)s).

Thus it is true that

(32) squedity entails square-and redity

and (33) square-and-redity entails squedity.

Definitional equivalence is easily introduced into the example: squedity and square-and-redity are definitionally equivalent if and only if (28) is inferred directly from (29). Given my reconstruction of concepts, definitional equivalence could be introduced by means of a similar notion for predicates (in this case :squed:s and :square and red:s); but nothing would be gained in the present context by doing so.

Is it true that

(34) squedity = square-and-redity?

On my view the answer is no. Neither the mutual entailment of squedity and square-and-redity nor their definitional equivalence is sufficient for the truth of (34).

Essentially, (34) is false because :squed:s are not :square and red:s and :square and red:s are not :squed:s. All :square and red:s have a complexity that is due to the logical connective I call "predicate conjunction." A tokening of a :square and red: is also a tokening of a :square: and a :red:. But :squed:s lack this complexity.

Notice another very important way in which the complexity of :square and red:s is manifested <u>directly in inference</u>. Given the account of conjunctive predicates in subsection A(ii),

(35) a is square

follows from

(36) a is square and red

as shown by:

a is square and red
hence, a is square and a is red
hence, a is square.

However, (35) follows from

(37) a is squed

only by (28) (or by (30)). Thus (37) is one step further removed from (35) than (36) is.

This point is not affected by the fact that we can derive the rules

(38) (INDCON)((:square: INDCON)s may be inferred from (:square and red: INDCON)s)

and (39) (INDCON)((:square: INDCON)s may be inferred from (:squed: INDCON)s).

Rule (38) gives us a one-step derivation of (35) from (36); rule (39), a one-step derivation of (35) from (37). But :square and red:s and :squed:s still differ in complexity in that the derivation of rule (39) requires (28) (or (30)) while the derivation of rule (38) does not.

Are there, on my view, any identities like (34) which are true? Suppose 'ruare' is defined as 'square and red'. Then what has been said about :squed:s and squedity also holds for :ruare:s and ruareness. Further, the core of ruareness is given by its definition, and this core is exactly the same as the core of squedity. Thus it is true that

ruareness = squedity

and :ruare:s are :squed:s and vice versa

though, of course, --ruare--s are not --squed--s.

Before returning to triangularity and trilaterality, I want to point out that the above remarks do not commit me to any view of the conditions under which one is justified in offering a definition. But I shall offer one observation on this subject. The logician's notion of definability is such that a term is definable by another term if and only if an appropriate equivalence involving both terms is derivable from a set of sentences. In certain circumstances, the analog of definability in my account provides a necessary, but not sufficient, condition for offering a definition. Thus as we shall see, the equivalence between triangularity and trilaterality is not sufficient justification by itself for offering of definition of one in terms of the other.

I turn now to my preferred reconstruction of triangularity and trilaterality. In this reconstruction, the cores of these concepts are given by explicit definition. For simplicity's sake, let us suppose that 'triangular' is defined as 'three-angled and plane-figured' and 'trilateral' as 'three-sided and plane-figured'. Assuming that being three-angled and plane-figured is not the same as being three-sided and plane-figured, I conclude that the cores of triangularity and trilaterality are not the same and, by the sort of reasoning illustrated above, that

(40) triangularity = trilaterality,

(41) :triangular:s are :trilateral:

and (42) :trilateral:s are :triangular:s

are all false.

The falsity of (40), (41), and (42) can also be seen directly in the inferences involving :triangular:s and :trilateral:s. The statement

(43) a is three-angled

may be inferred from

a is triangular

by definition and the rules of logic. But (43) may be inferred from

a is trilateral

only by invoking the derived equivalence

(44) (x)(x is triangular if and only if x is trilateral)

and the rules of logic or by invoking the derived rule which is the reconstruction of

(45) trilaterality entails triangularity.

Thus the inferential "mediation" illustrated in this example shows that :triangular:s and :trilateral:s do not have the same properties with respect to inference and thus that triangularity and trilaterality are not identical.

Further, as in the case of :squed:s and :square and red:s, the fact that we can derive the rules

(INDCON)((:three-angled: INDCON)s may be inferred from (:triangular: INDCON)s)

and (INDCON)((:three-angled: INDCON)s may be inferred from (:trilateral: INDCON)s)

does not affect the above point. The same reasons apply in this case as in the previous case.

The rules that reconstruct the entailments 2E(11) and (45) guarantee that :triangular:s and :trilateral:s have, in the sense characterized in the case of :squed:s and :square and red:s, the same inferential powers. But these rules are derived rules which are not derived from the rules of logic alone; moreover, the equivalence (44), is a derived equivalence which is not derived solely and directly from a truth of logic. Thus triangularity and trilaterality are not even definitionally equivalent.

No doubt being angled and being sided may themselves be reconstructed as complex concepts with cores. In such a case the cores of being sided and being angled might contain exactly the same simple concepts. However, even if this were the case, it would not follow that being angled and being sided were identical and thus that triangularity and trilaterality were identical, since cores are different if their simple concepts are combined differently. Thus suppose 'sred' is defined as 'square or red'. Then sredity is not identical to squedity even though their cores have exactly the same concepts. This nonidentity is reflected directly in inferences and would not be altered, for reasons of the sort given above, even if it were demonstrable that

(x)(x is square if and only if x is red).

There are other reconstructions of triangularity and trilaterality which preserve their cores and yet do not define them. In these cases the cores are preserved by the primitive rules of inference. For example, in the case of triangularity, its core is preserved if it is possible by primitive rules alone to infer

a is triangular

from a is three-angled and plane-figured

and vice versa. Similar remarks hold for trilaterality and being three-sided and plane-figured. Under these conditions the above remarks about triangularity and trilaterality still obtain. Even the differences in inferential mediation noted before are still present.

There are other reconstructions of our geometrical concepts that do not preserve what I have taken (for simplicity's sake) to be the cores of triangularity and trilaterality. Such reconstructions, though perhaps justified for certain purposes, are not, it seems to me, reasonably faithful to our concepts. Notice, though, that in a reconstruction in which triangularity does not have the core, being three-angled and plane-figured, what has been said about triangularity in the previous reconstructions is, in the present reconstruction, true of some concept with the core, being three-angled and plane-figured. The relations between the cores of the complex concepts are kept unless the reconstruction abandons the simple concepts which appear in the cores or the logical means of assembling these simple concepts.

We must pursue this topic a bit further for an obvious objection arises from the observation that a complex concept embodied in our ordinary language may have different cores in different reconstructions of the same concepts. For example, suppose we have two different reconstructions, R1 and R2, of our ordinary geometry. In both R1 and R2, cores are given for triangularity. The question is whether triangularity in R1 (call it "triangularity R1") is the same as triangularity in R2 (call it "triangularity R2"). It would appear that by my own principles the answer must be that triangularity R1 is not the same as triangularity R2 since the cores, being in different reconstructions, must be different. This conclusion may seem strange since R1 and R2 are, ex hypothesi, both reconstructions of the same concepts, those concepts which are part of our ordinary geometry. This objection, while it has some point, assumes uncritically several notions which are essential to an understanding of the issues it broaches. For example, how are we to understand the idea that R1 and R2 are "two different reconstructions of the same concepts?"

To clarify this matter, a few simple points must be made clear. First, there is a reasonably well determined system of predicates embodied in ordinary language which we would all agree to call "geometric." It would be quite a task indeed to set out in detail the exact features which distinguish geometric predicates from others. These distinguishing features are features of the system of inferential connections involving these predicates. In general, these features divide into two groups. One group is concerned with only those inferential connections which are formulated by rules which treat solely of the predicates which we wish to mark off as "geometric." Let us say that this group specifies the "internal structure" of the system of predicates. The other group specifies the inferential relationship of this system of predicates to other parts of the total conceptual scheme. These "external connections" are formulated by rules which inferentially connect the predicates we intend to call "geometric" with ones that are not geometric (e.g., color predicates).

Second, what I am saying when I claim that R1 and R2 are reconstructions of the same concepts is that

[i] R1 and R2 have the same internal structure

and [ii] R1 and R2 have the same inferential place in the total conceptual scheme.

Sameness of the total structures of R1 and R2 is determined through the rules (many of which might conveniently be stated as rules of unconditional assertion). R1 and R2 have the same internal structure if and only if, given a matching of the concepts of the two reconstructions, the rules of one reconstruction can be demonstrated to be a rearrangement of the rules of the other. Of course, a defined concept in R1 might be matched with a primitive concept in R2. Thus, under the matching of the concepts, the counterpart of a primitive rule in one reconstruction might be a derived rule in the other.

Condition [ii] is necessary because the satisfaction of condition [i] alone is not sufficient in all cases to insure that we have two reconstructions of the same concepts. For example, as is well known, the concepts of the real number system can be matched with geometrical concepts in such a way that any reconstruction of our geometric concepts can be shown to have the same internal structure as the real number system. It is in cases of this sort that condition [ii] becomes important. In the case we are considering, it is clear that the concepts of the real number system do not have the necessary external connections (e.g., with color concepts). That the real number system and Euclidean geometry can be shown to have the same internal structure given a particular matching of their concepts is sufficient and necessary for demonstrations in one system to be transferable to the other. Indeed it is just this important fact that modern "abstract algebra" has formulated so rigorously. But this matter should not be confused with what I am explicating.

Third, I must explain what is being said when I say that R1 and R2 are "different reconstructions" of the same concepts. That R1 and R2 are different reconstructions obviously cannot be explained with reference to the internal structures or the external connections of the R1 and R2 as a whole. Rather, what distinguishes R1 and R2 are features of the predicates and the rules they take as primitive. R1 and R2 are different reconstructions of the same concepts if and only if, given that R1 and R2 are reconstructions of the same concepts, i.e., that [i] and [ii] are satisfied, either

[iii] the primitive rules of R1 and the primitive rules of R2 are not rearrangements of each

other (under the matching of concepts required for [i])

or [iv] if condition [iii] is satisfied, the primitive predicates of R1 and the primitive predicates of R2 do not have the same external inferential connections.

In most cases, it is not difficult to determine that condition [iii] is not satisfied. For example, if two reconstructions of the same concepts have different numbers of primitive concepts, it will almost certainly not be possible to match the predicates so that the rules of one transform into the rules of the other.

But now let us return to the original question: Is triangularity R1 the same as triangularity R2? Suppose, upon clarification, this question is really the question: Given that R1 and R2 are reconstructions of the same concepts, are triangularity R1 and triangularity R2 matched to each other in the matching that is part of the demonstration that R1 and R2 satisfy condition [i]? I think that the answer is yes under certain conditions. Given that R1 and R2 have been constructed with what I have taken to be the core of our concept of triangularity as a guide, then one would think that triangularity R1 and triangularity R2 are just those concepts that it would be natural to match. However, it is not impossible for someone to convince us that there are good reasons for ignoring the core of our concept of triangularity in framing a reconstruction. Then, though triangularity R1 and triangularity R2 will be matched with some concepts, it may be that they are not matched with each other.

Suppose, though, upon clarification, our original question really is the question: Given that R1 and R2 are different reconstructions of the same concepts, are triangularity R1 and triangularity R2 the same? Then we could say no for there is a sense in which they are not the same. They are not the same in that they are in different reconstructions and the primitive concepts which appear in the definition of one are not the same as the primitive concepts which appear in the definition of the other.

Another line of thought leads to the same conclusion. Both R1 and R2 contain each other as subsystems. Thus in R1, by beginning with the concepts which are matched with the primitive concepts of R2, we could mimic in R1 all the definitions of R2. And in doing this, we would define a concept which has a definition exactly like, <u>from a certain step</u>, the definition of triangularity R2. Clearly even this concept is not the same concept as triangularity R1, though indeed this concept, like trilaterality R1, must mutually entail triangularity R1. Further investigation would show, I think, that this new complex concept is very closely related to triangularity R1 and then it would be possible on this basis to show how closely related triangularity R2 is to triangularity R1. But such rarified matters need not detain us, for I think that I have said enough to indicate that there is nothing very disturbing, upon reflection, about the senses in which triangularity R1 and triangularity R2 are different.

Though much more of general interest could be said about the matter of reconstructions and the identity of concepts, one more remark must suffice for the present.

We have already noted that our language is unlike a reconstruction of it in many ways. But a much more important reason for distinguishing so sharply between our language and reconstructions of it is that any reconstruction of our language is a reconstruction of the concepts it embodies at some time. Put another way, our language is something that develops and changes, and part of this development and change is conceptual. Thus, any part of our language might undergo such conceptual change and development that two reconstructions of that part made at different times would not be reconstructions of the same concepts. Such cases occur when we come to accept or reject primitive rules of inference, i.e., when, in the language of chapter 2, our language ceases to embody the same linguistic roles (though we may continue in our tokenings of the new roles to produce exactly the same natural linguistic objects, sometimes detrimentally).

The mention of rejecting and accepting rules of inference brings us handily back to a matter concerning rules like 2E(18.1). Such rules are derivative rules of inference. Put intuitively, these rules manifest the fact that we "draw out" inferential connections between complex concepts, inferential connections which are "built into" them with their cores. Demonstrating 2E(18.1) is a matter of giving arguments which utilize the rules pertaining to the concepts in the cores of triangularity and trilaterality and the principles of logic. Thus, our reliable inclination is to say that by demonstrating 2E(18.1) we are not changing the two concepts. Unlike accepting a primitive rule of inference which would alter the concepts our language embodies, accepting 2E(18.1) does not change anything but our grasp of the concepts. This is so because 2E(18.1) follows from rules pertaining to the concepts in the cores of triangularity and trilaterality and the rules of logic. Of course, abandoning 2E(18.1), in the face of its demonstration, would have profound conceptual repercussions since we should have to alter our primitive rules or perhaps give up certain rules of logic. The remarks on rules and conceptual change in subsections B(iii) and B(iv) of this chapter should be read with these qualifications in mind.

I do not want to give the impression that I think that knowledge of inferential connections between complex concepts is uninteresting or unimportant. The case of triangularity and trilaterality is not very interesting because the concepts are not very complex and they appear as the sole concepts in statements which are mutually inferrible. In the more interesting cases of mutual inferribility, the logical form of the statements that are mutually inferrible is not so simple and more than two concepts are involved. There can be no question of the informativeness of, and the better understanding provided by, demonstrations of mutual inferribility in these cases. On the other hand, changes in the concepts themselves and great advances in understanding are not brought by showing mutual (or one way) inferribility. Real conceptual changes, as opposed to changes only in our understanding of certain concepts, occur when some primitive concepts have to be altered and hence when any complex concept whose core contains these primitive concepts is also altered.

Chapter 4: The Reconstruction of the Natural Numbers

A. Preliminaries

(i) The Goal and Plan of This Chapter

The reconstructions given in this chapter parallel those given for other abstract entities such as redness and triangularity. Hence, metaphysical problems concerning the natural numbers are displayed as special cases of metaphysical problems concerning abstract entities in general. As I intimated at the end of chapter 1, numerical quantifiers are the primary material in the reconstruction of the natural numbers.

What is the extent of the reconstruction in this chapter? Primarily, I provide reconstructions of statements concerning addition and multiplication. With the reconstructions of these statements in hand, it is a trivial task to reconstruct statements with arithmetical predicates such as 'even' and 'prime'. Substantial attention is also given to the statements which correspond, in my reconstruction, to the so-called Peano axioms for arithmetic.

The chapter is divided into three sections, A, B, and C. Section C contains that part of the reconstruction which is on a par with the reconstruction of _triangularity_ as an individual in sections 2C and 2E. Section B contains the reconstruction of natural numbers as universals. Subsection B(i) reconstructs general classificatory statements involving natural numbers and explains what parts of the reconstruction belong to section B and what parts to section C. Subsection B(ii) reconstructs some of the statements which contain the phrase 'the number of'. Subsection B(iii), in continuing the reconstruction of such statements, provides the reconstruction of 'plus'. Subsection B(iv) discusses some properties of 'plus'. Subsection B(v) turns to the reconstruction of 'times'. Finally, subsection B(vi) discusses those statements which correspond, in the reconstruction of section B, to the "Peano axioms." This subsection also argues that I do not reconstruct arithmetical truths(falsehoods) as falsehoods(truths). Section A, which contains introductory material, has three further subsections. Subsection A(ii) deals with the notations for numerical quantifiers and other quantifiers, the definitions of numerical quantifiers, and the inferences and truths numerical quantifiers appear in essentially. Subsection A(iii) deals with distributive singular terms (DSTs); subsection A(iv), with certain statements containing the term 'true' and others containing 'true of' and with the rules for DSTs in these statements.

To save space, the terminological meticulousness of chapter 2 was not continued in chapter 3 and will not be in this and later chapters. Thus the reader will find that, as I have continued to use ordinary single quotes for several different jobs, so I shall loosely employ such terms as 'expression', 'term', and so forth. Were it necessary, I could unpack my remarks in the philosophically more correct terminology of chapter 2.

The reader should note that on several occasions the discussion in this chapter turns to the construction of special "notation." A notation is a system of materials designed for an embodiment of certain roles of Human Language and devised for special purposes. These notations, some of which were adopted in chapter 2, augment the natural linguistic objects provided by English.

Reconstructions such as the one in this chapter carry with them no commitments one way or the other about the actual process of learning elementary mathematical concepts. On this matter, the claim of the reconstruction is that, however and in whatever order we learn the concepts of elementary mathematics, what we learn is what the reconstruction shows them to be. Suppose (what I, indeed, think is true) that we pick up the workings of abstract singular terms like :triangularity:s and :redness:s right along with the workings of the corresponding predicates, :triangular:s and :red:s. This supposition is in no way inconsistent with my reconstruction of 'triangularity' and 'redness' as metalinguistic terms that are concerned with the role of these corresponding predicates. What follows from my account together with this supposition is that while learning to make statements about triangular things and red things, we are also learning to speak about the workings of the predicates 'triangular' and 'red'. Such learning is part of the process through which while we are learning to speak and reason about the world, we are also learning to talk about inferences and reasoning.

(ii) Numerical Quantifiers, Other Quantifiers, and Inference

In order to deal with the definitions of numerical quantifiers and to illustrate inferences with them, I must, first, discuss and comment further on quantifiers written in English and quantifiers in the notation adopted in 3A(iii).

In 3A(iii) I suggested, with certain reservations, that the matrix

(1) (Ex)Fx

written in technical notation has as its English correspondent

(1.1) something is (a) F.

This suggestion requires the amendment, noted then, that (1) corresponds not only to (1.1) but also to

(1.2) something was (a) F

and (1.3) something will be (a) F.

The matrix '(Ex)Fx' carries no indication of tense whatsoever and is best understood as corresponding, with respect to being E-quantified, to all three of the above statement matrices (and, indeed, to even others in other tenses).

For reasons of simplicity, I wish to have English notations for such quantified statements which carry no tense indication. Hence I shall employ the term 'be' and write

(1.4) something be (a) F.

By this stipulation I do not mean to commit myself to the claim that statements are, at bottom, tenseless or to any similar claim. The contrived expression (1.4) has a role in virtue of its introduction in terms of full-fledged statements which are tensed. It is important to note that (1.4) is not introduced as the conjunction of (1.1), (1.2), and (1.3) or as their disjunction. The role of (1.4) is exactly that of (1.1), (1.2), and (1.3) (and other such tensed statements) save in the matter of tense.

What has been done in the case of (1.1), (1.2), and (1.3) also must be done in the case of numerical quantifiers which I write in English as

(2) there is one ..., there are two ..., there are three ..., etc.,
there was one ..., there were two ..., there were three ..., etc.,
there will be one ..., there will be two ..., there will be three ..., etc.,

minimal quantifiers which I write in English as

(3) there is at least one ..., there are at least two ..., etc.,
there was at least one ..., there were at least two ..., etc.,
there will be at least one ..., there will be

at least two ..., etc.,

and maximal quantifiers which I write in English as

(4) there is at most one ..., there are at most two ..., etc.,
there was at most one ..., there were at most two ..., etc.,
there will be at most one ..., there will be at most two ..., etc.

Thus we shall have

(2.1) there be one ..., there be two ..., there be three ..., etc.,

(3.1) there be at least one ..., there be at least two ..., etc.,

and (4.1) there be at most one ..., there be at most two ..., etc.

where these contrived expressions are explained as (1.4) is. Remember two things: [i] I have illustrated only some tensed quantifiers; [ii] none of the quantifiers in (2.1), (3.1), and (4.1) can be unpacked as conjunctions or disjunctions of tensed quantifiers. The importance of these points will become clear in later examples.

Consider the following lists of quantifiers which I shall call "exact" quantifiers:

(2.2) (Ex one)Fx, (Ex two)Fx, (Ex three)Fx, etc.;

"min" quantifiers:

(3.2) (Ex least one)Fx, (Ex least two)Fx, (Ex least three)Fx, etc.;

and "max" quantifiers:

(4.2) (Ex most one)Fx, (Ex most two)Fx, (Ex most

three)Fx, etc.

All of the exact, min, and max quantifiers can be defined solely in terms of the universal and E-quantifiers, statement connectives, and identity.

I have intentionally called the quantifiers which appear in (2.2) ((3.2), (4.2)) by another name than the quantifiers that appear in (2.1) ((3.1), (4.1)), for some statements containing the quantifiers in (2.2) ((3.2), (4.2)) do not correspond to ones with quantifiers from (2.1) ((3.1), (4.1)). The reason for their divergence is that numerical, minimal, and maximal quantifiers do not form statements with any predicates whatever, but only with sortal predicates (what I also call "general terms" or "kind predicates"). For example,

there be two reds

is not acceptable. Using 'K' as a variable for kind terms, numerical quantifier statements must be of the following sort:

there be ... K.

On the other hand, exact, min, and max quantifiers, because of their unrestricted definitions in terms of the ordinary quantifiers and statement connectives, can form statements with any predicates whatsoever. I ought to note that I do not think that the distinction between kind terms and other predicates is a grammatical one in the nonphilosophical sense of this word.

But statements which are exact (min, max) quantifiers combined with kind terms do correspond to statements with numerical (minimal, maximal) quantifiers. Thus exact quantifiers, restricted to kind terms, are numerical quantifiers. In

(Ex two)cow x,

for example, the quantifier is a :there be two:. Put the other way around, the role of numerical quantifiers is the role which exact quantifiers have in statements in which they are combined with kind terms rather than with just any predicate. I shall, therefore, let convenience dictate whether I give my examples in ordinary English or technical notation or in an augmented English which mixes English natural linguistic objects and natural linguistic objects of the technical notation.

What must be done now is to provide a recipe for the definition of any numerical quantifier. Those and only those quantifiers which can be defined in the way set down in the recipe are numerical quantifiers.

Examples, written in augmented English, will guide us in framing the recipe: '(Ex one)Kx' is defined as

(Ex)(Kx and (z)(if Kz, then x = z))

and '(Ex two)Kx' is defined as

(Ey)(Ex)(Kx and Ky and not(x = y) and (z) (if Kz, then x = z or y = z)).

In accordance with 3C, such definitions are reconstructed as rules which permit the direct inference of a universally quantified biconditional from a truth of logic. In the case of the definition of '(Ex one)Kx', the biconditional is

(K)((Ex one)Kx if and only if (Ex)(Kx and (z)(if Kz, then x = z)))

and the truth of logic is

(K)((Ex)(Kx and (z)(if Kz, then x = z)) if and only if (Ex)(Kx and (z)(if Kz, then x = z))).

Clearly the definition of any numerical quantifier is completely determined by the description of a logically complex E-quantified statement matrix which, for simplicity, I call the "definiens of a numerical quantifier."

In order to make what follows a little easier, I state several properties of all definientia of numerical quantifiers. They are E-quantified and thus have as a first quantifier an E-quantifier. They have at most one universal quantifier. They contain a statement matrix which is conjunctive, which occurs in no other statement or statement matrix but ones which are E-quantified, which has at least and at most one kind term variable, and which has as a conjunct a universally quantified conditional. Besides the kind term variable, they contain only individual variables. No variable of a quantifier of any definiens is of the same type as the variable of another quantifier of the same definiens. In light of these properties, I speak, in the recipe, of "the universal quantifier," "the universally quantified conditional," and "the kind variable." The phrase

> the ... variable is different from (the same as) the variables ___

is short for

> the individual variable token in the (of the) ... is of a different type from (the same type as) the individual variable tokens ___.

The phrase

> with the variable of ___

is short for

> with a token of the type of variable, another token of which is in the ___.

I also employ obvious grammatical variants of these phrases.

Given the description of the definiens of a numerical quantifier (the "old" definiens), the description of the definiens of another numerical quantifier (the "new" definiens) is obtained as follows:

The new definiens is an E-quantified statement

[i][a] whose first quantifier variable is different from the variables of the quantifiers in the old definiens and

[b] whose remaining quantifiers and quantifier variables are the same as those of the old definiens and

[ii] whose conjunctive statement matrix is the same as the one in the old definiens except that it contains as a conjunct

[a] a statement matrix which is the kind variable combined with the variable of the E-quantifier not in the old definiens,

[b] any statement matrix which is the negation of an identity statement matrix which contains the variable of the E-quantifier not in the old definiens and the variable of an E-quantifier of the old definiens and

[c] a universally quantified conditional which is the same as the one in the old definiens except that it contains as a disjunct in its consequent the identity statement matrix which contains the variable of the E-quantifier not in the old definiens and the variable of the universal quantifier.

Consider the first definition in the example. The definiens of the numerical quantifier 'there be one' is an E-quantified statement with at most one E-quantifier and whose conjunctive statement matrix contains only

[i] a statement matrix which is the kind variable combined with the variable of the E-quantifier

and

[ii] whose universally quantified conditional has

[a] as an antecedent a statement matrix which the kind variable combined with the variable of the universal quantifier and

[b] as a consequent an identity statement which contains the variable of the universal quantifier and the variable of the E-quantifier.

With this description of the definiens of 'there be one', all the remaining definientia are available through the recipe.

From the above recipe it is possible to compile instructions for constructing a new definiens from an old definiens. Of course, in order to be able to apply these instructions in a given embodiment, one has to know how E-quantifying, conjoining, and disjoining are handled in that embodiment. The instructions are:

[i] E-quantify the old definiens with an E-quantifier which contains a variable different from the variables in the old definiens,

[ii] conjoin to the conjunctive statement matrix

[a] a statement matrix which is the kind variable combined with the variable of the E-quantifier not in the old definiens and

[b] all the statement matrices which are negations of identity statement matrices which contain the variable of the E-quantifier not in the old definiens and a variable in an E-quantifier in the old definiens and

[iii] disjoin to the consequent of the universally quantified conditional the identity statement

matrix which contains the variable of the E-quantifier not in the old definiens and the variable of the universal quantifier.

Since the definition of 'there be one' is given, all the remaining numerical quantifiers can be constructed from these instructions. Similar recipes and instructions can be given for minimal and maximal quantifiers.

I now turn to the task of illustrating matrices for permitted inferences involving numerical quantifiers essentially. All the inferences considered are derivative inferences. The variables 'H', 'I', 'J', and 'K' are kind term variables. The sign '/' has the same function as 'therefore'; inference matrices

--- // ___

are abbreviations for the conjunctive matrices

--- / ___ and ___ / ---.

The first list of examples involves maximal and minimal as well as numerical quantifiers:

(5) there be one K / there be at least one K,
there be two K / there be at least two K,
there be three K / there be at least three K,
etc.

there be one K / there be at most one K,
there be two K / there be at most two K,
there be three K / there be at most three K,
etc.

there be one K // there be at least one K and there be at most one K,
there be two K // there be at least two K and there be at most two K, etc.

I now illustrate inferences with '... fewer ... than ...', '... more ... than ...', and '... as many ... as ...'.

(6) there be one K, there be one H / there be as many Ks as Hs (or, there be as many Hs as Ks),

there be one K, there be two H / there be more Hs than Ks (or, there be fewer Ks than Hs).

An important feature of the statement matrices in the conclusions of the inference matrices in (6) is that their variables are not individual variables. Moreover,

there be more Hs than Ks

is an ellipsis for

(7) there be more Hs than there be Ks.

Since the appearance of the term 'more' before the 'H' is an irrelevant historical feature of English, the following would do as well:

(7.1) there be Hs more than there be Ks.

The matrix (7.1) suggests the thought that 'more than' is some sort of logical connective and hence that there should be some way of rendering (7.1) and the related statement matrices

(7.2) there be Hs as many as there be Ks

and (7.3) there be Hs fewer than there be Ks

to make this point explicit. The investigation of this suggestion in chapter 6 leads to an appreciation of the derivative status of the inferences illustrated in (6).

The most important inferences involving numerical quantifiers essentially are closely connected with logical truths of the sort given in section 1B. There the following statement was formulated:

> 1B(4) there are five things of a sort and there are three other things of the same or another sort if and only if there are eight things of some sort or other.

My first task is to reformulate 1B(4). Though 1B(4) sounds reasonable, it includes two different statements:

> there are at least five things of a sort and there are three other things of the same sort if and only if there are at least eight things of the same sort

and

> there are five things of a sort and there are three things of a different sort if and only if there are eight things of some sort or other.

The first of these statements is related to inference matrices (5) and will not concern us. The second is not entirely clear as it stands. What I offer as a true statement is (8), the conjunction of

> (8.1) (H)(I)(E J)(if no H be an I, then if there be five H and there be three I, then there be eight J)

and

> (8.2) (J)(E H)(E I)(if no H be an I, then if there be eight J, then there be five H and there be three I).

The truth of (8) hinges on the fact that the kind term variables in it are variables for logically complex as well as logically simple kind terms. Complex kind terms may be built by logical means from kind terms alone or from kind terms and ordinary predicates. For example, the kind term variables in (8) are variables for all of cow or horse,

cow in the field,

brown horse,

and cow in the field or brown horse.

Thus, given kind terms which satisfy the conditions in the antecedents of the conditional statement matrices in (8.1), any :there be eight: combined with the kind term which is the disjunction of these kind terms is a true statement. For example, given that no horse is a cow and there be five horses and there be three cows, there be eight horses or cows.

For simplicity's sake, I take an example in discussing (8.2). Suppose

(9) there be eight books on the table,

which I shall abbreviate to

(9.1) there be eight Bs.

By the definition of :there be eight:s, we obtain from (9.1) something of the following sort:

(9.2) (Er)(Es)(Et)(Eu)(Ev)(Ew)(Ey)(Ex)(Bx and ... and Br and not(x = y) and ... and not(x = r) and not(y = w) and ... and not(y = r) and not(w = v and ... and not(w = r) and not(v = u) and ... and not(v = r) and not(u = t) and ... and not(u = r) and not(t = s) and not(t = r) and not(s = r) and (z)(if Bz, then x = z or ... or r = z)).

In the conjunctive statement matrix of (9.2) there are twenty-eight negations of identities.

The strategy for getting the two needed predicates is intuitively straightforward. The negations of identities in (9.2) insure that each B is different from every other B.

Thus if a is a B and b is a B, then there is a property a has and b does not. The same is true of a and any other B. Let me write 'Pb' for the property that a has but b does not, 'Pc' for the property that a has but c does not and so on. Thus

B which is Pd and Pe and Pf and Pg and Ph

is not satisfied by d, e, f, g, and h. Similar properties are formulable for the Bs other than a.

Let me abbreviate the above phrase to

B which is --- defgh(for a).

The similar properties for b and c are:

B which is --- defgh(for b)

and B which is --- defgh(for c).

Only a, b, and c of all the Bs are

Bs which are --- defgh(for a) or which are --- defgh(for b) or which are --- defgh(for c).

Another predicate, formulated in an analogous manner, is true of only d, e, f, g, and h of the Bs. These two predicates are the ones needed in our example.

Done more rigorously, the argument from (9.2) to the appropriate instance of the conjunctive matrix in (8.2) follows the same lines but does not need the law of identity invoked in the intuitive discussion. For the following argument I write the negation of an identity statement matrix as a negated relational predicate statement matrix; for example,

(not(=y))x

is (not(x = y)).

Consider the statement matrix

(Er)(Es)(Et)(Eu)(Ev)(Bx and Bv and (not(=v))x and Bu and (not(=u))x and Bt and (not(=t))x and Bs and (not(=s))x and Br and (not(=r))x).

I abbreviate this matrix to

___ x ___.

It follows from (9.2) that

(Ew)(Ey)(Ex)(___ x ___ and ___ y ___ and ___ w ___ and not(x = y) and not(x = w) and not(y = w) and (z)(if ___ z ___, then x = z or y = z or w = z)),

i.e., (Ex three)(___ x ___).

Thus '___ x ___' is one of the matrices needed in the example. The other matrix is obtained in an analogous way. Notice that given (9.2), the disjunction of these matrices is extensionally equivalent to 'Bx'.

What inferences are closely associated with (8)? Of course, there are several sorts of inferences closely connected with (8). But, intuitively, the inferences most relevant to my enterprise are of the following sort:

.... There be five cows in the barn. There be three horses in the field. Hence, there be eight animals on the farm.

.... There be eight people in the room. Hence, there be five people near the table and there be three people around the desk.

The dots indicate that many other statements must be assumed as premises in order for the inferences to be correct.

Interesting though an account of the additional premises of these inferences may be, it is not needed for reconstructing arithmetical <u>statements</u>. It is statements like (8) that figure importantly in the reconstruction of arithmetical statements. Statements like (8) reflect a basic, logical feature of "numerousness," a feature concerning logical "togetherness" and "apartness." It is a logical feature (in a broad sense of 'logical') that such statements reflect for two reasons: first, they insure, as a matter of logic, that, under suitable conditions, certain numerical quantifier statements are true if and only if others are as well; second, they say nothing about what is physically possible or about our abilities or our opportunities. The metalinguistic statements which are important to the reconstruction, in particular the rules of inference formulated in section B, are easily seen to reflect the same sort of logical feature. Thus the detailed elucidation of the inferences which intuitively recommend themselves in connection with statements like (8) is not necessary for the work which follows.

As a final point, note that there are other inferences with numerical quantifier statements which, though interesting, are not closely related to the topics of this chapter. Suppose that there are twelve items appropriately characterized. With certain additional premises about the nature and relations of these items, it would be correct to infer that there are four pairs of eyeglasses. These inferences rest, in part, on inferences discussed in section B(v), but they are more intimately connected with the topic of "parts" and "wholes" than with the topics of this book.

(iii) DST Elimination

In section C, chapter 2, DSTs were introduced and the elimination of statements in which DSTs appear in favor of statements in which they do not appear was briefly discussed. The only principle of elimination given at that time was

2C(5) 'the K is F' is equivalent to 'all Ks are F'!

where the exclamation mark indicates that 2C(5) can be used only if a condition is satisfied. The condition is that for any instance of 'all Ks are F' to be used in 2C(5), it must state a truth "essential to the meaning" of the kind term which appears in the instance. The restriction on 2C(5) is necessary because many generalizations involving kind terms in an appropriate fashion are not equivalent to statements with DSTs.

Fortunately, I am not obliged to provide a general theory of DSTs. Even in chapter 2 the ordinary cases of DSTs were not dwelt on; rather, our attention was turned to other singular terms not usually said to be DSTs. Yet it was the claim of chapter 2 that these other singular terms, i.e., abstract singular terms, are DSTs. Part of the point of the reconstructions of chapter 2 is to make clear just what sort of DSTs abstract singular terms are. According to those reconstructions, abstract singular terms are metalinguistic DSTs which contain a special sort of kind term, viz., a Sellarsian general germ (SGT). This chapter, too, does not contain ordinary DSTs: all the DSTs which appear in this chapter are metalinguistic DSTs, and the predicate and relation tokens with which they combine are also metalinguistic.

The statements in which DSTs appear in this chapter (with one exception discussed in the next subsection) are of two kinds. The one kind is classificatory. An example is:

> the :there be five cows: is a numerical quantifier statement.

Such a classificatory statement is eliminated in favor of a generalization. In this example the generalization is:

> all :there be five cows:s are numerical quantifier statements.

The other kind is rules of inference. The elimination

of DSTs in rules of inference is taken care of by the expedient of assimilating 'may be inferred from' to a relation word. Thus instances of

the STAT may be inferred from the STATA

are equivalent to instances of

STATs may be inferred from STATAs.

Any further unpacking of statements of the latter sort awaits an investigation of practical discourse.

My position on DST elimination in the two sorts of statements just discussed is that these statements satisfy the restriction which was placed on 2C(5) as that restriction must be understood in light of the discussions in chapters 2 and 3. For rules of inference, my position was defended, though I did not say so explicitly at the time, in 3B. That my position is tenable for the classificatory statements found in this chapter is, it seems to me, a consequence of the fact that these classificatory statements follow from the characterizations of statements, predicates, and so on in chapters 2 and 3 and the definitions of numerical quantifiers in the last subsection. Thus that these classificatory statements say something which is "essential to the meaning" of the kind terms, i.e., the SGTs, in them comes to no more than that the predicates of these statements appear in the characterizations and definitions of the linguistic items the SGTs speak of.

The examples already given make clear the principles of DST elimination that will be employed in this chapter. These principles are used both when the SGT in the DST is logically simple and when it is logically complex. Further the principles are used on matrices and within molecular statements, but of course not within quotation.

(iv) DSTs and Truth

The reason for having a separate subsection on DST elimination in statements containing 'true' is that I do not wish to have to answer the question whether 'true' is a predicate. To assume that a statement like

the :snow is white: is true

can be handled as a classificatory statement is to assume that such a statement involves classification and thus predication. So I set out my account of such truth statements separately and do not commit myself to the claim that they are covered by what I have said about classificatory statements.

Beginning with the simplest matters, I note that statements of the following sort,

(10) ___ is true,

where the blank is a variable for abstract singular terms like 'that a is triangular' or 'that two plus two equals four', are reconstructed as statements containing metalinguistic DSTs. Thus, in the simplest case,

(10.1) that two plus two equals four is true

is reconstructed as

(10.2) the :two plus two equals four: is true.

To be consistent with the DST eliminations of chapter 2 and the previous subsection, (10.2) should become

(10.3) :two plus two equal four:s are true.

In order to insure this elimination, I shall say that the move from (10.2) to (10.3) and back is permitted by the following principle:

T1: instances of

the STAT is true

are equivalent to instances of

STATs are true.

Tl may be used in molecular statements.

In addition to the moves permitted by the application of Tl, the reconstruction will also require the more commonly discussed transition from

(11) that two plus two equals four is true

to (11.1) two plus two equals four

and the transition for (11.1) to (11). According to the reconstruction of (11) these transitions are from

(10.2) the :two plus two equals four: is true,

i.e., (10.3) :two plus two equals four:s are true,

to (11.1) and from (11.1) to (10.3). We can characterize these transitions by saying that given an instance of

STATs are true,

we are justified in tokening an instance of

P,

where the statement which is the instance of 'P' must be a <u>statement of the type which is encapsulated by the SGT in the instance of 'STATs are true'</u>. Thus, if the instance of 'STATs are true' is (10.3), the instance of 'P' must be a :two plus two equals four:.

Note that I do not say that these transitions are inferences. Whether there is a rule of inference which governs these truth transitions and, if there is, whether it is primitive or derivative, are questions that deserve careful scrutiny which cannot be given here.

It may seem, however, that there is hardly anything else these transitions could be but inferences. We are all familiar with cases in which a tokening either leads to another tokening or justifies another and yet in which we should be unlikely to claim that the two tokenings are inferentially related. For example, if I greet someone with that sort of tokening which is held by the customs of his society to be the only proper sort, then we are all justified in tokening the statement that I have discharged at least part of the social necessities properly. Or, for example, if I token an :I shall tell Jones that it is raining: and, thereafter, in conversation with Jones, I vocally token an :it is raining:, then I think that, given that we take the former tokening to express a decision or resolution, we can plausibly claim that the one tokening led to the other. I do not, of course, maintain that the truth case is exactly like either of these two cases. But I do claim that the phenomenon of linguistic transitions which are not inferences is familiar enough that it is not in the least absurd to prefer to leave open the question whether the truth transitions are inferences or not. So, for the purposes of this book, I shall simply insist that we are justified in using the transitions as I have characterized them.

In the contexts I have been discussing, 'true' appears in general statements or statements which reduce to general statements. It should not, however, be supposed that other senses of 'true' which require other sorts of contexts cannot be introduced. We sometimes wish to say that all the statements of a given type in a given natural language are true, e.g.,

> all *two plus two equals four*s (in English) are true

or that a particular statement in a given language is true, e.g.,

> this *two plus two equals four* (in English) is

true.

Both these contexts can be introduced by definition, thus:

all *two plus two equals four*s (in English) are true

is equivalent to

(E STAT)(*two plus two equals four*s are English STATs and STATs are true)

and this *two plus two equals four* (in English) is true

is equivalent to

(E STAT)(this *two plus two equals four* is an English STAT and STATs are true)

where 'STAT' is a variable for SGTs, not for asterisk-quote general terms.

The remaining task of this subsection is to introduce 'true of' in terms of the undefined sense of 'true' which I have been discussing. The precise manner in which I introduce 'true of' has a significance which will become clear with an example in B(i).

I do not intend to discuss whether being true of is a relation, for the answer to this question hinges on whether truth is property. If, however, being true of is a relation, it is not, on the Sellarsian account, a relation between linguistic items and other natural items (perhaps also linguistic). Some extended semantic formalists maintain that a language is a language, in part, because of sentences which say that the predicates of its syntactical system do, or do not, stand in the relation of being true of (or, being satisfied by) objects of a domain. My rejection of extended semantic formalism also includes the rejection of this claim. Thus, in the Sellarsian account, being true of is not a relation between "words" and "the world" except insofar as some such relation may be involved in truth itself.

I shall offer two principles, one for each context in which 'true of' appears in this chapter. In order to formulate these principles, we will require a variety of metalinguistic variables. We already have the variables

INDCON, INDCONA, INDCONB, etc.,

PREDCON, PREDCONA, PREDCONB, etc.,

and KINDPREDCON, KINDPREDCONA, KINDPREDCONB, etc.

In addition, I introduce the variable 'NUMQUANT', which is a variable for SGTs true of numerical quantifiers; i.e., it is a variable for

:there be one:, :there be two:, :there be three:, etc.

This variable also comes in various styles. The principles are:

T2: instances of

(E KINDPREDCONA)(E NUMQUANTA)(the (NUMQUANT KINDPREDCONA) is true of the (NUMQUANTA KINDPREDCON))

are equivalent to instances of

the (NUMQUANT KINDPREDCON) is true.

T3: instances of

(E INDCONA)(E PREDCONA)(the (PREDCON INDCONA) is true of the (PREDCONA INDCON))

are equivalent to instances of

the (PREDCON INDCON) is true.

As an example of T2,

(E KINDPREDCONA)(E NUMQUANTA)(the (:there be five: KINDPREDCONA) is true of the (NUMQUANTA :horses:))

becomes

the :there be five horses: is true.

As an example of T3,

(E INDCONA)(E PREDCONA)(the (:wise: INDCONA) is true of the (PREDCONA :Socrates:))

becomes

the :wise Socrates: is true.

For simplicity, I shall abbreviate the defined statements and statement matrices containing 'is true of'. Thus instead of what is above, I shall write:

the :there be five: is true of the :horses:

and the :wise: is true of the :Socrates:.

B. Numbers as Universals

(i) Numerical Quantifiers and Sellarsian General Terms

The reconstruction of triangularity as a universal hinges on the role of :triangular:s; nevertheless, my reconstruction of statements that speak of triangularity reflects the fact that the role of :triangular:s is found in their contributing in a certain way to statements. Thus the reconstruction of triangularity comes, in 2E, to involve the compound term

(:triangular: INDCON)

rather than simply the SGT

:triangular:.

Similarly, :there be one:s, :there be two:s, :there be three:s, etc., are all numerical quantifiers, and the reconstruction of numbers as universals depends on the role of these quantifiers. However, the role of numerical quantifiers, like those of all other kinds of linguistic items, is to be found in what they contribute to the statements in which they appear. Thus what is needed are metalinguistic terms which are, for numerical quantifiers, what

(:triangular: INDCON)

is for :triangulars:s.

As I have already noted, not just any predicate will do in a numerical quantifier statement. For example,

there be one red

is not acceptable. What is satisfactory are predicates for kinds, i.e., predicates like :horse:s. Thus

there be one horse

is acceptable. Consequently, the sort of metalinguistic terms needed are

(:there be one: KINDPREDCON)

and similar ones for the other numerical quantifiers.

In chapter 2, abstract entities were reconstructed both as universals and as abstract individuals. So, in addition to ML terms that pertain to numbers as universals, there must be MML terms that figure in the discussion of numbers as abstract individuals. Thus we need analogs to

:the :triangular::,

:the (:triangular: INDCON):

and (<u>PREDCON</u> :the (:triangular: INDCON):).

The sort of terms needed are easily illustrated:

:the :there be one::, :the :there be two::, :the :there be three::, etc.,

:the (:there be one: KINDPREDCON):, :the (:there be two: KINDPREDCON):, :the (:there be three: KINDPREDCON):, etc.,

and (PREDCON :the (:there be one: KINDPREDCON):),
(PREDCON :the (:there be two: KINDPREDCON):),
(PREDCON :the (:there be three: KINDPREDCON):), etc.

It will help in understanding the reconstruction of the natural numbers that I propose to remember the rough outline of the Whitehead-Russell construction of the numbers. Roughly speaking, on their account, natural numbers are classes of classes. Consequently, their view recognizes a distinction of three levels in the construction of natural numbers: individual objects, classes of objects, and classes of classes of objects. This trichotomy is mirrored in my account in an unusual way. In the discussion of abstract entities in chapter 2, a threefold distinction was also made. Thus in the case of 'triangularity', I distinguished triangular things, the universal triangularity, and the abstract individual triangularity. The second and third items in this list were reconstructed, after considerable discussion, by means of the following DST-matrices, respectively:

the (:triangular: INDCON)

and the (PREDCON :the (:triangular: INDCON):).

The most natural reconstructions of the statements

2C(6) triangularity is a universal

and 2C(7) triangularity is an abstract individual

are, respectively,

2C(6.1) the :triangular: is a predicate,

i.e., 2C(6.2) :triangular:s are predicates,

and the :the :triangular:: is an ML !predicate! DST,

i.e., 2C(7.5) :the :triangular::s are ML !predicate! DSTs.

(The exclamation marks are explained near the end of 2C.)

A similar situation holds for numbers as universals and numbers as individuals. Thus, analogs of 2C(6) and 2C(7) are:

(13) THREE is a number universal

and (14) <u>THREE</u> is a number individual.

The most natural move would be to adopt the following as the reconstructions of (13) and (14):

(13.1) the :there be three: is a numerical quantifier,

i.e., (13.2) :there be three:s are numerical quantifiers,

and (14.1) the :the :there be three:: is an ML !numerical quantifier! DST,

i.e., (14.2) :the :there be three::s are ML !numerical quantifier! DSTs.

These rough and ready reconstructions of (13) and (14) present a striking parallel in <u>form</u> to the Whitehead-Russell analysis. THREE is the distributive object corresponding to the classes of three objects and <u>THREE</u> is the distributive object corresponding to the class of all classes of three objects.

But just as the natural reconstruction of 2C(6), i.e., 2C(6.1), gives way to

2E(6.5) (INDCON)(the (:triangular: INDCON) is a statement),

i.e., 2E(6.6) (INDCON)((:triangular: INDCON)s are statements), so (13.1) is superseded by a reconstruction which employs 'the (:there be three: KINDPREDCON)':

(13.3) (KINDPREDCON)(the (:there be three: KINDPREDCON) is a numerical quantifier statement),

i.e., (13.4) (KINDPREDCON)((:there be three: KINDPREDCON)s are numerical quantifier statements).

Statement (13.4) gives such true statements as

:there be three horses:s are numerical quantifier statements.

Thus on this reconstruction of (13), it speaks about all statements which are kind terms combined with a certain numerical quantifier.

It is to the reconstruction of other statements about number universals to which I now turn, leaving all further remarks on numbers as individuals (and on (14)) to section C of this chapter.

(ii) Number Universals and 'the number of'

The actual work of reconstructing mathematical phrases and statements begins with the use of numerical words in connection with kinds. Most numerical statements involving kinds are token reflexive and hence essentially connected with the conditions in which they are made. I shall overlook this fact whenever nothing of any importance hinges on it. To further the generality of my account I also frame my examples in the contrived "be" idiom

In effect, a small part of the talk involving numerical words has already been worked out. Thus

(15) five books be red

and (16) Jones be to the right of three men

become, respectively,

(15.1) there be five books and they be red

and (16.1) there be three men and Jones be to the right of them.

And in general (with the reservations made below)

(17) ... Ks be F

and (18) S Rs ___ Ks

become, respectively,

(17.1) there be ... Ks and they be F

and (18.1) there be ___ Ks and S Rs them.

Of course, the above strategy does not provide the last word in the case of some predicates. For example, we might have the following as an instance of (17):

(17.2) five numbers be prime.

This would become on the above strategy

(17.3) there be five numbers and they be prime.

Clearly (17.3) is a mathematical statement in a more interesting sense than (15.1). I shall return to (17.3) near the end of section B.

The next statement matrices also involve kind terms. But since they contain numerical words which appear to be singular terms, I write them in the manner established in the last subsection: e.g.,

(19) the number of Ks equals FIVE.

An instance of (19) is:

(20) the number of horses equals FIVE.

4B(ii)

The first step in the investigation of (20) is to ask, "What sort of role does 'horses' have in (20)?" The role of 'horses' in (20) is, I suggest, not a predicative role. Were the role of 'horses' in (20) predicative, (20) would, in one way or another, be capable of being rendered as a statement in which 'horse' appears as a predicate. Thus

(21) horses be four legged,

though it does not appear to have 'horses' in a predicative role, is correctly rendered as

if anything be a horse, it be four legged,

which does have 'horse' as a predicate. No such rendering of (20) would seem to do justice to the appearance in it of the phrase 'the number of'. I suggest that the correct route to the reconstruction of (20) begins with recognizing that 'the number of', like 'the father of', ought to be combined with a singular term. Thus (20) becomes:

(22) the number of horsekind equals FIVE.

This rendering of (20) as (22) makes it clear that, on my account, (20) cannot be reconstructed as

there be five horses

or as any other object language statement which speaks directly of horses. The appearance of an abstract singular term, according to my account, insures that (22) is a metalinguistic statement. Hence, even though (22) may well prove to be true if and only if there be five horses, the latter statement could not very well be the reconstruction of (22).

The abstract singular term which is appropriate to (22) is one in which it is true that

(23) horsekind is a many,

rather than an individual. I suggest that (23) is

(24) horsekind is a kind

which can be reconstructed, at a first approximation, as

(24.1) the :horse: is a common noun (kind term, general term),

i.e., (24.2) :horse:s are common nouns.

Both (24.1) and (24.2) must be replaced by statements which incorporate, respectively, the terms

the (:horse: INDCON)

and (:horse: INDCON).

Thus the reconstruction of (24) is:

(24.3) (INDCON)(the (:horse: INDCON) is a common noun statement),

i.e., (24.4) (INDCON)((:horse: INDCON)s are common noun statements).

What relationship, in a broad sense of this term, might there be between the number universal FIVE and horsekind? Though my discussion of (20) and (21), in effect, dismissed the notion that FIVE is a property of <u>horses</u>, there remains the possibility that FIVE is a property of <u>horsekind</u>; or if not a property of horsekind, then at least something which might bear to horsekind a relationship of the sort which a property bears to an individual which has the property. Adapting a traditional philosophical term, I shall say that

horsekind exemplifies FIVE

and that, in general, kinds exemplify number universals. Using 'exemplifies', I can produce an intuitive rendering of (22):

(22.1) the number universal which horsekind exemplifies equals FIVE.

The old adage about skinning cats proves to have its point in pursuits other than taxidermy. Of the ways to skin (22.1), I choose one which is most direct in making use of the resources I already have. I begin by dealing with the simpler statement

(25) some number universal which horsekind exemplifies equals FIVE.

If I first reconstruct

(26) horsekind exemplifies FIVE,

then the relative clause in (25) will present no difficulties. I suggest

(26.1) the :there be five: is true of the :horses:

as the reconstruction of (26). According to A(iv), (26.1) is an abbreviation for a statement which is equivalent to

the :there be five horses: is true,

i.e., :there be five horses:s are true.

Notice, first, that the appropriate ML DSTs, those discussed in B(i), appear in the statement for which (26.1) is an abbreviation. Second, though (26.1) reconstructs (26), it is not correct to say that 'exemplifies' (or, more accurately, 'is exemplified by') is reconstructed as 'is true of'. Though all exemplification statements are reconstructed by statements containing 'is true of', only some, not all, statements containing 'is true of' are reconstructions of exemplification statements. Third, though numerical quantifiers are not predicates of kind terms, there can be no doubt that, on this reconstruction of (26), numerical quantifiers bear a relationship, in a very broad sense of this term, to kind terms which is a relationship that predicates bear to singular terms.

A statement matrix of which (26.1) is an instance is:

(27) the NUMQUANT is true of the :horses:.

The matrix (27), in virtue of what it is an abbreviation for, is equivalent to

the (NUMQUANT :horses:) is true,

i.e., (NUMQUANT :horses:)s are true.

It is the matrix (27) which appears in the reconstruction of (25). Thus (25) must begin

(E NUMQUANT)(the NUMQUANT is true of the :horses:....

The remainder of (25) requires the reconstruction of the phrase 'equals FIVE'. There are two possible reconstructions of 'equals'. The primary reconstruction is modeled on the reconstruction of entailment. The secondary reconstruction is in terms of truth. Though I think of the primary reconstruction as the most important, I shall give both.

The primary reconstruction of

N equals FIVE

is

(KINDPREDCON)(the (NUMQUANT KINDPREDCON) may be inferred from the (:there be five: KINDPREDCON) and the (:there be five: KINDPREDCON) may be inferred from the (NUMQUANT KINDPREDCON)).

I shall abbreviate the above as:

the NUMQUANT mi the :there be five:

(where 'mi' is supposed to suggest "mutually inferrible").

Thus the primary reconstruction of (25) is:

(25.1) (E NUMQUANT)(the NUMQUANT is true of the :horses: and the NUMQUANT mi the :there be five:).

Of course, (25.1), as explained in A(iii), is equivalent to a statement without DSTs.

For the secondary reconstruction, I introduce an equivalence relation which I call "material equivalence" and write 'meq'. For the time being, I explain material equivalence only for numerical quantifiers.

(28) the NUMQUANTA meq the NUMQUANTB

is equivalent to

(29) (KINDPREDCON)(the NUMQUANTA is true of the KINDPREDCON if and only if the NUMQUANTB is true of the KINDPREDCON),

i.e., (29.1) (KINDPREDCON)(the (NUMQUANTA KINDPREDCON) is true if and only if the (NUMQUANTB KINDPREDCON) is true).

Speaking intuitively, I would say that (28) is true if and only if certain numerical quantifiers are true of the same things.

I note, for later reference, that, given the present stage of my account, the only instances of (28), (29), and (29.1) that are true are ones that have two tokens of the same SGT in the positions of the variables 'NUMQUANTA' and 'NUMQUANTB'. Thus, in the present example, the only available true instance of (28) is:

the :there be five: meq the :there be five:.

Indeed, (28) is true if and only if

(x)(x is a NUMQUANTA if and only if x is a NUMQUANTB).

As far as my account has gone, there is nothing in these cases which parallels the the following:

the :triangular: meq the :trilateral:

is true (on the obvious definition) as well as

(x)(triangular x if and only if trilateral x),

but (x)(x is a :triangular: if and only if x is a :trilateral:)

is, as I argued in 3C, false. (A similar point holds for 'mi'.)

The secondary reconstruction of (25) is:

(25.2) (E NUMQUANT)(the NUMQUANT is true of the :horses: and the NUMQUANT meq the :there be five:).

The reconstructions of (22.1) include the conjuncts which appear in the reconstructions of (25) and, in addition, another conjunct reminiscent of a conjunct found in the Russellian unpacking of statements with definite descriptions. I give the two reconstructions with the primary first:

(22.2) (E NUMQUANT)(the NUMQUANT is true of the :horses: and

the NUMQUANT mi the :there be five: and

(NUMQUANTA)(if the NUMQUANTA is true of the :horses:, then the NUMQUANT mi the NUMQUANTA)).

(22.3) (E NUMQUANT)(the NUMQUANT is true of the :horses: and

the NUMQUANT meq the :there be five: and

(NUMQUANTA)(if the NUMQUANTA is true of the :horses:, then the NUMQUANT meq the NUMQUANTA)).

The arrangement of the conjuncts has no significance; it simply sets them off for easier reading.

The reconstructions of

(30) the number of K-kind equals FIVE,

which are (30.1) and (30.2), are obtained by reproducing (22.2) and (22.3), respectively, with the variable 'KINDPRED-CON' where (22.2) and (22.3) have the SGT ':horses:'. Similarly, the reconstructions of

(31) the number of K-kind equals N,

which are (31.1) and (31.2), have yet one more variable, say 'NUMQUANTB', where (30.1) and (30.2) have the SGT ':there be five:'.

(iii) Addition and Order for Number Universals

Though the reconstruction of (31) is a propitious start, there are other matrices containing 'the number of' which must be reconstructed:

(32) the number of Ks plus the number of Hs equals the number of Js,

(33) the number of Ks is greater than the number of Hs,

(34) the number of Ks is smaller than the number of Hs

and (35) the number of Ks equals the number of Hs.

It is appropriate that (32), (33), (34), and (35) have 'equals', 'is greater than', and 'is smaller than' rather than 'as many as', 'more than', and 'fewer than'. The latter, I have suggested, are connectives and may appear in object language statements, whereas the former, if my subsequent account is correct, appear only in metalinguistic statements.

Consider the following instance of (32):

(36) the number of horses (in the barn) plus the number of cows (in the field) equals the number of animals (on the farm).

The phrases in parentheses remind us of the token-reflexive nature of statements like (36) and that (36) is not saying anything, tout court, about the number of horses, the number of cows, and the number of animals. However, having made this point to avoid possible confusion, I shall return to my policy of treating statements like (36) without the modifying phrases.

According to the previous subsection, (36) should first become

(37) the number of horsekind plus the number of cowkind equals the number of animalkind

and then

(37.1) the number universal which horsekind exemplifies plus the number universal which cowkind exemplifies equals the number universal which animalkind exemplifies.

Similar reductions can be made in the task of reconstructing (33), (34), and (35). For example, consider the following instance of (33):

(38) the number of horses is greater than the number of cows.

Paraphrased in the same fashion as (36), (38) becomes

(39) the number universal which horsekind exemplifies is greater than the number universal which cowkind exemplifies.

What is needed in order to reconstruct (37.1) is an account of such statements as

(40) FIVE plus THREE equals EIGHT.

In the case of instances of (33), (34), and (35), the sorts of statements which must be investigated are:

(41) FIVE is greater than THREE,

(42) THREE is smaller than FIVE,

and (43) FIVE equals FIVE.

All of these statements will, in line with my practice in the previous subsection, be given a primary and a secondary reconstruction. I begin with (40), for an account of (40) provides the resources to handle the rest.

Subsection A(ii) appealed to our intuitive appreciation of what sorts of inferences were connected with (8), the conjunction of

(8.1) (H)(I)(E J)(if no H be an I, then if there be five H and there be three I, then there be eight J)

and (8.2) (J)(E H)(E I)(if no H be an I, then if there be eight J, then there be five H and there be three I).

The rules of inference I shall now set out are formulated with these inferences and (8) in mind and should be viewed against the background of the primary reconstruction of 'N equals FIVE' in B(ii).

The rules are conditional rules and the condition is the ML analog of 'no H be an I'. Stated intuitively, the ML condition is that the kind predicate which is combined with a :there be five: and the kind predicate which is combined with a :there be three: are true of different things. Consider the kind predicates, the :horse: and the :cow:. Corresponding to the condition that no horse is a cow is the ML condition:

(44) not(E INDCON)(the :horse: is true of the INDCON and the :cow: is true of the INDCON).

The statement for which (44) is an abbreviation is equivalent to:

not(E INDCON)(the (:horse: INDCON) is true and the (:cow: INDCON) is true).

The statement matrix needed for the primary reconstruction of (40) is:

(45) not(E INDCON)(the KINDPREDCONA is true of the INDCON and the KINDPREDCONB is true of the INDCON).

I abbreviate (45) to

the KINDPREDCONA disj the KINDPREDCONB

and (44), correspondingly, to

the :horse: disj the :cow:.

The primary reconstruction of (40) is (46), the conjunction of

(46.1) (KINDPREDCONA)(KINDPREDCONB)(E KINDPREDCON) (given the KINDPREDCONA disj the KINDPREDCONB, the (:there be eight: KINDPREDCON) may be inferred from the (:there be five: KINDPREDCONA) and the (:there be three: KINDPREDCONB))

and (46.2) (KINDPREDCON)(E KINDPREDCONA)(E KINDPREDCONB) (given the KINDPREDCONA disj the KINDPREDCONB, the ((:there be five: KINDPREDCONA) :and: (:there be three: KINDPREDCONB)) may be inferred from the (:there be eight: KINDPREDCON)).

I abbreviate (46) to (47), the conjunction of

(47.1) the :there be eight: mbif the :there be five: and the :there be three:

and (47.2) the :there be five and there be three: mbif the :there be eight:

(where 'mbif' is supposed to suggest "may be inferred from").

Several observations are in order. First, the singular term conjunction in (46.1) and (47.1) must be understood as the one in the example in 3A(ii). Thus the matrix within (46.1), without the condition, is <u>not</u> equivalent to

> the (:there be eight: KINDPREDCON) may be inferred from the (:there be five: KINDPREDCONA) and the (:there be eight: KINDPREDCON) may be inferred from the (:there be three: KINDPREDCONB).

Second, the arguments for (46.1) and (46.2) are ML analogs of the arguments for (8.1) and (8.2). The key to these arguments is in the kind predicates characterized in the cases of (8.1) and (8.2). For example, if we have ':horse in the field:' and ':cow in the barn:', then the SGT necessary for (46.1) is ':horse in the field or cow in the barn:'.

The secondary reconstruction of (40) also utilizes techniques developed in the reconstructions of B(ii). In the present case, however, there is no way to use material equivalence and there is no reason to employ 'is true of', rather than 'is true'. The secondary reconstruction of (40) is no more than a direct ML analog of (8) which contains 'is true'. The secondary reconstruction of (40) is (48), the conjunction of

(48.1) (KINDPREDCONA)(KINDPREDCONB)(E KINDPREDCON) (if the KINDPREDCONA disj the KINDPREDCONB, then if the (:there be five: KINDPREDCONA) is true and the (:there be three: KINDPREDCONB)

is true, then the (:there be eight: KINDPREDCON is true)

and (48.2) (KINDPREDCON)(E KINDPREDCONA)(E KINDPREDCONB) (if the KINDPREDCONA disj the KINDPREDCONB, then if the (:there be eight: KINDPREDCON) is true, then the ((:there be five: KINDPREDCONA) :and: (:there be three: KINDPREDCONB)) is true).

I shall abbreviate (48) as (49), the conjunction of

(49.1) the :there be five: and the :there be three: mimp the :there be eight:

and (49.2) the :there be eight: mimp the :there be five and there be three:

(where 'mimp' is to suggest "material implication" and is intended to remind one of its relationship to 'meq').

Using the abbreviations I have given, it is simple to state the reconstructions of

(50) N plus M equals L.

The primary reconstruction of (50) is the conjunction of

(50.1) the NUMQUANTA mbif the NUMQUANTB and the NUMQUANTC

and (50.2) the (NUMQUANTA :and: NUMQUANTC) mbif the NUMQUANTA.

The secondary reconstruction of (50) is the conjunction

the NUMQUANTB and the NUMQUANTC mimp the NUMQUANTA

and the NUMQUANTA mimp the (NUMQUANTB :and: NUMQUANTC).

As the reconstructions of (32) use the reconstructions of (50), so the reconstructions of (33), (34), and (35) use, respectively, the reconstructions of

(51) N is greater than M,

(52) N is smaller than M,

and (53) N equals M.

Since (52) can be defined in terms of (51) and (53), I shall deal with (51) and not (52). The matrix (51) can be defined using (50); (51) is equivalent to

(54) (E L)(M plus L equals N).

Thus the instance of (51) I gave earlier, namely,

(41) FIVE is greater than THREE,

is equivalent to

(E L)(THREE plus L equals FIVE).

The reconstructions of (54) come from the reconstructions of (50) by the appropriate E-quantification.

The reconstructions of (53) are:

the NUMQUANTA mi the NUMQUANTB

and the NUMQUANTA meq the NUMQUANTB.

With these reconstructions, I am in a position to reconstruct (32), (33), (34), and (35). Consider (36), the instance of (32) which I had paraphrased as

(37.1) the number universal which horsekind exemplifies plus the number universal which cowkind exemplifies equals the number universal which animalkind exemplifies.

I give only the primary reconstruction of (37.1); the secondary reconstruction can easily be worked out using the primary as a model.

The primary reconstruction of (37.1) requires the matrix

[i] the NUMQUANTA is true of the :horses: and

the NUMQUANTB is true of the :cows: and
the NUMQUANT is true of the :animals:

and a matrix [ii], like [i], except in having 'NUMQUANTC', 'NUMQUANTD', and 'NUMQUANTE' where [i] has, respectively, 'NUMQUANT', 'NUMQUANTA', and 'NUMQUANTB'. The reconstruction is

(E NUMQUANT)(E NUMQUANTA)(E NUMQUANTB)([i] and

the NUMQUANT mbif the NUMQUANTA and the NUMQUANTB and

the (NUMQUANTA :and: NUMQUANTB) mbif the NUMQUANT and

(NUMQUANTC)(NUMQUANTD)(NUMQUANTE)(if [ii], then
the NUMQUANT mi the NUMQUANTC and
the NUMQUANTA mi the NUMQUANTD and
the NUMQUANTB mi the NUMQUANTE)).

The reconstructions of the matrix (32) are obtained from the reconstructions of (37.1) by dropping the SGTs, ':horses:', ':cows:', and ':animals:' and adding ML variables. The procedures for handling the reconstructions of (33), (34), and (35) are the same.

(iv) <u>Some Properties of 'plus' and Further Reconstructions</u>

Several properties of addition are easily shown to be preserved by my reconstructions of 'plus'. According to our intuitive understanding of addition, it is commutative and associative. Thus, on my reconstructions, it should be true that

FIVE plus THREE equals EIGHT

if and only if

THREE plus FIVE equals EIGHT

and that

FIVE plus (THREE plus TWO) equals TEN

if and only if

(FIVE plus THREE) plus TWO equals TEN.

That my reconstructions of 'plus' preserve these properties rests on similar properties of conjunction. Take commutativity as an example. The truth (8) is clearly equivalent to a truth which has

there be three I and there be five H

instead of

there be five H and there be three I

and which has the quantifiers with the variables 'H' and 'I' switched in order. Similarly, there are rules equivalent to (46.1) which have the phrase

the (:there be three: KINDPREDCONB) and the (:there be five: KINDPREDCONA)

instead of the phrase

the (:there be five: KINDPREDCONA) and the (:there be three: KINDPREDCONB)

and ones equivalent to (46.2) which have the phrase

the ((:there be three: KINDPREDCONB) :and: (:there be five: KINDPREDCONA))

instead of the phrase

the ((:there be five: KINDPREDCONA) :and: (:there be three: KINDPREDCONB)).

Similar claims are true of the matrices (50.1) and (50.2). Analogous points can be made about associativity with the help of logical truths and rules which involve two :and:s instead of one.

It is also easily shown that my reconstruction can accomodate an "identity element" for 'plus' and hence such statements as

FIVE plus ZERO equals FIVE.

The possibility of introducing an identity element reflects that fact that statements of the sort of which the following is an example are true:

(H)(I)(E J)(if no H be an I, then if there be five H and there be no I, then there be five J)

and (J)(E H)(E I)(if no H be an I, then if there be five J, then there be five H and there be no I).

The DST matrix

the (:there be no: KINDPREDCON)

appears in the reconstructions of statements containing 'ZERO'. With this term, reconstructions of

N plus ZERO equals N

can be worked out from the reconstructions of (50).

Notice that if I were to keep 'ZERO' in my reconstruction of number universals, I should have to alter part of my earlier account. For example, with 'ZERO',

(51) N is greater than M

is equivalent to

(E L)(M plus L equals N and not(L equals ZERO)),

not to (54). Further, my list of quantifiers would have to begin with :there be no:s and my reconstructions would be of, not the natural numbers, but what is usually called the "non-negative integers." But since it is clear that I can add to my reconstructions of number universals a reconstruction of

'ZERO' and since the complications bequeathed by the inclusion of 'ZERO' are not very enlightening, I shall return to a consideration of the natural numbers.

The following statements are analogous to some of Peano's axioms for arithmetic:

(55) ONE is a natural number

and (56) (N)(M)(N plus M is a natural number).

In 4B(vi), I shall consider other analogs of Peano's axioms.

The reconstruction of (55) is straightforward and obviously true:

(55.1) (KINDPREDCON)(the (:there be one: KINDPREDCON) is a numerical quantifier statement).

A similar reconstruction of (56) is also satisfactory if one grants, as I am prepared to, that conjunctions of numerical quantifier statements are numerical quantifier statements:

(56.1) (NUMQUANTA)(NUMQUANTB)(KINDPREDCONA)(KINDPREDCONB)(the ((NUMQUANTA KINDPREDCONA) :and: (NUMQUANTB KINDPREDCONB)) is a numerical quantifier statement).

I do, however, have several other options with regard to (56). One of them is simply to replace it with a statement that the sum of any natural numbers is equal to a natural number:

(57) (N)(M)(E L)(N plus M equals L and L is a natural number).

On this option, addition would not, as mathematicians say, be "closed" under addition. But given that equality is an equivalence relation (a point to be discussed in this subsection), every sum would be "equivalence-related" to a natural number. I find nothing objectionable with this state of affairs and thus would be satisfied with this option.

Another option is simply to alter my reconstructions of (55) and (56) so that instead of the predicate 'is a numerical quantifier statement', they have the predicate 'is a numerical quantifier statement or a conjunction of numerical quantifier statements'. This option, too, seems satisfactory to me. It is important to notice that this option does not require any tampering with variables. In particular, the variables 'N', 'M', 'L', and so on are still variables for singular terms in which 'plus' does not occur.

An interesting variant on this option is made possible by the introduction of a new notation which makes certain abbreviations possible. Something of the sort has been done in the abbreviations of the previous subsections. What I have in mind now, though, is much more thoroughgoing: it begins with numerical quantifier statements themselves. Another reason for devoting space to this matter is that devices of the sort employed in this subsection are helpful in treating multiplication for number universals in the next subsection.

I shall introduce "additive" quantifiers by means of "conjunctive" numerical quantifiers. The introduction of conjunctive numerical quantifiers requires a little care: I cannot introduce

(there be five & there be three)K

as there be five K and there be three K,

for the latter matrix is logically inconsistent. The conjunctive statement matrix which must be used is:

(58) there be five H and there be three I.

I introduce

(59) (there be five & there be three)(H, I)

as equivalent to (58). Notice that in this notation it is

the facts of left-to-right order which are significant in determining which kind variable goes with which numerical quantifier.

I then introduce

(five && three)(H, I)

as equivalent to (59). And for uniformity of notation, I introduce

eight J

as equivalent to

there be eight J.

With quantifiers like 'five && three', which I shall call "additive" quantifiers, at my disposal, I am in a position to rewrite such truths as (8).

Further, SGTs like

:five && three:

and :eight:

can be used in ML reconstructions. Once again, care is required. It will not do to write

(:five && three: KINDPREDCON).

The following is correct:

(:five && three: (KINDPREDCONA, KINDPREDCONB)).

Moreover, it is necessary to have new ML variables (e.g., 'ADDQUANT', 'ADDQUANTA', etc.).

With these ML terms, it is possible to produce reconstructions of statements containing 'plus'. For example, the primary reconstruction of (40), abbreviated in a manner similar to that in which I did abbreviate the previous primary reconstruction of (40), is:

the :eight: mbif the :five && three: and
the :five && three: mbif the :eight:.

The new primary reconstruction of (50) is (in abbreviated form):

the NUMQUANT mbif the ADDQUANT and
the ADDQUANT mbif the NUMQUANT.

The reconstruction of (56) becomes:

(56.2) (ADDQUANT)(KINDPREDCONA)(KINDPREDCONB)(the (ADDQUANT (KINDPREDCONA, KINDPREDCONB)) is a numerical quantifier statement or an additive quantifier statement).

Of course, the reconstruction of (55) has the same disjunctive predicate as (56.2):

(55.2) (KINDPREDCON)(the (:one: KINDPREDCON) is a numerical quantifier statement or an additive quantifier statement).

The final matter of this subsection concerns 'equals'. The reconstructions of this section handle two sorts of equality statements. One sort is reconstructed with 'mi' or with 'meq'. As I pointed out in B(ii), the only true instances of this sort of equality statement are all instances of

N equals N.

So, for these equality statements, it is quite clear that

(N)(N equals N)

(N)(M)(if N equals M, then M equals N)

and (N)(M)(L)(if N equals M and M equals L, then N equals L).

An example of the other sort of equality statement is (40). These equality statements involve 'plus'. It is true for these statements that

(N)(M)(L)(if N plus M equals L, then L equals N plus M)

because the reconstructions of

L equals N plus M

have the same conjuncts as the reconstructions of

(50) N plus M equals L.

That transitivity obtains for these statements is a consequence of the transitivity of 'mbif' and 'mimp'. That reflexivity holds for these statements can be seen from the primary reconstruction of

(N)(M)(N plus M equals N plus M)

which is:

(KINDPREDCONA)(KINDPREDCONB)(E KINDPREDCONC)(E KINDPREDCOND)(given the KINDPREDCONA disj the KINDPREDCONB, the ((NUMQUANTA KINDPREDCONC) :and: (NUMQUANTB KINDPREDCOND)) may be inferred from the (NUMQUANTA KINDPREDCONA) and the (NUMQUANTB KINDPREDCONB))

and (KINDPREDCONC)(KINDPREDCOND)(E KINDPREDCONA)(E KINDPREDCONB)(given the KINDPREDCONA disj the KINDPREDCONB, the ((NUMQUANTA KINDPREDCONA) :and: (NUMQUANTB KINDPREDCONB)) may be inferred from the ((NUMQUANTA KINDPREDCONC) :and: (NUMQUANTB KINDPREDCOND))).

The secondary reconstruction is similar and is also true. Finally, note that if the reconstructed equality statements allow what logicians call "replacement", then those abbreviated statements which are instances of

--- mbif ... and ... mbif ---

or --- mimp ... and ... mimp ---

also allow it.

(v) Multiplication

As the reconstructions of statements like (40) are crucial to the last subsection, so the reconstructions of statements like

(60) TWO times THREE equals SIX

are the key to all others in this subsection. I shall not, however, once (60) is reconstructed, bother to reconstruct other statements involving 'times' (e.g., those with both 'times' and the phrase 'the number of'). The reconstructions of (60) fit into these other reconstructions as the reconstructions of (40) fit into the others of the last subsection.

What statement corresponds to (60) as (8) corresponds to (40)? The search for an answer to this question is aided by reflection on a sort of inference which might justifiably, I think, be called "multiplicative."

Consider the obviously enthymatic inference:

(61) ....There be two automobiles. Hence, there be eight wheels.

What statements must be added to the premise of (61) in order to make a valid argument which is not enthymatic?

An obvious addition is the statement

every automobile has four wheels

which is

(62) for every automobile, there be four wheels (which are of that automobile).

The importance of the material in parentheses is easily brought out. Suppose that the automobiles spoken of by the premise of (61) are George and Harry. Given (62) <u>without</u> the parenthetical material, it follows that

there be four wheels and there be four wheels.

Unfortunately, this conjunction is not sufficient for the conclusion that there be eight wheels. What is sufficient follows from (62):

(63) there be four wheels of George's and there be four wheels of Harry's.

Then, given that nothing is both a wheel of George's and a wheel of Harry's, it is correct to infer from (63) that there be eight wheels (of the automobiles).

A reformulation of the argument incorporating what has been discussed is:

(64) (x)(if Hx, then there be four I which have R to x)

(x)(y)(if Hx and Hy and not(x = y), then no I which has R to x be an I which has R to y)

there be two H

hence, there be eight J,

where the variable 'J' is restricted to the disjunctions of the predicates which appear in the consequent of instances of the first premise and to predicates materially equivalent to these disjunctions.

The distinctive feature of the argument (64) is that its premises permit the inference of a conjunction of numerical quantifier statements (e.g., (63)) which have the same numerical quantifier (in this case, the :there be four:) and are such that any kind term in these statements is disjoint from any other kind term in these statements. I shall call these conjunctions "multiplicative" conjunctions. Other arguments, besides (64), may sanction multiplicative conjunctions. But I intend neither to investigate which arguments these are and whether they are justly called "multiplicative" nor to consider what else, if anything, must be added to (64) in order to insure its correctness. What I do intend to do is to focus on what I have called "the distinctive feature" of such arguments as (64) and to build my account of multiplication around that. Thus, on my view, multiplications are, ultimately, special additions, additions which involve multiplicative conjunctions. Multiplicative inferences are those inferences whose premises, whether they resemble (64) or not, insure that multiplicative conjunctions may be inferred.

Similarly, divisions of natural numbers involve "breakings up" of a numerical quantifier statement into a multiplicative conjunction. Divisional inferences are those inferences which have premises which insure such a conjunction. For example, a divisional inference is involved in the enthymatic inference from

there be eight wheels

to there be two cars.

In this case, the conjunction which must be obtained from the given premise and the other statements suppressed in the enthymeme has, as in the case of the multiplicative inference already discussed, numerical quantifier statements with the numerical quantifier, the :there be four:.

From the point of view of the preceding discussion, there is no difficulty about which truth corresponds to (60) as (8) does to (40); it is (65), the conjunction of

(65.1) (H)(I)(E J)(if no H be an I, then if there be

three H and there be three I, then there be six J)

and (65.2) (J)(E H)(E I)(if no H be an I, then if there be six J, then there be three H and there be three I).

In (65), the multiplication of THREE <u>by</u> TWO is manifested only in the conjunction

(66) there be three H and there be three I.

But more can be done by means of definitions which are, in many ways, similar to the abbreviations discussed in the last subsection. These definitions introduce terms by means of multiplicative conjunctions like the instances of (66). For example,

(66.1) two(there be three)(H, I)

is equivalent to (66). Thus (65) is equivalent to (67), the conjunction of

(67.1) (H)(I)(E J)(if no H be an I, then if two(there be three)(H, I), then there be six J)

and (67.2) (J)(E H)(E I)(if no H be an I, then if there be six J, then two(there be three)(H, I)).

Numerical words appearing with numerical quantifiers, e.g., 'two' in (66.1) and (67), are not abbreviations of numerical quantifiers, though their roles are explained by means of numerical quantifiers. For example, a statement in which there is one numerical quantifier and one kind term and the numerical quantifier appears with a :one: is equivalent to a statement with the same numerical and the same kind term. Given any numerical quantifier and a kind term and another kind term disjoint from the former kind term, any statement which has that numerical quantifier appearing with a :two:

and has both kind terms is equivalent to a multiplicative conjunction in which there are two conjuncts and that numerical quantifier is the quantifier of all the conjuncts and one kind term is in one conjunct and one kind term is in the other conjunct. It is possible to set down a recipe, like the one for numerical quantifiers, for the descriptions of statement matrices which are the definientia of the numerical words in matrices like (66.1). I shall call these numerical words "multiplicative numerical words" and the entire quantifiers they appear in "multiplicative quantifiers."

It can be seen from the examples in the preceding paragraph that all the numerical words which appear in the ML descriptions of the definientia of multiplicative numerical words are in numerical quantifiers or in contexts which can be handled as were (17) and (18) in B(ii). Further, the metalinguistic characterizations of the roles of multiplicative numerical words stand in the same general relationship to the statements containing those words as metalinguistic characterizations of logical connectives and ordinary quantifiers stand to statements containing these logical terms (see 3A(ii)).

Multiplicative numerical words permit the formulation of truths, e.g., (67), which, though equivalent to ones concerning addition, are distinctly multiplicative. Previously I said that what is distinctive of multiplicative inferences is that their premises permit the inference of multiplicative conjunctions. The metalinguistic statements which describe these conjunctions and which thus state the multiplicative features of these conjunctions are not, and cannot be, part of a multiplicative inference itself. But multiplicative numerical words can be part of such inferences. And the statements which introduce multiplicative numerical words incorporate directly and without change the descriptions of multiplicative conjunctions. Thus though multiplicative numerical words do not make statements in which they appear metalinguistic statements, they have roles which are characterized by metalinguistic statements that include descriptions of the conjunctions which are distinctive of multiplication.

Reconstructions of (60) contain SGTs, like

:two(there be three):,

which are true of multiplicative quantifiers. One such reconstruction, a primary reconstruction of (60), is (68), the conjunction of

(68.1) (KINDPREDCONA)(KINDPREDCONB)(E KINDPREDCON) (given the KINDPREDCONA disj the KINDPREDCONB, the (:there be six: KINDPREDCON) may be inferred from the (:two(there be three): (KINDPREDCONA, KINDPREDCONB)))

and (68.2) (KINDPREDCON)(E KINDPREDCONA)(E KINDPREDCONB) (given the KINDPREDCONA disj the KINDPREDCONB, the (:two(there be three): (KINDPREDCONA, KINDPREDCONB)) may be inferred from the (:there be six: KINDPREDCON)).

A secondary reconstruction of (60) is easily worked out from (68).

It is possible to formulate other acceptable reconstructions of (60); these reconstructions do not contain the SGT ':two(there be three):'. An additional piece of terminology is helpful: a :there be three: multiplicative conjunction is a multiplicative conjunction in which the numerical quantifier is the :there be three:. Of these reconstructions of (60) the primary is (69), the conjunction of

(69.1) (KINDPREDCONA)(KINDPREDCONB)(E KINDPREDCON) (the (:there be six: KINDPREDCON) may be inferred from the :there be three: multiplicative conjunction in which there be two :there be three:s and the KINDPREDCONA and the KINDPREDCONB are the kind terms)

and (69.2) (KINDPREDCON)(E KINDPREDCONA)(E KINDPREDCONB) (the :there be three: multiplicative conjunction in which there be two :there be three:s and the KINDPREDCONA and the KINDPREDCONB are the kind terms may be inferred from the (:there be six: KINDPREDCON)).

It should be remembered that a numerical quantifier statement must contain a kind term and that the definition of 'multiplicative conjunction' includes the condition that the kind terms of the conjunction are disjoint.

Notice that the phrase

(70) :there be three: multiplicative conjunction in which there be two :there be three:s

is true of just those conjunctions which are equivalent by definition to statements with the multiplicative quantifier, the :two(there be three):. Statement (69) incorporates the description of these conjunctions, whereas (68) has the multiplicative numerical word which is introduced by means of these conjunctions.

Though (69) is satisfactory as a reconstruction of (60), in one way it is not quite as good as (68). Consider, as a parallel, (65) and (67). It is (67), not (65), which contains a linguistic item, viz., a multiplicative numerical word, whose role is directly connected with the fact that (60) is about the multiplication of TWO by THREE. Similarly, (69) also lacks a linguistic item of this sort. By contrast, (68) does have such an item since the SGT

:two(there be three):

is true of multiplicative quantifiers which must contain a

multiplicative numerical word. This state of affairs stands out even more clearly in the matrices of which the above multiplicative quantifier SGT is an instance. Thus using the ML variable 'MULTNUMWORD', I can write the SGT matrices

(MULTNUMWORD :there be three:)

and (71) (MULTNUMWORD NUMQUANT).

The next task, the reconstructing of

(72) N times M equals L,

presents a hazard I shall not attempt to negotiate till chapter 6. The reconstructions of (72) which follow the lines of (68) will clearly have the matrix (71). Thus these reconstructions of (72) will have, within the metalinguistic quantifiers, conditional statement matrices which are of the sorts illustrated by the following:

(73.1) given ..., then the (NUMQUANT KINDPREDCON) may be inferred from the (MULTNUMWORD NUMQUANTA (...))

and (73.2) given ..., then the (MULTNUMWORD NUMQUANTA (...)) may be inferred from the (NUMQUANT KINDPREDCON).

The hazard which must be negotiated in filling out (73.1) and (73.2) arises because the definitions of multiplicative numerical words insure that what appears in the places marked by the blanks in (73.1) and (73.2) is different for instances of (72) which differ in the multiplicative numerical word SGT needed in their reconstructions. Thus since the multiplicative numerical word SGT needed for the reconstructions of (60) is ':two:', there are two ML variables with the SGT ':two(there be three):'. If the SGT needed is ':three:', then there must be three ML variables with the multiplicative quantifier SGT.

A similar obstacle can be described in the case of reconstructions of (72) which are patterned on (69).

For the present, it will suffice that there is no difficulty in reconstructing all the instances of (72) in an orderly fashion. There is an obvious recipe, devised by considering the definientia of multiplicative numerical words, that enables one to proceed from the reconstructions of

ONE times M equals L

to the reconstructions of

TWO times M equals L

and so on. Consequently, I can reconstruct every instance of

(M)(E L)(N time M equals L).

The points of the preceding paragraph are important for the reconstruction of a statement which is for multiplication what (56) is for addition:

(74) (N)(M)(N times M is a natural number).

The options in the case of (74) are similar to those in the case of (56). I restrict myself to two points. First, one satisfactory move is to reconstruct 'natural number' by means of the disjunction 'numerical quantifier or additive quantifier or multiplicative quantifier'. Second, another satisfactory move is to replace (74) by the true statement which corresponds to (57):

(75) (N)(M)(E L)(N times M equals L and L is a natural number).

The reconstruction of (75) is by means of the predicate 'numerical quantifier', not the disjunctive predicate just mentioned.

However, either of these options requires surmounting the obstacle which stands in the way of reconstructing (72).

For the moment, then, all I can say is that I have reconstructions of every instance of both

(76) (M)(N times M is a natural number)

and (77) (M)(E L)(N times M equals L and L is a natural number).

The truth of the instances of (77) assures us that every multiplicative quantifier statement stands in the familiar inferential and truth relationships to a numerical quantifier statement. So, given the instances of (77) and

(56) (N)(M)(E L)(N plus M equals L and L is a natural number),

it is possible to deal with statements which are more complex than (40) and (60). For example, there are the statements

(78) TWO times (THREE times FOUR) equals TWENTY-FOUR,

(79) TWO times (THREE plus FOUR) equals FOURTEEN,

(80) (TWO plus THREE) times FOUR equals TWENTY,

(81) (TWO times THREE) times FOUR equals TWENTY-FOUR,

and (82) (TWO times THREE) plus FOUR equals TEN.

As examples of the employment of the instances of (77) and of (56), I offer the reductions of

TWO times (THREE times FOUR),

(TWO plus THREE) times FOUR,

and (TWO times THREE) plus FOUR

to, respectively,

TWO times TWELVE,

FIVE times FOUR,

and SIX plus FOUR.

These latter terms are all reconstructed on the pattern illustrated in the reconstructions of (40) and (60).

In light of these reductions, it seems to me to be satisfactory to decide to take, for example, as the reconstructions of (78) the reconstructions of

TWO times TWELVE equals TWENTY-FOUR,

as the reconstructions of (80) the reconstructions of

FIVE times FOUR equals TWENTY,

and as the reconstructions of (82) the reconstructions of

SIX plus FOUR equals TEN.

This decision would bring it about that every arithmetical statement involving 'plus' or 'times' and 'equals' would have reconstructions of one of two basic sorts, i.e., of the sort of which (40) is an example or of the sort of which (60) is an example.

It is possible, however, to provide statements (78) through (82) with reconstructions which are different from the reconstruction of statements like (40) and (60). To do this one begins, from scratch, with numerical quantifiers, additive quantifiers, multiplicative quantifiers, and multiplicative numerical words, and introduces rules for multiplicative numerical words which permit them to appear in other contexts than multiplicative quantifiers. These rules also introduce what I shall call "mixed quantifiers." For simplicity, I indicate the sort of rules required without attention to the now-familiar matters concerning notation for kind term variables and their quantifiers.

The first step is to arrange that multiplicative numerical words can appear with quantifiers which are not numerical quantifiers but which are introduced directly or indirectly in terms of numerical quantifiers. Thus, for example, a statement with the multiplicative numerical word 'two' combined with any such quantifier is equivalent to a conjunction in which there are two conjuncts having this quantifier. For example,

(78.1) two(three(there be four))

is introduced by means of

(78.2) three(there be four) ... and three(there be four) ___;

(79.1) two(three && four)

is introduced by means of

(79.2) (three && four) ... and (three && four) ___.

Notice that instances of (78.2) and (79.2) are not, strictly speaking, multiplicative conjunctions. Multiplicative conjunctions have conjuncts which are numerical quantifier statements. But the quantifiers of (78.2) (79.2) are not numerical quantifiers. These conjunctions are what I shall call "extended multiplicative conjunctions."

The mixed quantifiers of the above example are the basis for distinctive reconstructions of (78) and (79). Statement (78) is reconstructed with the SGT

:two(three(there be four)):

and (79) with

:two(three && four):.

The next step is to formulate rules for complex multiplicative numerical words. I illustrate these rules with two examples which also provide the mixed quantifiers necessary for the reconstructions of (80) and (81):

(80.1) (two and three)(there be four)

is introduced by means of

(80.2) two(there be four) ... and three(there be four) ___;

(81.1) (two(three))(there be four)

is introduced by means of

(81.2) three(there be four) ... and three(there be four) ___.

With these mixed quantifiers, reconstructions of (80) and (81) can be formulated with, respectively, the SGTs

:(two and three)(there be four):

and :two(three))(there be four):.

It should be noted that these new rules for multiplicative numerical words are very general and permit multiplicative numerical words to appear even with mixed quantifiers. This fact insures that, no matter how complex the context, the necessary mixed quantifier and corresponding SGT are defined.

Certain of the properties of multiplication are demonstrable from the introductions of mixed quantifiers. For example, since (78.1) and (81.1) are both introduced by means of the same conjunction, it follows that

(83) TWO times (THREE times FOUR) equals (TWO times THREE) times FOUR.

Similarly, the handling of (80.1) and its kin insures one sort of distribution. Of course, the introductions chosen are not the only possible ones. For instance, (81.1) could have been introduced by means of

(81.3) (three and three)(there be four).

Then it would have been a matter of demonstration, a simple one to be sure, that associativity held as in (83).

The important point is that whatever follows from the introductions of mixed quantifiers, there always are other things which are in need of demonstration. Thus, even though (83) is obtained directly from the rules for multiplicative numerical words, it still must be shown that such an equality does not conflict with what is obtained by the reductions of

TWO times (THREE times FOUR)

and (TWO times THREE) times FOUR.

So, in the case of (83), it must also be the case that

TWO times TWELVE equals SIX times FOUR.

Similarly, since the introduction of (80.1) by means of (80.2) yields directly that

(TWO plus THREE) times FOUR equals (TWO times FOUR) plus (THREE times FOUR),

it must also be the case that

FIVE times FOUR equals EIGHT plus TWELVE.

Whether these and other properties of multiplication might be demonstrated from features of my reconstructions of 'times', as associativity and commutivity of addition were derived from my reconstruction of 'plus', is not a topic I wish to pursue. The next subsection settles these matters by giving an account of mathematical induction. With mathematical induction and complete recipes for the definientia of additive, multiplicative, and mixed quantifiers, the properties of multiplication and addition can be demonstrated in the usual fashion.

Finally, the reconstructions of (72) (provided in chapter 6) and the reconstructions of (50) provide the means for reconstructing statements with arithmetical predicates, i.e., those predicates, like 'prime', which are defined in terms of addition and multiplication. For example,

prime(L)

is equivalent to

(N)(M)(L does not equal ONE and if N times M equals L, then N equals L and M equals ONE or N equals ONE and M equals L).

(Statement (17.3) in subsection B(ii) can now be handled in the obvious way.) The account of mathematical induction in the next subsection provides the wherewithal to reproduce the usual arithmetical demonstrations concerning statements containing 'prime' and other arithmetical predicates.

(vi) Induction and Succession

The immediate purpose of this subsection is to give an account of succession and mathematical induction. In the process, I make explicit what has only been intuitively indicated previously: viz., the definition of the predicate 'numerical quantifier'.

The structure of the subsection is complicated. Part of my account parallels certain set-theoretic accounts of the natural numbers. It does not, however, actually involve what I would call "sets" (or, "classes"). The parallels are close enough to render it obvious that my account can be carried on in essentially the same vein as these set-theoretic ones. Consequently, it emerges from my account that the reconstructions of the previous subsections do not reconstruct truths (falsehoods) as falsehoods (truths). I also show that I can, with a few additions, get a result which is not found in set-theoretic treatments which are formalist. Finally, I consider some statements which adequately relate my account of succession to my reconstructions of addition and multiplication.

The definition of 'the successor of' for numerical quantifiers will be derived from what I earlier called "the recipe for numerical quantifiers." This last phrase, though convenient, is not quite accurate since the recipe is a recipe for the description of some but not all E-quantified statement matrices of a certain sort. All the matrices of this sort have, roughly, the properties mentioned just before the recipe in A(ii). I shall call these matrices "Q-matrices" and give a definition of them. Their characterization in A(ii), though satisfactory at the time, must be clearer for the work of this subsection.

The definition of 'Q-matrix' is as follows: something is a Q-matrix if and only if

[a] it is E-quantified,

[b] it is such that any E-quantified statement matrix it contains which appears within statement matrices appears only within E-quantified statement matrices,

[c] it contains only quantifiers with individual variables and every quantifier has a different variable from every other quantifier,

[d] it contains exactly one conjunctive statement matrix which appears within no statement matrices except ones that are E-quantified and which contains as a conjunct a universally quantified conditional statement matrix,

[e] it has exactly one universal quantifier,

[f] it has exactly one kind term variable and no other variables but individual variables,

and [g] the antecedent of its universally quantified

conditional statement matrix contains only a statement matrix with a kind term variable combined with the variable of the universal quantifier.

An intuitive idea of what this definition accomplishes can be obtained by considering the following expression:

***(... and (   ) and ...).

Q-matrices written in the notation adopted in 3C have the structure illustrated in the above expression. The asterisks stand where E-quantifiers are in a Q-matrix. The dots stand where the conjunctive statement matrix is; one conjunct of this conjunctive matrix, indicated in the above expression by parentheses enclosing no expressions, is a universally quantified conditional statement matrix that has an antecedent which is described in [g] in the definition. The definition of Q-matrix places, one might say, rather rigid restrictions on the logical structure of Q-matrices, but is rather lax about what may appear within that structure.

Several points about the definition of 'Q-matrix' are important. First, though the forthcoming definition of 'numerical quantifier' relies on the predicate 'Q-matrix', the appearance of the numerical quantifier, the :there be one:, in the definition of 'Q-matrix' causes no difficulties. This appearance of the :there be one: is simply for convenience and can be eliminated in favor of 'at least and at most one' or by means of the matrix described in A(ii).

Second, the definition of 'Q-matrix' in no way makes use of or refers to an ordering of E-quantifiers. Conditions [a] and [b] in the definition make reference to quantifier order unnecessary.

Finally, other predicates besides 'Q-matrix' would be satisfactory for the work which follows. At a later stage of this subsection it will be clear why the predicate 'Q-matrix' is the most convenient choice.

Because of conditions [d], [e], and [f] in the definition of 'Q-matrix', I continue to employ the phrases 'the conjunctive statement matrix', 'the universal quantifier', 'the universally quantified conditional', and the 'kind term variable'.

I define 'succeeds' for Q-matrices. The intuitive import of 'a Q-matrix succeeds another Q-matrix' is that these Q-matrices are related as the descriptions derived from the recipe in A(ii) say they are. However, it is important to notice that, though the recipe in A(ii) contains the phrase 'the first E-quantifier', the definition of 'succeeds' (like the definition of 'Q-matrix') does not appeal to quantifier order. A Q-matrix (the latter) succeeds another Q-matrix (the former) if and only if

[i] every quantifier and quantifier variable of the former is the same as some quantifier and quantifier variable of the latter and there is one E-quantifier and one quantifier variable of the latter that are not in the former

and [ii] the conjunctive statement matrix of the latter is the same as that of the former except that the latter's contains as a conjunct

[a] the statement matrix which is the kind variable combined with the variable of the E-quantifier that is not in the former,

[b] any statement matrix which is the negation of an identity statement matrix which contains the variable of the E-quantifier that is not in the former and the variable of an E-quantifier of the former, and

[c] a universally quantified conditional which is the same as that of the former except that it contains as a disjunct in its consequent the identity statement matrix which has the variable of the E-quantifier that is not in the former and the variable of the universal quantifier.

Notice, once again, that the appearance of :there be one:s in this definition causes no problems.

Under the definition of sameness for Q-matrices which I shall presently give, it will be clear that every Q-matrix has a unique Q-matrix which succeeds it. Consequently, I speak of "the successor of a Q-matrix."

The upcoming definitions are stated in terms of kinds of what I call "elements" of Q-matrices. The list of kinds of elements derives in an obvious way from the definition of 'succeeds'. The kinds of elements are:

E-elements. . .E-quantifiers with individual variables;

K-elements. . .statement matrices which are the kind variable combined with the variable of an E-element;

NI-elements. . .statement matrices which are the negations of identity statement matrices which contain the variable of an E-element and the variable of a different E-element;

I-elements. . .identity statement matrices with the variable of an E-element and the variable of the universal quantifier.

The elements of a Q-matrix are either E-, K-, NI-, or I-elements.

Notice that the definition of 'succeeds' describes a difference between Q-matrices which depends only on elements. In fact, with the terminology of elements, the definiens of that definition can be restated as follows:

[i] every E-element of the former is the same as some E-element of the latter and there is one E-element of the latter that is not an E-element of the former (call it the "new" E-element)

and [ii] the conjunctive statement matrix of the latter is the same as that of the former except that the latter's contains as a conjunct

[a] a K-element which has the variable of the new E-element,

[b] any NI-element which has the variable of the new E-element and the variable of an E-element of the former, and

[c] a universally quantified conditional which is the same as that of the former except that it contains as a disjunct in its consequent the I-element which has the variable of the new E-element.

The following definitions also depend only on elements. The first is a definition of 'is a part of' for Q-matrices: A Q-matrix (the former) is a part of a Q-matrix (the latter) if and only if

(x)(Ey)(if x is an E- (K-, NI-, I-) element of the former, then y is an E- (K-, NI-, I-) element of the latter and (z)(Eu)(not(z is an E- (K-, NI-, I-) element of the former not identical to x and not(u is an E- (K-, NI-, I-) element of the latter not identical to y)))).

If, and only if, a Q-matrix is part of a Q-matrix and the latter is part of the former, the former is the same Q-matrix as the latter. A Q-matrix is a proper part of another Q-matrix if and only if the former is a part of the latter and the former is not the same Q-matrix as the latter.

Q-matrices are not, as I indicated before, all of the sort which I shall want as definientia of numerical quantifiers. The definition of 'Q-matrix' is not restrictive enough. The next move is to define a predicate which is supposed to be true of just those Q-matrices which qualify as definientia of numerical quantifiers.

Any predicate which satisfies the following conditions, I shall call a "successor"predicate in mimicry of common set-theoretic definitions of 'successor set'. To state the first condition, I must reformulate the description (given in A(ii)) of a Q-matrix which is intended to be the definiens of the numerical quantifier, the :there be one:. I shall call this Q-matrix the "Q-matrixA." The Q-matrixA is the Q-matrix

[i] which has at most one E-element

and [ii] whose conjunctive statement matrix has as conjuncts only

[a] at least and at most one K-element and

[b] a universally quantified conditional whose consequent is an I-element with the variable of the universal quantifier and the variable of the E-element.

(Notice that under the relation of being the same Q-matrix as, any Q-matrix which satisfies [i] and [ii] is the same Q-matrix as any other which satisfies [i] and [ii]; that is the justification for the 'the' in 'the Q-matrixA'.) The first condition is:

(84) the Q-matrixA is (an) F.

The second condition is:

(85) (X)(if X is (an) F, then the successor of X is (an) F)

(where 'X' is restricted to singular terms for Q-matrices). Which predicates are successor predicates is not very important, though it is clear that 'Q-matrix' is a successor predicate.

The next step is to define the predicate 'inductive Q-matrix' (which I shall write "IQ-matrix"). 'IQ-matrix' is defined as the conjunction of all the successor predicates. Notice that any other predicate defined from this same conjunction is, by the commutativity and associativity of 'and', materially equivalent to 'IQ-matrix'.

Many philosophers would object to such a definition on the grounds that there might be infinitely many successor predicates and if that is the case, there is no conjunction of them. This objection rests on one of the restrictions usually found in semantic formalist accounts of syntactical systems. I do not, since I have rejected extended semantic formalism, find any reason to be bound by such restrictions. Conjunctions with more than finitely many conjuncts are governed by the same rules as other conjunctions: a conjunction may be inferred from all of its conjuncts and each of its conjuncts may be inferred from it. In any case, since my account of quantification allows quantification with predicates, I can define 'IQ-matrix' by such quantification. Thus, if 'S' is a variable restricted to successor predicates, then

X is an IQ-matrix

is equivalent to

(S)(X is (an) S).

Of course, most semantic formalists would have objections to such a definition as well. My reply to those objections is in 3A. For convenience, my subsequent remarks take 'IQ-matrix' to be the conjunction of all the successor predicates.

Intuitively speaking, the predicate 'IQ-matrix' should be such that the true instances of the matrix

X is an IQ-matrix

are just those statements which have the singular term 'the Q-matrixA' or a singular term for an "ancestor" of the Q-matrixA under the relation of succession. What can be shown at this stage of the account is that 'IQ-matrix' is, in one sense, the "smallest" successor predicate. The "smallness" of the predicate 'IQ-matrix' surely fulfills part of our intuitive desires about the predicate 'IQ-matrix'.

Consider any successor predicate. Since 'IQ-matrix' is defined by the conjunction of all successor predicates, this successor predicate is a conjunct of that conjunction. Therefore, everything the conjunctive predicate is true of, this successor predicate is true of. Thus the conjunctive predicate, and hence 'IQ-matrix', materially implies the successor predicate. With the help of this conclusion, it can be shown that

(87) (F)(if (X)(if X is (an) F, then X is an IQ-matrix) and (84) and (85), then (X)(X is (an) F if and only if X is an IQ-matrix)).

Intuitively speaking, no successor predicate is true of some, but not all, of the things 'IQ-matrix' is true of. So, 'IQ-matrix' is the "smallest" successor predicate.

Analogs of "Peano's axioms," stated in terms of IQ-matrices, can now be proven. The first is:

(88) the Q-matrixA is an IQ-matrix.

The next is:

(89) (X)(if X is an IQ-matrix, then the successor of X is an IQ-matrix).

Both (88) and (89) are easily proven from the definitions. The third is the principle of induction, (86), which has already been proven in the argument for (87).

The fourth says that no IQ-matrix which succeeds some IQ-matrix is the same Q-matrix as the Q-matrixA (or, as I shall also call it in light of (88), "the IQ-matrixA"):

(90) (X)(the successor of X is not the same Q-matrix as the IQ-matrixA).

The proof of (90) rests on the fact that the IQ-matrixA has no NI-elements. But, as can be seen from the definition of 'succeeds', any IQ-matrix which succeeds an IQ-matrix has some NI-elements.

The last is:

(91) (X)(Y)(if not(X is the same Q-matrix as Y), then not(the successor of X is the same Q-matrix as the successor of Y)).

The proof of (91) depends on some easily proven truths about IQ-matrices:

(91.1) (X)(Y)(if X is a proper part of the successor of Y, then X is the same Q-matrix as Y or X is a proper part of Y);

(91.2) (X)(Y)(Z)(if X is a proper part of Y and Y is a proper part of Z, then X is a proper part of Z);

(91.3) (X)(not(X is a proper part of X)).

Since all IQ-matrices are Q-matrices, no changes need be made in the definitions of the terms appearing in the above statements.

The proof of (91) begins with the assumptions

[i] not(X is the same Q-matrix as Y)

and [ii] the successor of X is the same Q-matrix as the successor of Y.

Let me write 'sX' for 'the successor of X' and 'sY' for 'the successor of Y'. Given the definition of 'succeeds', it follows that

X is a proper part of sX

and Y is a proper part of sY.

Given the definitions of 'is the same Q-matrix as' and 'is a proper part of', it follows from [ii] that

X is a proper part of sY

and Y is a proper part of sX.

By invoking (91.1), it follows that

X is the same Q-matrix as Y or X is a proper part of Y

and Y is the same Q-matrix as X or Y is a proper part of X.

By assumption [i], it then follows that

X is a proper part of Y

and Y is a proper part of X.

And then by (91.2), it follows that

X is a proper part of X

and Y is a proper part of Y.

These conclusions are in contradiction to (91.3) and hence [ii] is false and hence

not(sX is the same Q-matrix as sY).

The proofs of (91.2) and (91.3) are obvious. The proof of (91.1) is inductive. The induction is on the matrix

(92) (Y)(if X is a proper part of sY, then X is the same Q-matrix as Y or X is a proper part of Y).

That (92) holds for the IQ-matrixA is a consequence of the fact that the IQ-matrixA is the same Q-matrix as itself and a proper part of any other IQ-matrix. Now I assume (92) and show that

(Y)(if sX is a proper part of sY, then sX is the same Q-matrix as Y or sX is a proper part of Y).

From

(93) sX is a proper part of sY,

it follows that

(94) X is a proper part of sY,

given the additional premise that

(X)(X is a proper part of sX).

The truth of this last statement can be determined, as I previously pointed out, from the definition of 'succeeds'. From (94) and (92), it follows that

X is the same Q-matrix as Y or X is a proper part of Y.

Suppose

X is the same Q-matrix as Y.

Then, since successors are unique under the relation of being the same Q-matrix as, it follows that sX is the same Q-matrix as sY.

However, this contradicts (93). Thus it must be the case that

X is a proper part of Y.

But then the definition of 'is a proper part of' assures us that it is not the case that there is a different E-element of X for every E-element of Y. Therefore, it follows that

(95) if x is the E-element of sX which is not in X, then (Ey)(y is an E-element of Y and (z)(Ew) (if z is an E-element of X and of sX, then w is an E-element of Y and y is different from w)).

Using (95), it is possible to show that one condition of the definition of 'is a part of' is satisfied. Similar arguments, all originating from

X is a proper part of Y,

can be given to show that the conditions on K-, NI-, and I-elements are also satisfied. (Certain results relevant to these arguments are, for convenience, given later.) Thus we have:

sX is a part of Y

and hence

sX is the same Q-matrix as Y or sX is a proper part of Y.

This completes the induction step of the proof of (91.1).

I have now completed the line of development which parallels, in many ways, one sort of set-theoretic account of the natural numbers. Though my remarks have not been about numerical quantifiers, it is not difficult to show that the same line of development can be carried out in their case. The key move in this transfer is establishing the connection between IQ-matrices and numerical quantifiers: a numerical quantifier is a quantifier defined by at least and at most one IQ-matrix. The :there be one: is defined by the IQ-matrixA. A numerical quantifier succeeds another numerical quantifier if and only if the IQ-matrix which defines the former succeeds the IQ-matrix which defines the latter. Then, successor predicates are introduced for numerical quantifiers: something is a successor predicate for numerical quantifiers if and only if it satisfies

[i] the :there be one: is (an) F

and [ii] if any numerical quantifier is (an) F, then the successor of that numerical quantifier is (an) F.

Through the definitional connection of numerical quantifiers and IQ-matrices, it is possible to show that 'numerical quantifier' is the "smallest" of the successor predicates for numerical quantifiers. From this point proofs of analogs of the Peano axioms parallel those given above for IQ-matrices. Plainly, nothing stands in the way of giving an account of numerical quantifiers which is parallel to and parasitic on the account of IQ-matrices.

However, a somewhat different approach to the definientia of numerical quantifiers permits me to give a better account of these definientia and thus a better account of numerical quantifiers.

IQ-matrices have certain characteristics because successor predicates are defined in a way which, to some extent, reflects the intuitive notion that IQ-matrices are the Q-matrixA and all those Q-matrices which can be reached from the Q-matrixA "in a finite number of steps." If there were some way of handling the phrase 'in a finite number of steps', it would be possible to specify the definientia of numerical quantifiers as those Q-matrices which are either the Q-matrixA or a Q-matrix reached from the Q-matrixA "in a finite number of steps" of that sort described in the definition of 'succeeds'.

Certain possibilities are opened up by the observations of the previous paragraph. In particular, a closer look at the definition of 'succeeds' (or at the original recipe in section A) suggests the possibility that the sort of Q-matrix needed for the definitions of numerical quantifiers can be characterized independently of successor predicates. The basis for this suggestion is that, while the definition of 'Q-matrix' establishes a certain sort of "structure," the definition of 'succeeds' (or, the recipe in section A) tells us, in effect, what is allowed to appear within that structure.

I offer the following definition of 'NQD-matrix' (where 'NQD' is to suggest "numerical quantifier definiens"): an NQD-matrix is a Q-matrix which is such that

[i][a] if something is a conjunct of its conjunctive statement matrix and is not the universally quantified conditional, then it is a K-element or an NI-element and

[b] the consequent of its universally quantified conditional is a disjunction which has only I-elements as disjuncts

and [ii][a] for each of its E-elements, there is one K-element in its conjunctive statement matrix which has the variable of that E-element and

[b] (x)(y)(if x is an E-element of it and y is an E-element of it and x is not the same as y, then in its conjunctive statement matrix there is one NI-element with the variables

of x and y) and

[c] for each of its E-elements, there is one I-element in the consequent of the universally quantified conditional which has the variable of that E-element and the variable of the universal quantifier.

NQD-matrices, being Q-matrices, require no new definitions of 'is a part of', 'is a proper part of', or 'is the same Q-matrix as'. Further, the description of the Q-matrixA is such that the Q-matrixA is clearly an NQD-matrix. (So, I shall speak of "the NQD-matrixA.") These points bring out the convenience of using the predicate 'Q-matrix'.

The issue of "finiteness" arises in connection with NQD-matrices for the following reasons. I have already admitted the possibility of statements which are, in some sense, "infinite" (e.g., a statement with an "infinite" conjunctive predicate). There is nothing in the definition of 'NQD-matrix' which insures that all NQD-matrices are "finite." However, given the earlier intuitive reflections on IQ-matrices, the matrices needed for the definitions of numerical quantifiers must be "finite." So, I must provide some characterization of "finiteness" for NQD-matrices.

Though several characterizations suggest themselves, the only one which appears to be independent of my work with IQ-matrices is the definition which depends on the notion of entities' being in 1-1 correspondence with a "part" of themselves. In set theory, such a notion is explicated by taking "parts" as "subsets." In my case, no sets (or, classes) are involved; it is the elements of an NQD-matrix which are, or are not, in 1-1 correspondence with some but not all of themselves.

Thus consider the following condition:

(96) (x)(y)(z)(if Rxy and Rxz, then y is the same as z and if Ryx and Rzx, then y is the same as z).

Given that (96) is satisfied, an NQD-matrix is finite if and only if

(97) not(E R)((x)(Ey)(if x is an element of it, then Rxy and y is an element of it) and (Ez)(w)(z is an element of it and if w is an element of it, then not(Rwz))).

For example, the NQD-matrixA is finite. The proof of this depends on the fact that, according to the description of the NQD-matrixA, its elements are one E-element, one K-element (with the variable of the E-element), and one I-element (with the variable of the E-element and the variable of the universal quantifier). Thus there are three elements in the NQD-matrixA. Consider any two-place predicate which satisfies both (96) and the first conjunct of the conjunctive statement matrix in (97). In the case of the NQD-matrixA, this supposition insures that one of the following conjunctions is true (where 'a', 'b', and 'c' are singular terms for the elements of the NQD-matrixA):

Raa and Rbc and Rcb;
Raa and Rbb and Rcc;
Rab and Rbc and Rca;
Rab and Rba and Rcc;
Rac and Rbb and Rca;
Rac and Rbc and Rcb.

In each of these conjunctions, no element of the NQD-matrixA is such that it does not stand in the relation to some element of the NQD-matrixA. Thus the other conjunct within (97) cannot be true. Therefore, in the case of the NQD-matrixA, no two-place predicate satisfies both conjuncts of the conjunctive statement matrix within (97). Hence, the NQD-matrixA is finite. (Again, the appearance of :there be one:s, :there be two:s, and :there be three:s in this proof is for convenience and does not show the definition of 'finite' to be in any difficulty.)

A moment ago I said that earlier definitions, framed for Q-matrices, would work without change for NQD-matrices. Since NQD-matrices are Q-matrices, this is what one would expect. However, the definition of 'succeeds', though it is applicable to NQD-matrices, leaves two important questions to be answered. Is the Q-matrix which succeeds a finite NQD-matrix an NQD-matrix? Is it a finite NQD-matrix?

The answer to the first question is affirmative because the definition of 'NQD-matrix' was framed with the definition of 'succeeds' in mind. Thus the difference between a Q-matrix and its successor is solely a matter of elements, as is the difference between two NQD-matrices. Secondly, the new elements in the Q-matrix which succeeds another Q-matrix clearly satisfy [ii] in the definition of 'NQD-matrix'.

With the fact that the Q-matrixA is an NQD-matrix, the result of the previous paragraph gives the conclusion that the predicate 'NQD-matrix' is a successor predicate. Therefore, all IQ-matrices are NQD-matrices. From this result follow numerous truths about IQ-matrices and their parts, proper parts, and so on.

Is the Q-matrix which succeeds a finite NQD-matrix finite? The demonstration that it is finite has two parts. The parts are determined by the definition of 'succeeds'. The NQD-matrix which succeeds a finite NQD-matrix must differ from the latter by having exactly one E-element, one K-element, and one I-element the latter does not have. The succeeding NQD-matrix also differs from the finite NQD-matrix in having NI-elements the latter does not have. The "new" NI-elements, i.e., those which the former has and the latter does not, are in 1-1 correspondence with the "old" E-elements, i.e., those which the latter has. The 1-1 relation is that of having the variable of. So, for the first part of the demonstration I assume that the "old" elements, i.e., the elements of the finite NQD-matrix, together with the new NI-elements are not in 1-1 "proper" correspondence with themselves, i.e., in 1-1 correspondence with some but not all of themselves. On this assumption, I then show that the old elements and the new NI-elements <u>together with</u> the new E-element (the new K-element, the new I-element) cannot be in 1-1 proper correspondence with themselves. The second part of the demonstration is the proof of the assumption used in the first part. Both parts together thus show that the NQD-matrix which succeeds a finite NQD-matrix is finite.

Suppose, to commence the first part, that the old elements together with the new NI-elements are not in 1-1 proper correspondence with themselves. Further, suppose that these elements together with the new E-element are in 1-1 proper correspondence with themselves. Hence, at least one of these elements does not stand in the relation of the 1-1 correspondence to any of these elements. Let us call any such element an "excluded" element. Either the new E-element is an excluded element or it is not.

> Case A: Suppose the new E-element is an excluded element. Then the old elements and the new NI-elements with the new E-element are in 1-1 correspondence with just old elements and the new NI-elements. Therefore the new E-element is related under the correspondence to either an old element or a new NI-element. Hence the remaining elements, i.e., the old elements and the new NI-elements, are in 1-1 proper correspondence with them-

selves. This contradicts the assumption of the first part.

Case B: Suppose that the new E-element is not an excluded element. Then it is related under the correspondence to itself or to an old element or a new NI-element.

Subcase [a]: Suppose that the new E-element is related to itself. Then the remaining elements must be in 1-1 proper correspondence with themselves because there is at least one excluded element and, by the assumption of this case, it is not the new E-element. Again there is a contradiction with the assumption of the first part.

Subcase [b]: Suppose that the new E-element is related to an old element or a new NI-element. Then some old element or some new NI-element is related to the new E-element. From this point, the key to this subcase is the description of the definiens of a new two-place predicate. This definiens utilizes the 1-1 proper correspondence which has been assumed at the beginning of this part. In order to make the description easier to follow, I give an example, written in augmented English, of the <u>sort</u> of matrix needed:

(98) if not(y is the new E-element), then Rxy, or x is the element which Rs the new E-element and y is an excluded element

(where 'R' is the expression for the 1-1 proper correspondence and it is false that (y)(Ex)(if y is an old element or a new NI-element or the new E-element and x is an old element or a new NI-element or the new E-element, then Rxy)).

The description of the definiens of the new two-place predicate is as follows: the definiens is a disjunction, one disjunct of which is a conditional and the other a conjunction. The antecedent of the conditional is the negation of an identity statement matrix which has a variable and a singular term for the new E-element. The consequent is a relational statement matrix with the relational expression of the 1-1 proper correspondence combined with the variable of the antecedent and another variable, where it is important that a certain condition is satisfied. The condition is that a certain universally quantified statement is false. The statement in question has the relational expression of the 1-1 proper correspondence with the variables of the consequent of the conditional in the very same places they occupy in the consequent of the conditional. The variable which is <u>not</u> both in the antecedent and the consequent is E-quantified. The universally quantified statement which is false is the universal quantification of the remaining variable of the relational predicate containing the E-quantifier. The other disjunct is a conjunction, one conjunct of which is an identity statement matrix which has the variable that appears in the conditional only in its consequent and which has a singular term for the element which is related under the 1-1 proper correspondence to the new E-element. The other conjunct is also an identity statement matrix and it has the variable of the antecedent of the conditional and a singular term for an excluded element.

The new relation which is defined in the way described insures a 1-1 proper correspondence of the old elements and the new NI-elements and the new E-element with themselves. The new relation is so arranged that the new E-element is an excluded element. Therefore, it has been shown that the assumption of this subcase leads to the satisfaction of the assumption of case A and hence to a contradiction by the argument of case A.

So, having obtained a contradiction in both cases A and B, I conclude, given the assumption of this part, that the old elements and the new NI-elements with the new E-element cannot be in 1-1 proper correspondence with themselves. Parallel arguments can be given for the same claim about the old elements and the new NI-elements and the new E-element with the new K-element and about the old elements and the new NI-elements and the new E-element and the new K-element with the new I-element. Therefore, I conclude, given the assumption of this part, that the old elements and the new NI-elements with the new E-element and the new K-element and the new I-element cannot be in 1-1 proper correspondence with themselves. This completes the first part of the demonstration.

The second part of the demonstration depends on several facts. First is a fact I mentioned several paragraphs back: the new NI-elements are in 1-1 correspondence with the old E-elements. Second, there is no 1-1 proper correspondence between the old E-elements and themselves. Suppose there were. Then all the old elements would be in 1-1 proper correspondence with themselves. The necessary 1-1 proper correspondence is the disjunction of the supposed 1-1 correspondence of the old E-elements with themselves (restricted to the old E-elements) and of the identity relation (restricted to the remainder of the old elements). But if the old elements, i.e., the elements of the finite NQD-matrix, were in 1-1 proper correspondence with themselves, the finite NQD-matrix would not, contrary to the assumption of the whole demonstration, be finite. Third, a consequence of these points is that the new NI-elements cannot be in 1-1 proper correspondence with themselves.

The strategy of this part is to show that the supposition that the old elements with the new NI-elements are in 1-1 proper correspondence with themselves leads to a contradiction, given the premise that the old elements are not in 1-1 proper correspondence with themselves. The crux of the argument is an extension of the technique used in formulating a definition of a new relation in subcase [b] of case B in the first part.

Supposing that the old elements and the new NI-elements are in 1-1 proper correspondence with themselves, we obtain two cases: case A in which no old elements are related under the 1-1 proper correspondence to the new NI-elements and case B in which some old elements are so related to new NI-elements.

In case A, there are two subcases.

Subcase [a] is that in which new NI-elements are related only to new NI-elements. Since, as I showed earlier, the new NI-elements cannot be in 1-1 proper correspondence with themselves, any excluded element is an old element. Since there is at least one excluded element, the 1-1 proper correspondence of the supposition (restricted to old elements) is a 1-1 proper correspondence of the old elements with themselves. This is in contradiction with the main premise of this part.

Subcase [b] is that in which some new NI-elements are related to old elements. Given the supposition of case A, it follows that some new NI-elements are excluded elements. Whether some old elements are excluded elements or not, it follows that the 1-1 proper correspondence of the supposition (restricted to the old elements) is a 1-1 proper correspondence of the old elements with themselves. Again there is a contradiction with the main premise.

Notice that the subcases could have been handled differently. The subcases could have been: subcase [a] in which no new NI-elements are excluded elements and subcase [b] in which some new NI-elements are excluded elements. In subcase [a], given the assumption of case A and the fact that the new NI-elements cannot be in 1-1 proper correspondence with themselves, it follows that some old element must be an excluded element. In subcase [b], the same fact about new NI-elements shows that some new NI-elements are related under the 1-1 proper correspondence to old elements. In either case, we obtain a 1-1 proper correspondence of the old elements with themselves and thus a contradiction.

Case B employs the sort of argument used in subcase [b] of case B in the first part of the demonstration. Remember that, under the supposed 1-1 proper correspondence, every new NI-element must be related to some old element or new NI-element, and different new NI-elements, to different elements. Then since the new NI-elements cannot be in 1-1 correspondence with themselves, for every old element which is related under the supposed 1-1 correspondence to a new NI-element, there is a new NI-element so related to an old element.

It is now possible to describe the definition of a new relation which leads to a 1-1 proper correspondence of the old elements with themselves. This relation is parasitic on the supposed 1-1 proper correspondence.

The definition has a definiens like (98). For convenience, I state, in intuitive terms, what the parts of the definiens say, and I do not bother to write out descriptions which are long and tedious. One disjunct of the definiens says that the defined relation agrees with the supposed relation except on any old element that is related, under the supposed relation, to a new NI-element. An example of this disjunct written in augmented English is:

(99.1) if not(x is an old element and y is a new NI-element), then Rxy

(where the same condition obtains as in the case of (98)). Disjoined to the disjunct just discussed is a conjunction part of which says that any old element that is related under the supposed relation to a new NI-element is, under the defined relation, related to an old element to which, under the supposed relation, a new NI-element is related. An example of this is:

(99.2) x is an old element such that (Ez)(z is a new NI-element and Rxz) and y is an old element such that (Ew)(w is a new NI-element and Rwy)

(where, of course, the same condition still obtains). The other part of the conjunction says that different old elements of the former sort are related, under the defined relation, to different old elements of the latter sort. An example of this part of the definiens is obvious. The relations defined as described are 1-1 proper correspondences of the old elements and the new NI-elements with themselves.

The conclusion that such a defined relation leads to a 1-1 proper correspondence of the old elements with themselves follows from the fact that no old element is related, under the defined relation, to a new NI-element. Thus the supposition of case A of this part is satisfied. Therefore, case B of this part also leads to a contradiction with the main premise of the demonstration, viz., that the NQD-matrix of which the old elements are the elements is finite.

Having derived contradictions in both cases of the second part of the demonstration, I conclude that the Q-matrix which succeeds a finite NQD-matrix is not only an NQD-matrix, but also finite. Further, under the relation 'is the same Q-matrix as', successors of finite NQD-matrices are obviously unique. Therefore the successor of a finite NQD-matrix is a finite NQD-matrix.

This last truth, in conjunction with the previously established claim that the Q-matrixA is a finite NQD-matrix, insures that 'finite NQD-matrix' is a successor predicate. Hence, all IQ-matrices are finite NQD-matrices.

Once again I turn to the proof of analogs of the Peano axioms. The first is:

(100) the Q-matrixA is a finite NQD-matrix.

The second is:

(101) (X)(if X is a finite NQD-matrix, then the successor of X is a finite NQD-matrix).

Both (100) and (101) have been demonstrated in showing that 'finite NQD-matrix' is a successor predicate. The proof of

(102) (X)(if X is a finite NQD-matrix, then the successor of X is not the same Q-matrix as the NQD-matrixA)

is similar to the proof of (90).

The analog of the principle of induction is:

(103) (F)(if the NQD-matrixA is (an) F and (X)(if X is (an) F, then the successor of X is (an) F), then (X)F(X))

(where 'X' is restricted to singular terms for finite NQD-matrices). A proof of (103) is obtained from a stronger result.

First, I show that every finite NQD-matrix, except the NQD-matrixA, is the successor of some finite NQD-matrix. From the definition of 'NQD-matrix', it follows that every finite NQD-matrix, except the NQD-matrixA, has at least two E-elements. With the E-elements, it must also have the K-, NI-, and I-elements set down in the definition. But the elements which go with an E-element according to the definition of 'NQD-matrix' are just those which are described in the definition of 'succeeds'. Thus the elements spoken of in the definition of 'succeeds' are in every finite NQD-matrix except the NQD-matrixA. Consider the Q-matrix which has all and only those elements of such a finite NQD-matrix with the exception of at least and at most one E-element and of the K-, NI-, and I-elements which must accompany that E-element. This Q-matrix must satisfy the definition of 'NQD-matrix'; otherwise the finite NQD-matrix by which this Q-matrix is characterized would not satisfy the definition of 'NQD-matrix'. Further, this new NQD-matrix must be finite since the original finite NQD-matrix contains the new one as a proper part. This new finite NQD-matrix is the one of which the other finite NQD-matrix is the successor.

Given this result and what was demonstrated earlier, viz., that the successor of a finite NQD-matrix is a finite NQD-matrix, if follows that

(X)(X is a finite NQD-matrix if and only if X is the NQD-matrixA or the successor of some finite

NQD-matrix).

So, restricting 'X' to the singular term 'the NQD-matrixA' and singular terms for successors of finite NQD-matrices, we may infer

(X)F(X)

from all the instances of

F(X)

since we know that a singular term for each finite NQD-matrix appears in the instances of 'F(X)'. The principle of inference just defended is the analog of the so-called principle of "infinite induction." The principle of induction, (103), follows directly from the principle of infinite induction.

With (103), it is possible to demonstrate

(104) (X)(Y)(if not(X is the same Q-matrix as Y), then not(sX is the same Q-matrix as sY))

(where 'X' and 'Y' are restricted as above) along the same lines as (91) was demonstrated.

A variety of other interesting results can also be easily demonstrated; for example:

(X)(Y)(if X is a finite NQD-matrix and Y is a finite NQD-matrix, then if Y is a proper part of X, then not(X is a part of Y));

and the finite NQD-matrices which are proper parts of X are not in 1-1 proper correspondence with themselves.

A direct consequence of (103) is that

all finite NQD-matrices are IQ-matrices.

So, it follows, given the earlier result which is the converse of the above, that something is a finite NQD-matrix if and only if it is an IQ-matrix. Speaking intuitively, I would summarize these results by saying that finite NQD-matrices are all and only those Q-matrices which can be "generated in finitely many steps by succession" from the Q-matrixA (including, of course, the Q-matrixA).

The connection between 'numerical quantifier' and 'finite NQD-matrix' is easily made. In fact, it is, mutatis mutandis, the same as that which was explained in the case of 'numerical quantifier' and 'IQ-matrix'. Since something is a finite NQD-matrix if and only if it is an IQ-matrix, taking finite NQD-matrices as the definientia of numerical quantifiers cannot conflict with the earlier account in terms of IQ-matrices. Thus my account of the predicate 'numerical quantifier' is essentially complete. I have, I think, given justification, independent of the work in the other subsections of this section, for my practice of talking about "all numerical quantifiers," "some numerical quantifiers," and so on.

Preparatory to the final topic of this subsection, I shall deal with some minor points. First, the metalinguistic talk of this subsection has been accomplished with nonillustrating metalinguistic terms. The bridge to the illustrating terms of the earlier sections is effected by reflecting on the sort of embodiment, i.e., augmented English, which has appeared in the reconstructions of these sections. For example, given the natural linguistic objects employed by augmented English, the :there be one: is the numerical quantifier which is defined by the NQD-matrixA, and all the tokens of the numerical quantifier which is defined by the NQD-matrixA are :there be one:s (though not all, of course, need be *there be one*s, i.e., augmented English :there be one:s).

Second, the final topic of this subsection is related to a topic in more common treatments of arithmetic: viz., the "inductive definition" of addition and multiplication. What must be entirely clear is that my account differs in several ways from any account which involves the inductive definition of addition and multiplication. One major difference, of course, is that such accounts are usually formalist. More important, I am in no need of a "definition" of addition or multiplication and certainly not in need of an inductive definition of them. Moreover, there is no question on my account of having to prove the existence of a function (i.e., a set of a certain sort) which has been defined inductively. No function (or, set) is involved in explaining 'plus' and 'times' in terms of the phrase 'may be inferred from' (or, secondarily, 'is true of') and of quantification of a special sort. All that remains for me to do is to show that my explanation ensures certain properties of addition and multiplication.

Consider addition. Suppose that there is a phrase in the idiom of number universals which is reconstructed by the phrase 'the successor of' as it applies to numerical quantifiers. (Actually, it is numerical quantifier statements which appear in the reconstructions; but my present simplification is unimportant, since succession for numerical quantifier statements can be defined by succession for numerical quantifiers.) For example,

s(FIVE)

is reconstructed by means of

the successor of the :there be five:;

s(N),

by the successor of the NUMQUANT.

More complicated contexts, such as

s(FIVE plus THREE),

have a reconstruction which is introduced by proving inductively the reconstructions of

(N)(M)(E L)(N plus M equals L).

The successor of a conjunctive numerical quantifier is the successor of that numerical quantifier which is such that it and the conjunctive numerical quantifier are mutually inferrible.

Two things which should be true on my account are the reconstructions of:

(105) (N)(N plus ONE equals s(N))

and (106) (N)(M)(M plus s(N) equals s(M plus N)).

The point of arguing for the truth of the reconstructions of (105) and (106) is that it shows that reconstructing 's' by 'the successor of' preserves the intuitive relationships between addition and succession which are reflected in inductive definitions of addition.

To prove (105) it must be shown, as can be seen from the primary reconstruction of (105), that from a certain conjunction of numerical quantifier statements may be inferred a numerical quantifier statement and vice versa. My proof that these inferences are correct is a sketch of the steps needed to show that these are derivative inferences. Some of these steps appeal to the structure of NQD-matrices.

Let us consider the inference from the conjunction to the numerical quantifier statement. In A, it was shown that the correctness of such inferences depends on handling the kind terms in the premise and the conclusion correctly. In the inference under consideration, the kind terms of the conjunction disjoined are the kind term of the numerical quantifier statement. For the next point, one must remember that the definiens of the :there be one: has one E-element and that the successor of a numerical quantifier has in its definiens one E-element which the definiens of that numerical quantifier does not have. Thus the rules of E-quantifier inference allow us to infer a statement with some of the needed features, viz., with all the E-elements of the definientia of both conjuncts of the conjunction and with a kind term which is the disjunction of the kind terms of the conjunction. The new NI-elements needed for the numerical quantifier statement are obtained by making use of the condition which is appended to the rule of inference being proved, viz., the condition that the kind terms of the conjuncts are disjoint. Finally, the new I-element needed in the universally quantified conditional of the numerical quantifier statement is obtained directly from the universally quantified conditionals of the conjuncts.

The other inference, the one to the conjunction from the numerical quantifier statement, also depends on the correct handling of the kind terms needed in the conjunction. These kind terms are of the sort illustrated in A(ii). Each is the kind term of the numerical quantifier statement conjoined with NI-elements. In the present case, the kind term which is combined with :there be one: is the conjunction of the kind term of the numerical quantifier statement with the NI-elements of that statement which are such that

these NI-elements have one variable which is the variable of an E-element in the definiens of the numerical quantifier whose successor is in the numerical quantifier statement

and the other variable of every such NI-element is the variable of the E-element which is not in the definiens of that numerical quantifier, but is in the definiens of its successor

and every variable of an E-element of the definiens of

that numerical quantifier is in at least and at most one of these NI-elements.

The conjunctive statement matrix just described is E-quantified with an E-quantifier for every individual variable except the one which appears in each of these NI-elements. The kind term for the other conjunct is built in a similar fashion, but requires only one NI-element and one E-quantifier. The E-elements work out correctly for the same reason they did in the other case: the numerical quantifier in the conjunction with the :there be one: is the numerical quantifier whose successor appears in the numerical quantifier statement. The definiens of the successor of a numerical quantifier has exactly one E-element the numerical quantifier does not have; it is this E-element which is essential to the derivation of the conjunct with the :there be one:. The NI-elements of the conjuncts come directly from the NI-elements of the numerical quantifier statement. Finally, the I-elements of the conjuncts are derived from the disjunction of I-elements in the numerical quantifier statement by using the NI-elements in the conjunctive kind terms of the conjuncts.

The proof of (106) is an induction on

(M)(M plus s(N) equals s(M plus N)).

The argument in the basis step and in the inductive step is of the same sort as that given above for (105). The only new matters are dealing with s(ONE) in the basis step and the successor of a successor in the inductive step. A little reflection will convince the reader that neither of these matters is any difficulty.

Analogs of (105) and (106) for multiplication are:

(107) (N)(ONE time N equals N)

and (108) (N)(M)(s(N) times M equals (N times M) plus M).

The argument for (107) arises directly from the definition of the multiplicative numerical word 'one'. It was said in B(v) that a statement with 'one' combined with any numerical quantifier is equivalent to a conjunction with one conjunct which has the numerical quantifier which is combined with 'one'. Clearly, then, no difficulty attends the demonstration of (107).

The argument for (108) is an induction on

(M)(s(N) times M equals (N times M) plus M).

But it is not possible to give this argument now for two reasons. First, the reconstructions of statements like (108) were not finished in B(v) and will not be till chapter 6. Second, since (108) requires succession for multiplicative numerical words and since the universal quantification to be gained by induction is a quantification with a variable for multiplicative numerical words, induction and succession must be shown to obtain for multiplicative numerical words. However, showing this, it turns out, requires that the questions about the reconstructions of statements like (108) be answered. So, the completion of these matters must be postponed till chapter 6. For the moment, however, I do wish to point out that given the sort of reconstructions of statements like (108) which were suggested in B(v) and which will be presented in chapter 6 and given succession and induction for multiplicative numerical words, no impediment appears to the demonstration of (108). Given that the successor of the :one: is the multiplicative numerical word, the :two:, the basis step of the argument is straightforward:

(M)(s(ONE) times M equals (ONE times M) plus M).

The inductive step adds only the complication of dealing with the successor of a successor of a multiplicative numerical word; reflection on the connection between multiplicative numerical words and multiplicative conjunctions (discussed in B(v)) shows that the argument for the inductive step is also no problem.

C. Numbers as Individuals

(i) Introduction

The reconstruction of number individuals on which I embark in this section could be orchestrated with a variety of different technical accompaniments, each recapitulating different earlier developments. However, from the perspective of the general strategy I am pursuing and the philosophical points at issue, the technical accompaniments are largely uninteresting and tedious. Consequently, the music of variables, quantifiers, and quotes in this section is a plain song.

Along with this abridgement of the details, there is a rearrangement of the order of development presented in sections A and B. The progress in sections A and B is from introductory material about DSTs, truth, and numerical quantifiers though reconstructions of specific arithmetical contexts to, finally, a rather lengthy account of induction and succession. The line of development in section C is considerably different.

No space is given in section C to the discussion of the extension of the material on DSTs and truth in A(iii) and A(iv). The needed new principles are easily formulated from the examples presented in the following subsections.

What would correspond in section C to the informal treatment of numerical quantifiers in A(ii) is omitted in favor of a discussion of induction and succession which is the analog of the treatment of the predicate 'numerical quantifier' in B(vi). This discussion is in C(iii). The subsection after this present one, C(ii), gives a treatment of the MML DSTs necessary for the reconstructions of this section. The remainder of section C, subsections (iv) and (v), is devoted to reconstructions of arithmetical statements.

(ii) MML Distributive Singular Terms

The first step is an investigation of terms like

(109) the :the :there be one::,

(110) the :the (:there be one: KINDPREDCON):,

and (111) the (PREDCON :the (:there be one: KINDPREDCON):).

These singular terms do not figure equally in what follows, but a careful study of them is essential.

Any statement containing (109) reduces to one with the MML SGT

(112) :the :there be one::.

Hence, since

(113) :the :there be one::s are individual constants,

it is also true that

(113.1) the :the :there be one:: is an individual constant.

In particular, following the previous notational conventions, we have

(113.2) :the :there be one::s are ML !numerical quantifier! DSTs

and (113.3) the :the :there be one:: is an ML !numerical quantifier! DST.

Thus we could offer (113.3) and hence (113.2) as a tentative reconstruction of

(114) ONE is a number individual.

While (113.3) is a start in the right direction, it is not a very satisfying start. The strategy at the level of number individuals is dictated by the same considerations which influenced the reconstruction of number universals. Number universals are reconstructed by reflecting on the role of numerical quantifiers. Thus for the ML reconstruction of number universals, terms like :the :there be one::s were found inadequate and terms of the following sort were introduced instead:

the (:there be one: KINDPREDCON).

So, to keep the present reconstruction on the right line, we must investigate (110) and its kin.

Consider any token which is a :the (:there be one: KINDPREDCON):, e.g.,

(115) the (:there be one: KINDPREDCON).

Clearly (115) is not a DST, but a DST matrix. An instance of (115) is

the :there be one horse:.

Since

the :there be one horse: is a numerical quantifier statement,

i.e., all :there be one horse:s are numerical quantifier statements,

is true,

(115.1) all (:there be one: KINDPREDCON)s are ...

should be completed as follows:

(115.2) all (:there be one: KINDPREDCON)s are numerical quantifier statements, i.e., (115.3) the (:there be one: KINDPREDCON) is a numerical quantifier statement.

Given (115.3) and remembering that :the (:there be one: KINDPREDCON):s are not DSTs, but only DST matrices, we have

(116) the :the (:there be one: KINDPREDCON): is an ML !numerical quantifier statement! DST matrix

which reduces to

(116.1) :the (:there be one: KINDPREDCON):s are ML !numerical quantifier statement! DST matrices.

First, there can be no doubt that :the (:there be one: KINDPREDCON):s are ML matrices, rather than singular terms, for they contain a variable. Second, :the (:there be one: KINDPREDCON):s are matrices for DSTs, for the instances of these matrices are DSTs. The phrase 'numerical quantifier statement' flanked by exclamation marks reminds us that any DST which is an instance of such a matrix appears as the subject term of a true ML statement which has the phrase 'numerical quantifier statement' as its predicate. This phrase is taken directly from (115.2) and (115.3), as the phrase 'numerical quantifier', which appears in exclamation marks in (113.2) and (113.3), is taken from

the :there be one: is a numerical quantifier,

i.e., all :there be one:s are numerical quantifiers.

So, (116) may be offered as a more acceptable reconstruction of (114). However, further scrutiny of (116) and (116.1) would prove that, though (116) is much closer to what we should require for a final reconstruction of (114), it fails in a now familiar way: namely, the term that is its subject contains no variable. Thus in the reconstruction of certain statements containing the term '<u>ONE</u>', it would be impossible to indicate interconnections by quantification.

It may seem that there is a variable in (110), namely, 'KINDPREDCON'. But this is not so. A sign design which is a --KINDPREDCON-- appears within Sellarsian quotes in (110). This sign design is not, because of the quotation, produced in the tokening of a variable. In fact, according to the principles relating to the composition of SGTs,

(117) :the (:there be one: KINDPREDCON):

is (117.1) (:the:)(:(:there be one: KINDPREDCON):),

which is

(117.2) (:the:)(::there be one::)(:KINDPREDCON:).

Thus (117) contains an SGT, viz., ':KINDPREDCON:', which is true of a certain kind of ML variable, i.e., an ML variable for SGTs true of kind terms. The term ':KINDPREDCON:' is an MML SGT built on the illustrating principle, and what it illustrates is a sign design which is produced in my notation in tokenings of certain ML variables.

Consequently, as I added a variable to

:there be one:

and :triangular:

to get

(:there be one: KINDPREDCON)

and (:triangular: INDCON),

so I must add to (117) an MML variable (which I shall write in the fashion of ML variables with the addition of underlining). Putting the variable in PMese position, we have

(118) (PREDCON :the (:there be one: KINDPREDCON):)

where 'PREDCON' is an MML variable. With (118) we can construct

(111) the (<u>PREDCON</u> :the (:there be one: KINDPRED-CON):).

What reconstruction of (114) can be made with (111)? In attempting such a reconstruction of (114) we must remember that (111) contains a variable and that we shall therefore need quantification; thus we have

(119) (<u>PREDCON</u>)(the (<u>PREDCON</u> :the (:there be one: KINDPREDCON):) is an "ML !numerical quantifier statement! DST matrix" statement

which reduces to

(119.1) (<u>PREDCON</u>)(all (<u>PREDCON</u> :the (:there be one: KINDPREDCON):)s are "ML !numerical quantifier statement! DST matrix" statements.

From (119.1) by universal quantifier elimination, we get as an example,

all ((:odd:) :the (:there be one: KINDPREDCON):)s are "ML !numerical quantifier statement! DST matrix" statements,

i.e., all :odd (:there be one: KINDPREDCON)):s are "ML !numerical quantifier statement! DST matrix" statements.

The phrase within the double quotes is <u>taken directly from (116)</u> and serves to indicate what type of statements we are talking about. <u>The only significance of the double quotes in this case</u> is that they mark off the phrase taken from (116).

In sum, the number individuals

(120) <u>ONE</u>, <u>TWO</u>, <u>THREE</u>, <u>FOUR</u>, etc.,

would be reconstructed in finished form by means of

(121) the (PREDCON :the (:there be one: KINDPRED-CON):),

the (<u>PREDCON</u> :the (:there be two: KINDPRED-CON):),
the (<u>PREDCON</u> :the (:there be three: KINDPRED-CON):),
the (<u>PREDCON</u> :the (:there be four: KINDPRED-CON):), etc.

That is, statements containing numerical words for number individuals are reconstructed as statements containing the logically complex MML DST matrices in (121) (along with, of course, quantification over the variable '<u>PREDCON</u>'). I shall not, however, make very great use of the DST matrices in (121) for, as I said at the beginning of this section, the practical (in the ordinary sense) problems of reconstruction on the MML level prevent pursuit of the reconstructions in any detail.

(iii) <u>Induction and Succession</u>

My main claim in this subsection is that the task of explaining induction and succession on the MML level is like that of explaining them on the ML level. The only important difference is in the sort of items treated. In B(vi), the items were, of course, numerical quantifiers. In this subsection, they are, as subsection (ii) has made clear, ML !numerical quantifier statement! DST matrices. I discuss two accounts of induction and succession for these ML items in this subsection. Both accounts are parasitic, though in different ways, on other accounts of induction and succession.

Both these accounts rely on its being shown that ML !numerical quantifier statement! DST matrices are approachable by means of other ML items which I shall call "ML !numerical quantifier! SGTs." For example,

(122) :there be one:

is an ML !numerical quantifier! SGT. The phrase within the

exclamation marks is taken from such statements as

the :there be one: is a numerical quantifier,

i.e., all :there be one:s are numerical quantifiers.

All ML !numerical quantifier statement! DST matrices contain at least and at most one ML !numerical quantifier! SGT. For example,

(115) the (:there be one: KINDPREDCON)

contains a ::there be one::. Given this correspondence between ML !numerical quantifier statement! DST matrices and ML !numerical quantifier! SGTs, an account of induction and succession for the former can easily be derived from such an account for the latter.

The first of my two accounts gives a treatment of ML !numerical quantifier! SGTs which is directly parasitic on the ML treatment of numerical quantifiers in B(vi). Since each ML !numerical quantifier! SGT appears in at least and at most one ML DST for a numerical quantifier, 'SUCCEEDS' for ML !numerical quantifier! SGTs can be introduced by means of 'succeeds' for numerical quantifiers:

an ML !numerical quantifier! SGT SUCCEEDS an ML !numerical quantifier! SGT

is introduced as

(E X)(E Y)(X is the ML DST which contains only the former ML !numerical quantifier! SGT and Y is the ML DST which contains only the latter ML !numerical quantifier! SGT and X succeeds Y).

Thus it is true that

The ML !numerical quantifier! SGT ':there be two:' SUCCEEDS the ML !numerical quantifier! SGT ':there be one:'

because it is true that 'the :there be two:' contains only ':there be two:' and 'the :there be one:' contains only ':there be one:' and

the :there be two: succeeds the :there be one:.

Similar definitions can be given for 'is the SAME ML !numerical quantifier! SGT as', 'is a PART of', and 'is a PROPER PART of'.

Under these definitions, analogs of all the theorems of subsection B(vi) can be proven except those concerning addition and multiplication for number individuals. However, the forthcoming accounts of addition and of multiplication given, respectively, in subsections C(v) and C(vi) are also parasitic on those of section B and it will be clear that the account just given in this subsection is in line with the accounts in C(v) and C(vi).

The account just given, though satisfactory, does not reflect the fact that what an ML !numerical quantifier! SGT is true of is defined. A more penetrating treatment of induction and succession on the MML level, the second account aluded to above, therefore begins with a treatment of ML SGTs true of NQD-matrices and then forges the obvious connection to ML !numerical quantifier! SGTs. This second account is parasitic on the account in B(vi), but in only a trivial way. The key to the second account is showing how to produce on the MML level an analog of the entire ML treatment in B(vi). Thus this more penetrating account discusses ML SGTs true of NQD-matrices from scratch by characterizing their "structure" and their "elements" in imitation of what was done for Q-matrices, IQ-matrices, and NQD-matrices. I wish to indicate how this would be done.

Consider an ML SGT which is true of every token of the Q-matrixA, viz.,

(123) :(Ex)(Kx and (z)(if Kz, then x = z)):.

This SGT has a certain sort of complexity which can be brought out by considering its composition from other SGTs. The composition of SGTs depends, of course, on the SGTs being composed. In the case of (123), one composition is that of

:(Ex):

with

:(Kx and (z)(if Kz, then x = z)):.

In the notation I have been using, this is written thus:

(:(Ex):)(:Kx and (z)(if Kz, then x = z)):).

Of course,

(124) :(Ex):

is itself composed of

:E: (or, better perhaps, :(E):)

and :x:.

The first point about such compositions is that they are not to be understood on what appears to be the appropriate model for

x is a white horse.

This predicate is apparently the predicate

x is white and a horse

and thus "composed" by conjunction. By contrast,

x is an :(Ex):

is not equivalent to

x is an :(E): and an :x:.

Similarly, as I argued in chapter 2,

x is a :triangular a:

is not equivalent to

x is a :triangular: and an :a:.

This first point is made clearer, and my second point made, by replacing illustrating SGTs with nonillustrating SGTs. The nonillustrating SGT in the case of ':(E):' is the predicate 'E-quantifier'. In the case of ':x:', it is the predicate 'variable'--or, rather, since the Q-matrices that (123) is true of require two variables which are different (though not, of course, necessarily of the style of --x--s and the style of --z--s), we shall have the predicates 'variableA' and 'variableB'. Whether

:x:s are variableAs

or :x:s are variableBs

is unimportant so long as, given the notion adopted in 3A, not both of these statements are true. (Remember that, as I pointed out in 3A, all variables have the same generic role and are differentiated only in the context of statements involving more than one variable.)

The special nature of the predicate composition in (123) is apparent if I write (123) in a partially "decomposed" form which mixes illustrating and nonillustrating SGTs:

(125) (E-quantifier)(variableA)((:K:)(variableA)
(:and (z)(if Kz, then:)(variableA)(: = z:)).

Understanding this sort of composition of predicates is no more difficult than understanding the special significance of, say, a matrix's being E-quantified rather than universally quantified. A statement matrix is of a sort of matrix in virtue of being E-quantified; similarly, certain SGTs are of a sort of SGT in virtue of containing the predicate 'E-quantifier'. I shall call such SGTs "E-quantifier SGTs." There is an explanation of what this sort of SGT is which parallels, in a certain way, the explanation of what E-quantified statements and statement matrices are. (Notice that given my convention about exclamation marks, !E-quantifier! SGTs, i.e., those SGTs true of E-quantifiers, can be construed as the limiting case of E-quantifier SGTs: viz., as those E-quantifier SGTs which are composed only with themselves.)

The explanation of the role of E-quantifiers employs the ML predicate 'E-quantifier'; similarly, the explanation of the role of the predicate 'E-quantifier' and its special function in SGT composition must employ an MML predicate. The obvious MML predicate to employ is ':E-quantifier:'. (If I had not transferred my attention to nonillustrating ML predicates, but continued with illustrating ML predicates like ':(E):', then the MML explanation would use the predicate '::(E)::'.)

What should be said about the role of the predicate, the :E-quantifier:? Well, being a predicate, it must, like other predicates, have its role explained in terms of what it contributes to the inferential connections of statements and statement matrices in which it appears. Thus we can inquire about the inferential connections of the statements which are instances of

x is an E-quantifier

much as we inquired about the inferential connections of instances of

x is triangular.

What is to be said about the inferential connections of the former statements? The answer to this question has been, to some degree, supplied in 3A. (Although greater attention was lavished on the predicate 'universal quantifier' in 3A, nothing but convenience and space prevents a thorough account of 'E-quantifier' along the lines begun there.) The question asked in 3A was phrased in the traditional form, "What are E-quantifiers?" It was, however, understood that this question was to be taken as a request for an account of the predicate 'E-quantifier'. Thus though I said that a statement which is an E-quantified predicate may be inferred from each statement which is that predicate combined with a singular term, I could have formulated my remarks in 3A as rules of inferences pertaining to statements with the predicate, the :E-quantifier: (or, the adjective, the :E-quantified:). The same thing could be done for illustrating SGTs like ':(E):', save that the rules of inference would have terms with double Sellarsian quotes.

Once the accounts of 'E-quantifier', 'universal quantifier', 'variable', 'statement matrix', 'identity', 'conjunction', 'negation', 'and 'junction' (for want of a better term, I employ 'junction' as the nonillustrating counterpart of ':if ___, then ...:'), are set out, the different sorts of complex SGTs can be explained. These explanations are like the explanations given in a discussion of quantified statements. Thus, just as a universally quantified statement and an E-quantified statement differ in what the rules of inference permit one to infer from them and to infer them from, so E-quantifier SGTs differ inferentially from universal quantifier SGTs. Roughly speaking, an SGT is an E-quantifier SGT only if from statements having that SGT as a predicate it follows that the items of which the SGT is predicated have the inferential characteristics formulated by the rules of inference discussed in 3A.

These matters must not be confused with the way in which the materials of my notation provide an embodiment for complex SGTs. One of the significant features of my notation is that ML predicates, whether illustrating or nonillustrating, are strung together from left to right, as are the materials of the items of which the complex SGTs are true. Having such a similarity between the notation for complex SGTs and the items of which the SGTs are true is, of course, a great convenience. It is not, however, necessary to these SGTs, and it is not a part of the characterization of what it is to be a complex SGT of a certain sort.

Given the machinery of a theory of complex SGTs, it is clearly possible to characterize a kind of such SGTs, ones which would be called (in imitation of "Q-matrix") "Q-SGTs." One of these can be singled out as the "Q-SGTA" (in imitation of the "Q-matrixA"). Then an account of the ELEMENTS of Q-SGTs can be given; and with the ELEMENTS characterized, the definition of 'SUCCEEDS' for Q-SGTs is easily set out. From this point the way is open to repeating the development of B(vi) by giving the definitions of 'is the SAME Q-SGT as', 'is a PART of', 'is a PROPER PART of', and then 'IQ-SGT' and 'NQD-SGT'. In fact, the MML development is step by step parallel to the ML development and the arguments of B(vi) are transferable to the MML treatment simply by switching from "elements" to "ELEMENTS" and so on.

The relationships investigated in the beginning of this subsection are preserved under these definitions of the MML level. For example, a Q-SGT SUCCEEDS another Q-SGT if and only if the Q-matrix of which the former Q-SGT is true succeeds the Q-matrix of which the latter Q-SGT is true.

Finally, the appropriate connection with addition and multiplication for number individuals is correctly made by my reconstructions of statements with 'PLUS' and 'TIMES' a subsection hence.

(iv) Number Individuals and 'the NUMBER of'

The reconstruction of

(126) the NUMBER of Ks EQUALS N

is important, not so much for itself, but for its being a

simple example of the general strategy I shall follow in dealing with addition and multiplication for number individuals. Insight into this general strategy is indirectly furnished by noting that the reconstruction of (126) cannot be obtained directly from the reconstruction of

the number of Ks equals N.

Or, to use an example, the reconstruction of

(127) the NUMBER of horses EQUALS <u>FIVE</u>

cannot be obtained directly from the reconstruction of

(20) the number of horses equals FIVE.

One foot of my claim about these two reconstructions is on the fact that the reconstruction of (20) contains, as a conjunct within the quantifier '(E NUMQUANT)', the matrix

(27) the NUMQUANT is true of the :horses:.

The matrix (27) is equivalent to

the (NUMQUANT :horses:) is true

which, given that the matrix

(128) the NUMQUANT mi the :there be five:

is also a conjunct in the (primary) reconstruction, is obviously what is needed in the reconstruction of (20). The matrix (27) is, according to A(iv), an abbreviation of

(E KINDPREDCONA)(E NUMQUANTA)(the (NUMQUANT KINDPREDCONA) is true of the (NUMQUANTA :horses:)).

And, of course, it is an instance of

the (NUMQUANT KINDPREDCONA),

viz., the (:there be five: KINDPREDCONA),

which reconstructs 'FIVE'.

I ignore the terms in (121) since it will not affect the

following points and assume, for simplicity, that '<u>FIVE</u>' is reconstructed by means of

(129) the :the (:there be five: KINDPREDCON):.

With this assumption, another foot of my claim is on the fact that there is no way of working (129), or an MML variable for it, into (27) or into (128). The SGT in

the :there be five:

is true of numerical quantifiers, whereas the SGT in (129) is true of ML DST matrices. Statements made by combining such ML DST matrices and :horses:s have no direct connection with there being five horses.

However, this example illustrates one sort of connection between (27) and (129): (129) contains the SGT ':the (:there be five: KINDPREDCON):' which is true of just those DST matrices that are, given (27) and (128), important for the reconstruction of (20). This suggests that (127), among other things, says something about these DST matrices. Combining this suggestion with the point that the MML statement which reconstructs (127) must say something about the ML level leads to the obvious move of construing (127) as saying (roughly) that

the only instance of the reconstruction of
(130) the number of horses equals N
that is true is the reconstruction of (20).

This move in reconstructing (127) has several merits. It allows (127) to say something intelligible and important about the DST matrices, :the (:there be five: KINDPREDCON):s, while keeping (127) connected with

there be five horses

through the mediation of (20). We shall see in the next subsection how this dual advantage is carried on in the case of

'PLUS' and 'TIMES'.

A more complete account of (127) requires that I introduce MML variables. The SGT ':the (:there be five: KINDPREDCON):' is, as we know from (116.1), true of ML !numerical quantifier statement! DST matrices. Let us introduce the MML variable '<u>ML!NQST!DSTMAT</u>' for these general terms. The SGT '::there be five::' is true of ML !numerical quantifier! SGTs. So, I introduce the MML variable '<u>ML!NQ!SGT</u>' for these SGTs. Finally, we must remember that the SGT in (129) is true of DSTs which contain ::there be five::s.

Instead of giving the complete reconstruction of (127), which must, among other things, incorporate the whole reconstruction of (20), I set out <u>part</u> of the reconstruction of (127) using <u>only one conjunct</u> of the reconstruction of (20), viz., (27), for illustration:

(127.1) (E <u>ML!NQST!DSTMAT</u>)(E <u>ML!NQ!SGT</u>)(all <u>ML!NQST!DSTMAT</u>s contain an <u>ML!NQ!SGT</u> and

((:the:) <u>ML!NQ!SGT</u> (:is true of the :horses::))s are true and

the <u>ML!NQST!DSTMAT</u> MI the :the (:there be five: KINDPREDCON):).

One item of the additional work necessary for completing the reconstruction of (127) is an account of 'MI' which does for 'EQUALS' what 'mi' does for 'equals'. This account is given in the next subsection. With this account of EQUALITY, a complete, though perhaps unexciting, reconstruction of (127) (and with a little additional effort (126)) would be in hand.

(v) <u>Addition for Number Individuals</u>

The main aim of this subsection is to reconstruct statements like

(131) FIVE PLUS THREE EQUALS EIGHT

The reconstructions of statements like (131) follow the pattern set down in the previous subsection: (131) is reconstructed as a statement which speaks about the truth of the statement which reconstructs

(40) FIVE plus THREE equals EIGHT.

In addition to reconstructing statements like (131), I shall give the reconstructions of

(132) N EQUALS M.

The matrix (132) is also reconstructed in conformity with the strategy of the previous subsection: it is reconstructed in such a way that each instance of it is a statement which speaks about the truth of the reconstruction of an instance of

(53) N equals M.

Since I shall begin the work of this subsection by considering an instance of (132), viz.,

(133) FIVE EQUALS FIVE,

I must remind the reader of the reconstructions of (53). The primary reconstruction of (53), in its abbreviated form, is

the NUMQUANTA mi the NUMQUANTB.

The secondary reconstruction of (53), in its abbreviated form, is

the NUMQUANTA meq the NUMQUANTB.

Thus the primary reconstruction of

(43) FIVE equals FIVE

is the :there be five: mi the :there be five:.

The primary reconstruction of (133) involves the truth of the primary reconstruction of (43); the secondary reconstruction of (133), the truth of the secondary reconstruction of (43). I shall give only primary reconstructions in this subsection; the secondary reconstructions are easily formulated by reflecting on the primary.

Using the same MML DSTs I employed in the previous subsection, I give the primary reconstruction of (133):

(134) (E ML!NQ!SGTA)(E ML!NQ!SGTB)(the :the (:there be five: KINDPREDCON): contains the ML!NQ!SGTA and

the :the (:there be five: KINDPREDCON): contains the ML!NQ!SGTB and

the ((:the:) ML!NQ!SGTA (:mi the:) ML!NQ!SGTB) is true).

The (primary) reconstruction of (132) is easily obtained from (134); it is:

(135) (E ML!NQ!SGTA)(E ML!NQ!SGTB)(the ML!NQST!DSTMATA contains the ML!NQ!SGTA and

the ML!NQST!DSTMATB contains the ML!NQ!SGTB and

the ((:the:) ML!NQ!SGTA (:mi the:) ML!NQ!SGTB) is true).

Before beginning the work on (131), I wish to make a change in the notation for the DSTs which figure in the reconstruction of number individuals. Consider

the :the (:there be three: KINDPREDCON):

which is the reconstruction of 'THREE'. Since 'KINDPREDCON' is caught within a pair of quotes, it is not, as I explained earlier, a variable and thus can play no part in any of the quantifications in MML reconstructions. So, I abbreviate it in such contexts to 'KN'.

The reconstruction of (131) involves the truth of the statement which reconstructs (40). What is needed for doing the reconstruction can, of course, be obtained from the reconstruction of

(50) N plus M equals L.

The reconstruction of (50), in its abbreviated form, is the conjunction of

the NUMQUANTA mbif the NUMQUANTB and the NUMQUANTC

and the (NUMQUANTB :and: NUMQUANTC) mbif the NUMQUANTA.

The reconstruction of (40) is obtained from this conjunction by putting a ::there be eight:: in place of the :NUMQUANTA:s, a ::there be five:: in place of the :NUMQUANTB:s, and a ::there be three:: in place of the :NUMQUANTC:s.

The (primary) reconstruction of (131) is:

(136) (E <u>ML!NQ!SGTA</u>)(E <u>ML!NQ!SGTB</u>)(E <u>ML!NQ!SGTC</u>) (the :the (:there be eight: KN): contains the <u>ML!NQ!SGTA</u> and the :the (:there be five: KN): contains the <u>ML!NQ!SGTB</u> and the :the (:there be three: KN): contains the <u>ML!NQ!SGTC</u> and

the ((:the:) <u>ML!NQ!SGTA</u> (:mbif the:) <u>ML!NQ!SGTB</u> (:and the:) <u>ML!NQ!SGTC</u>) is true and

the ((:the:) <u>ML!NQ!SGTB</u> (:and:) <u>ML!NQ!SGTC</u>) (:mbif the:) <u>ML!NQ!SGTA</u>) is true).

Intuitively speaking, what (131) says is that :the (:there be three: KN):s, :the (:there be five: KN):s, and :the (:there be eight: KN):s contain items which satisfy the conjunction of the rule matrices which reconstruct (50). And, of course, the instance of the rule matrices in question is (40).

The (primary) reconstruction of

(137) <u>N</u> PLUS <u>M</u> EQUALS <u>L</u>

is obtained from (136) by replacing ':the (:there be eight: KN):', ':the (:there be five: KN):', and :the (:there be three: KN):' by the appropriate MML variables.

At this juncture it is interesting to compare what I have done thus far with an intuitive explanation of a Russellian definition of addition for classes of classes.[1] The main idea behind the Russellian definition is that the class of classes, S, is the sum of two other classes of classes, M and N, if and only if S's members can be "split" into two disjoint parts, B and C, which are such that B is in M and C is in N. Because we are not working with classes we cannot talk of "splitting" the members of a number into two parts. But there are in the DSTs,

the :the (:there be five: KN):

and the :the (:there be three: KN):,

two SGTs,

:the (:there be five: KN):

and :the (:there be three: KN):,

which are true of ML items which contain, respectively,

::there be five::s

and ::there be three::s.

And though these ML items cannot in any literal sense be the "split" parts of yet other ML items, viz., the

::there be eight::s

in :the (:there be eight: KN):s, the conjunction of rules of inference in which :the (:there be five: KN):s and :the (:there be three: KN):s appear with :the (:there be eight: KN):s can be understood as achieving something analogous to "splitting." Thus, roughly speaking, the analog of "splitting" the members of a class of classes is finding two types of items which appear in certain sorts of rules with another type of item.

(vi) Multiplication for Number Individuals

Multiplication is handled by the strategy of the previous subsections. From a reconstruction of

(138) TWO TIMES THREE EQUALS SIX,

I obtain a reconstruction of

(139) N TIMES M EQUALS L.

However, I am not in a position to give the reconstruction of (138). The reason for this can be found by reviewing the reconstructions of the previous subsection. The (primary) reconstruction of

(131) FIVE PLUS THREE EQUALS EIGHT

is put together with the help of the (abbreviated) reconstruction of

(50) N plus M equals L.

Similarly, for the reconstruction of (138), it is necessary to make use of the reconstruction of

(72) N times M equals L.

The difficulty is that the reconstruction of (72) is not completed until chapter 6.

But though the reconstruction of (138) cannot be given at this time, it is simple enough, under an assumption about the reconstruction of (72), to give an MML statement which approximates the reconstruction reasonably well. Consider

(60) TWO times THREE equals SIX.

A reconstruction of (60) (not, as it will turn out, a completely finished one) is given in B(v). This reconstruction,

(68), I shall abbreviate to (140), the conjunction of

the :there be six: mbif the :two(there be three):

and the :two(there be three): mbif the :there be six:.

My assumption about the reconstruction of (72) is that its abbreviation will be such that (140) is an instance of that abbreviation. Consequently, using the variable 'MULTNUMWORD' introduced in B(v), I shall assume, for present purposes, that the abbreviation of the reconstruction of (72) is (141), the conjunction of

the NUMQUANT mbif the (MULTNUMWORD (NUMQUANTA))

and the (MULTNUMWORD (NUMQUANTA)) mbif the NUMQUANT.

With (141), the reconstruction of (138) follows the pattern of the reconstruction of (131).

Notice that to complement the MML variable '<u>ML!NQ!SGT</u>', which is a variable for such MML SGTs as

::there be six::

and ::there be three::,

we need a variable for such SGTs as

::two::

which are MML SGTs true of ML SGTs like

:two:

which are true of a multiplicative numerical word. Thus I introduce the MML variable '<u>ML!MNW!SGT</u>'. An instance of the general term matrix

<u>ML!MNW!SGT</u> <u>ML!NQ!SGT</u>

is (142) (::two::)(:(:there be three:):)

and (142) is equivalent to

:(:two:)(:there be three:):,

i.e., ::two(there be three)::.

Following the pattern of the reconstruction of (131), I give a reconstruction of (138):

(143) (E ML!NQ!SGTA)(E ML!NQ!SGTB)(E ML!MNW!SGT) (the :the (:there be six: KN): contains the ML!NQ!SGTA and

the :the (:two(there be three): (KNA, KNB)): contains the ML!NQ!SGTB and

the :the (:two(there be three): (KNA, KNB)): contains the ML!MNW!SGT and

the ((:the:) ML!NQ!SGTA (:mbif the:) ML!MNW!SGT ML!NQ!SGTB) is true and

the ((:the:) ML!MNW!SGT ML!NQ!SGTB (:mbif the:) ML!NQ!SGTA) is true).

A reconstruction of (139) is obtained from (143) by replacing ':the (:there be six: KN):' and ':the (:two(there be three): (KNA, KNB)):' by appropriate MML variables.

The properties of associativity and commutivity of addition and multiplication for number individuals can be demonstrated on the basis of the reconstructions of this subsection and the previous one. Using (131) and (139), we would have no trouble defining other arithmetical notions. Thus

(144) N IS GREATER THAN M

is defined as

(145) (E L)(M PLUS L EQUALS N).

From this definition it is possible to prove all the usual properties of the relation 'IS GREATER THAN'.

Further we can give definitions of the various mathematical properties that are of interest in elementary number theory. For example, the definition of

(146) PRIME (N)

is (147) N does not EQUAL ONE and (M)(L)(if M TIMES L EQUALS N, then either M EQUALS ONE or L EQUALS ONE).

Of course 'PRIME' could be introduced by the same strategy we employed in the case of 'PLUS' and 'TIMES'. However, it is clear that given the reconstructions of 'TIMES' and 'EQUALS', a number individual is PRIME if and only if the corresponding number universal is prime. Indeed such a remark could be made about all properties of number individuals. In a sense, it does not matter whether we work at the ML or the MML level: results proven on one level are mirrored by corresponding results on the other level. Were this not the case, I should hardly be able to claim that I had reconstructed addition and multiplication on both the ML and MML levels.

Chapter 5: Topics Pertinent to the Reconstructions

A. Logicism

The aim of this chapter, and part of the next, is to provide exposition and argument to clarify further what has gone before. Some of what I shall say (such as the remarks in this section) is no more than additional exposition of matters about which it is necessary that there should be no confusion. Other remarks attempt to point out the merits of the reconstructions and to fend off possible criticisms.

A natural question about the reconstruction of chapter 4 is to what extent it fulfills the logicist aim of construing mathematics, or at least that part of mathematics with which I have chosen to deal, on the basis of logic alone. There can be no clear-cut answer to this question without an exact formulation of logicism. However, I shall not attempt to sort through the disagreements about logicism and to give an accurate account of it. My remarks will, I hope clarify my position even if they are not wholly pertinent to the reader's view of logicism. (I shall use as examples statements which pertain to addition; more complicated examples would not importantly alter my remarks.)

Consider 4A(ii)(8), the conjunction of

4A(ii)(8.1) (H)(I)(E J)(if no H be an I, then if there be five H and there be three I, then there be eight J)

and

4A(ii)(8.2) (J)(E H)(E I)(if no H be an I, then if there be eight J, then there be five H and there be three I).

Is 4A(ii)(8) a truth of logic? Are the numerical quantifier statement inferences associated with 4A(ii)(8) valid in virtue of logic alone?

From my point of view, the so-called second-order quantification in 4A(ii)(8) does not remove it from logic. As 3A makes clear, the mechanisms necessary for quantification involving predicate variables are the same as those which are necessary for quantification involving individual variables. Thus, unlike many semantic formalists, I have no reason to think that quantification involving predicate variables removes 4A(ii)(8) from the province of logic to class theory (or, to a theory of properties and relations which is at least as strong as class theory). So, for me, the quantification in 4A(ii)(8) is entirely consistent with its being a truth of logic.

But there is another important consideration. I said in 4A(ii) that numerical quantifiers combine only with general terms (kind terms, sortal predicates), not with any predicates whatsoever. Thus numerical quantifiers and what I called in that subsection "exact quantifiers" are not, strictly speaking, the same. Of course, numerical quantifiers can be understood as exact quantifiers restricted to general terms. Indeed the definitions of exact quantifiers and numerical quantifiers differ only in that the predicate variables in the definientia of numerical quantifiers are kind term variables while those in the definientia of exact quantifiers are not. However, unless there is a characterization of kind terms solely in vocabulary agreed to be logical, it would appear that 4A(ii)(8) is formulatable only in a context wider than logic.

Let me put my point in a different way. In the vicinity of 4(ii)(8), there is what I would allow as a truth of logic. It is similar to 4A(ii)(8) except that it has exact quantifiers and ordinary predicate variables. If the restriction of these predicate variables to kind terms can be formulated solely in terms we would agree are logical terms, then 4A(ii)(8) would be a special case of this truth of logic. If not, then 4A(ii)(8) is not a special case of this truth of logic.

One more point on this matter is worth noting. The demonstration of 4A(ii)(8), though it must <u>speak</u> <u>of</u> kind terms (or, kind term variables) because it speaks of numerical quantifiers, does not make use of any principles of inference which are confined to statements with kind terms (or, statement matrices with kind term variables). The premises for this demonstration that are drawn from the definitions of numerical quantifiers involve only those features of the definientia of numerical quantifiers which are common to both the definientia of numerical quantifiers and the definientia of exact quantifiers. These features are, in fact, ones involving only logical terms, viz., the quantifiers, the statement connectives, and identity. Thus even if the formulation of 4A(ii)(8) should require a vocabulary wider than what we would be willing to accept as logical vocabulary, one might still be tempted to say that, in light of its demonstration, 4A(ii)(8) enjoys a status very much like a truth of logic. (Similar things can be said about the numerical quantifier statement inferences which depend on 4A(ii)(8).)

Related questions arise in connection with 4B(iii)(46) and 4C(v)(136). Statement 4B(iii)(46) is a rule of inference and 4C(v)(136), a statement (indirectly) about that rule of inference. So the natural questions to ask are: Is 4B(iii)(46) a rule <u>of</u> <u>logic</u>? Is 4C(v)(136) a statement about a rule <u>of</u> <u>logic</u>.

Note that the considerations about numerical quantifiers and kind terms just discussed have analogs in the cases of 4B(iii)(46) and 4C(v)(136). With this point in mind, I can answer the questions by saying that nothing prevents an affirmative answer to both save the resolution of the problem about the characterization of kind terms. There is no reason, on my view, why a rule of logic should not have the features and structure (allowing for some possible refinements) that 4B(iii)(46) has. Thus 4B(iii)(46) would turn out to be a rule of logic and 4C(v)(136) a statement about this rule if the difference between kind term and other predicates could be formulated solely in logical terms.

As in the case of 4A(ii)(8), it is of rather little interest to me whether the answer to these questions is yes or no. My reason for this indifference is simple: I accept no special theses about elementary mathematics which depend on the answers to these questions. Unlike Frege, I have no reason to believe that showing elementary mathematics to contain only "analytic" truths is of any real interest. It is true that one can think of several senses of 'analytic' (including 'truth of logic or rule of logic') in which 4A(ii)(8) and 4B (iii)(46) might turn out to be analytic. But such a result would have no bearing on any epistemological claims I might be tempted to make about elementary mathematics. (I shall have somewhat more to say about such epistemological claims when I return to a discussion of formalism later in this chapter.)

My only claim that depends on the features and structure of 4B(iii)(46) is that, whether or not it is a rule of logic, it is a rule of language. This claim would be true even if kind terms could not be distinguished from other predicates by means of logic; the distinction would still, on my view, be a linguistic one. Thus, in that broad sense of 'formal' which encompasses linguistic matters as well as logic, 4B(iii) (46) is a formal rule of inference and 4C(v)(136) is a formal statement about such a rule. Further, 4A(ii)(8) is a formal truth whose demonstration, as I pointed out, involves only formal matters which are also logical.

I also wish to emphasize that, on my view, the reconstructions of chapter 4 do <u>not</u>, in any way, utilize class theory. Of course, some of the arguments and notions found in these reconstructions look like those that are found in class theory. On my view, there are two reasons why this should be so. First, many notions in my reconstructions (such as being true of) must have important logical similarities to class-theoretic notions (such as being a member of); otherwise, my reconstructions would not have the sort of structure of levels they do in fact have. The second reason is one that is much more important. Class theory is not independent of the resources I have utilized in my reconstructions. Indeed, as we shall see in chapter 6, I obtain (the fundamentals of) class theory from exactly the same resource as my reconstructions in chapter 4. In short, classes are handled, on the view I am defending, just as other "abstract" entities are. Thus the sorts of arguments and notions in my reconstructions which appear to be from class theory are part of the, if you will, "linguistic theory" on which class theory and all other talk of "abstract" entities are constructed.

B. Nominalism and the Existence of Natural Numbers

The topic of this section, the existence of natural numbers, cannot be treated adequately without more elaborate remarks on existence, truth, and related notions than I have the space to give. My remarks are intended only to indicate the sort of position I defend. I shall frame my comments around the simplest examples; my points are unaffected by the complication of the example.

Chapter 4 provides a reconstruction for such statements as

4B(i)(13) THREE is a number universal.

The true statement provided as a reconstruction of 4B(i)(13) is

4B(i)(13.3) (KINDPREDCON)(the (:there be three: KINDPREDCON) is a numerical quantifier statement).

Neither universal nor E-quantification, according to my account in 3A, commits one to the existence of anything. So I turn to an even simpler statement that does not involve quantification:

4B(i)(13.1) the :there be three: is a numerical quantifier.

With this last example in mind, my first claim is that on my reconstructions, the statement

(1) there are numerical quantifiers

is true. It is statements like (1) which, in 3A, I called "garden-variety" existence statements. So my first claim is, in effect, that on my reconstructions a garden-variety existence statement about numerical quantifiers is true.

In 3A, I claimed that these garden-variety existence statements are not to be explicated as E-quantified statements and that E-quantified statements are not to be given a "reading" by means of garden-variety existence statements. I shall take this opportunity to elaborate this claim while providing support for my claim about (1). (My remarks should not, of course, be taken as an attempt at a complete account of garden-variety existence statements since such an account requires dealing with epistemological issues which cannot be included in this book.)

My rejection of the claim that (1) is the ordinary language counterpart of

(2) (Ex)(x is a numerical quantifier)

is, so to speak, conditional. I should not object to the suggestion to treat (1) as (2) _if_ this move were seen as one with restrictions. Statement (2) will do as a rendering of (1) _under certain conditions_, but not as a rendering of (1)

<u>simpliciter</u>.

Some of these conditions, as might be expected, arise because of my account of the E-quantifier. At least one other condition is one which I should wish to make independently of my account of quantification, though it is connected with the special features of my account of quantification. The import of this condition is that (2) is an adequate rendering of (1) only under (at least) the condition that the predicate in (2) is a sortal predicate belonging to a full-fledged classificatory scheme that allows true, singular classificatory statements (e.g., 4B(i)(13.1)) and true general classificatory statements (e.g., numerical quantifiers are defined by E-quantified matrices).

One consequence of appending this condition to the rendering of (1) by (2) is that the inferential relation of 4B (i)(13.1) and (2) is not what one would expect. In 3A, I allowed E-quantified statements like (2) to follow, <u>sans</u> condition, from statements like 4B(i)(13.1). But now insofar as (2) is treated as rendering (1), (2) does not follow from 4B (i)(13.1) except under (at least) the condition I have mentioned.

I shall restate my point without the background of the question of the relation of (1) and (2). Consider statements

(3) there exist numerical quantifiers

and (4) numerical quantifiers exist.

I shall understand both of these as garden-variety existence statements equivalent to (1). Statements (1), (3), and (4) do not have their truth assured by the truth of 4B(i)(13.1) <u>alone</u>. These statements are true only if 4B(i)(13.1) is true under (at least) the condition I have mentioned.

I think that chapter 4 is part of a good case for the claim that statements like 4B(i)(13.1) are true classificatory statements made within a full-fledged classificatory scheme. I have, of course, only sketched the basic outline of the whole scheme and filled in such parts as were necessary to the defense of statements like 4B(i)(13.1) and general statements about numerical quantifiers, Q-matrices, IQ-matrices, and NQD-matrices. Nonetheless, it is, I think, reasonably clear that 4B(i)(13.1) is couched in a conceptual setting with the sort of classificatory structure and articulation that is also found in the setting of other, more ordinary, singular and general classificatory statements (e.g., Socrates is a man, all men are animals). It is on such considerations that I would build a defense of the truth of (1) (and (3) and (4)).

The mild nominalism of my position is brought out by other considerations about my reconstructions. In 3A(iii), I said that, from a philosophical perspective, one's ontological commitments are not reflected by the totality of garden-variety existence statements one accepts. One's ontological commitments, I suggested, can involve only "simple," not "complex" entities. Further, to talk of the "complexity" of entities is to talk of the eliminability of the linguistic items for these entities within a tenable philosophical account of the relevant issues.

Part of the argument for the claim that garden-variety existence statement do not reflect one's commitments is that such statements are indifferent to all matters of complexity and simplicity. Given that houses of cards are made from cards, it can be true both that there **is** a house of cards and that there are cards out of which this house is built. Or, suppose that all statements about physical objects could be eliminated in favor of ones which spoke only of molecules. Under such a supposition, it could still be true that there are physical objects and that there are molecules, in particular those molecules which compose physical objects.

Even more complicated cases of complexity and simplicity are ignored by the garden-variety existence statement. Thus let us suppose that smiles are complex entities whose complexity is brought out by their "nominal" nature; thus

the cat is wearing a whimsical smile

is eliminated in favor of

the cat smiles whimsically.

Despite this elimination, it can still be true, given certain conditions, that

there is a whimsical smile which the cat is wearing.

A similarly complicated case is that of 4B(i)(13.1) and its kin. Though 4B(i)(13.1) and its kin are eliminable in favor of general statements like

4B(i)(13.2) :there be three:s are numerical quantifiers,

(1) is still true and its truth is justified, in part, by the truth of 4B(i)(13.1).

It is this indifference of garden-variety existence statements to the complexity of objects that, with other considerations, leads me to accept the claim that one's commitments are not reflected by the totality of garden-variety existence statements one would assent to. One's commitments are to be judged by statements which are not eliminable. Those statements like 4B(i)(13.1), which are introduced by statements like 4B(i)(13.2), can commit one to no more than what the statements which introduce them commit one to. And clearly _if_ 4B(i)(13.2) commits us to anything, it can be to _no more_ than tokens of some type, _not_ distributive objects or "abstract entities" in any traditional sense of this latter phrase.

I have been careful to say that statements like 4B(i)(13.2) can commit us to _no more_ than linguistic tokens. For the sake of the following argument, I shall assume that there is a sense of 'commit' which is such that statements like 4B (i)(13.2) and other uneliminable statements of my reconstructions commit one to linguistic entities. But I distinguish between being committed to linguistic entities in this sense and being committed to the garden-variety existence of linguistic tokens. The sorts of statements reconstructed in chapter 4 do not (with one kind of explicable exception) commit us to the garden-variety existence of linguistic tokens. In fact, the truth of these statements (once again with one sort of exception) does not depend on the garden-variety existence of linguistic tokens.

The argument for these claims, which I shall call the "main" claims of this section, are based on several other claims. The first is that for a general statement to be meaningful and true, it does not have to be the case that there are entities of which the general terms in the statement are true. Thus 4B(i)(13.2) is true whether or not there are any :there be three:s. Of course, it may well be that such general truths about tokenings would not in fact be made in ordinary circumstances, if the speaker did not believe that there are tokenings of which the SGTs in the general truths are true. This may well be a good point about the practical context in which saying goes on. But it in no way shows that such general statements themselves commit us to or depend for their truth on the existence of linguistic tokens.

The second claim is one that I have made repeatedly: quantification by itself does not bring about commitment. So, for example, 4B(i)(13.3) does not commit us to the existence of anything by virtue of the quantification in it, and no garden-variety existence statement follows from it by virtue of the quantification in it.

With these two claims in mind, consider the sorts of statements discussed in the previous section.

Statement 4A(ii)(8) is a conjunction of quantified, conditional statements. From my claim about quantification and some obvious points about the sort of conditionals in the conjuncts of 4A(ii)(8), it follows that 4A(ii)(8) does not commit us to the existence of anything and does not depend for its truth on the garden-variety existence of anything. Thus 4A(ii)(8) satisfies the main claims.

The statement 4B(iii)(46) is eliminable in favor of a conjunction of quantified, conditional rules. In each of these conditional rules, both the condition and the remainder of the rule are completely general. This fact along with my two claims shows that the main claims are again satisfied.

Similar remarks are true for the MML statement that reconstructs 4C(v)(131).

Thus I conclude that the statements which are uneliminable in my reconstructions and which figure into the reconstructions of statements involving addition do not commit one to, or depend on, the garden-variety existence of linguistic items. Though it would be tedious to show it in detail, the same is true for the uneliminable statements necessary to the reconstructions of statements involving multiplication and for the uneliminable statements in the accounts of induction and succession.

The only other statements I have reconstructed in chapter 4 are the exceptions I mentioned: these are numerical quantifier statements, statements that reconstruct statements like

4B(ii)(20) the number of horses equals FIVE

which contain 'the number of', and statements that reconstruct statements like

4C(iv)(127) the NUMBER of horses EQUALS <u>FIVE</u>

which contain 'the NUMBER of'. I shall confine myself to remarks on numerical quantifier statements. Statements like 4B(ii)(20) and 4C(iv)(127) are reconstructed in such a way that their reconstructions are true only if some numerical quantifier statement is true. Further, the uneliminable statements one reaches at the end of the reconstructions of 4B(ii)(20) and 4C(iv)(127) have no features, except their dependence on the truth of a numerical quantifier statement, that would commit one to, or make them dependent on, the existence of anything.

Since I have allowed that numerical quantifier statements are garden-variety existence statements, it is obvious that, in some cases, numerical quantifier statements depend on the garden-variety existence of linguistic tokens; such a numerical quantifier statement is

> (5) there are three numerical quantifier tokens (in Jones's statement).

This result about (5) is not a surprise. Moreover, it is not in any way damaging to my reconstructions or to the main claims of this section. The statements of my reconstructions in no way imply the truth of any numerical quantifier statement about linguistic tokens or imply that we should accept any numerical quantifier statement about linguistic tokens. This claim is supported by two points, one relatively unimportant and one very important.

The relatively unimportant one is that in the case of (5) and its kin (and as well in the case of 4B(ii)(20) and 4C(iv)(127)), chapter 4 tells one only how to reconstruct these statements, not that any of them is true or acceptable. These statements are thus treated in a way unlike that in which 4A(ii)(8), 4B(iii)(46), and 4C(v)(136) are treated. Arguments for the truth of these latter statements are given.

The more important point is that

(1) there are numerical quantifiers

and (6) there are numerical quantifier tokens

should not be confused. Statement (1), I have claimed, is justified, under my reconstructions, by 4B(i)(13.1). Statement (6) is not so justified. Moreover, (6) does not follow from (1). The truth of (6) is assured (once again, under (at least) the condition I mentioned earlier) by the truth of statements like

(7) this is a numerical quantifier token.

But such statements as (7) are not part of my reconstructions.

It is important that I forestall an objection against the main claims of this section. The objection rests on the apparently plausible claim that the garden-variety existence statement (1) must rest on some other statement which is not eliminable in my reconstruction. After all, the objection urges, since 4B(i)(13.1) is introduced by 4B(i)(13.2) and (1) is justified (under (at least) certain conditions) by 4B(i)(13.1), there must be a statement akin to 4B(i)(13.2) on which (1) depends. And surely this statement, the objection concludes, is a garden-variety existence statement about numerical quantifier tokens.

Though much might be said about this line of thought, I shall limit my remarks by admitting that (1) does depend on a statement which is uneliminable in the reconstructions. In fact, the statement is

(8) (E NUMQUANT)(the NUMQUANT is a numerical quantifier).

But, of course, on my view, nothing much follows from the admission I have made in the previous paragraph. First, I note, once again, that quantification does not by itself commit one to the existence of anything. Second, (8) is not a garden-variety existence statement. In particular, neither is it the statement (6), nor does (6) follow from (8). The truth of (8) does not depend on the existence of numerical quantifier tokens; and the acceptance of (8) does not commit one to the existence of numerical quantifier tokens.

I do, of course, agree that those who give the semantic formalist account of quantification cannot agree with what I have said about (8). This is also true of those who fall prey to the trap of "reading" (8) in English with either the phrase

there is a

or the phrase

there exists a.

In 3A, I rejected both the semantic formalist account of quantification and the above "readings" of the E-quantifier.

To conclude this subsection, I reply to another objection. Someone might suggest that the "linguistic" nature of my reconstructions is sure to lead to the consequence that the existence of numerical quantifiers and thus natural numbers is "only potential." It may seem to some that any "linguistic" account of natural numbers must, despite what I have already said, have this consequence.

I must confess that I do not find talk of the "potential" existence of numbers very enlightening or very clear. To say that a number exists "only potentially" seems to me to be a roundabout way of saying that there is no such number. But, apart from this point, the conclusion that there are no natural numbers of a certain description would follow from the claim that the existence of natural numbers depends on the existence of the linguistic tokens of a certain sort. This is so because, for natural numbers greater than a certain number, no one has tokened the appropriate numerical quantifiers. Thus it would follow that some natural number is the last; in particular, there is no successor of this natural number.

My direct reply to this objection I defer for the moment. The point I wish to make now is one that I hope will clear up a confusion. The objection may appear to be correct because statements like

4B(i)(13.1) the :there be three: is a numerical quantifier

and

4B(i)(13.2) :there be three:s are numerical quantifiers

contain the SGT

:there be three:.

The appearance of this SGT in these statements may seem to depend on the existence of at least one :there be three:, the one that <u>seems</u> to appear between the quotes of the SGT. This argument is one that I have criticized repeatedly: the natural linguistic object (which is a --there be three--) between the quotes is not produced in a tokening of a :there be three:. All that is <u>true</u> is what is explained in chapter 2: tokenings of ::there be three::s in English involve the production of natural linguistic objects of the same kind as tokenings of :there be three:s in English. But it is <u>false</u> that in tokening a ::there be three::, one tokens a :there be three:.

My direct reply to the objection is that in 4B(vi) I gave proofs of arithmetical statements which show that the conclusion the objection reaches is false. In particular, there is a successor for every numerical quantifier and thus for every natural number.

Of course, the proofs of these arithmetical statements about numerical quantifiers are parasitic on ones for finite NQD-matrices. Now with this admission the objection would seem to return to life slightly transformed. The existence of finite NQD-matrices, it says, surely depends on the existence of distributive objects like conjunction (the :and:), negation (the :not:), the E-quantifier, and so on. Moreover, the existence of these distributive objects in turn must depend on the existence of linguistic tokens (:and:s, :not:s, E-quantifier tokens, and so on). Therefore, the existence of numerical quantifiers does depend, in the end, on the existence of linguistic tokens.

My response to the resurrected form of the objection begins with the admission that the garden-variety existence of "complex" entities does indeed depend on the garden-variety existence of the "simple" entities which compose the "complex" ones. Thus if the objection is correct, it would show that the whole framework of linguistic distributive objects depends for its existence on linguistic tokens. I must admit that this conclusion concerning all the linguistic distributive objects, both "complex" and "simple," does not in some ways seem so objectionable to me. Nevertheless, the resurrected objection relies on the unsupported assertion that "simple" distributive objects exist only if linguistic tokens do. I see no reason to accept this assertion.

The garden-variety existence of conjunction seems to me to depend on the truth of statements like

(9) the :and: is a connective

and, perhaps, on

(10) some connective is identical to the :and:.

I see no reason to believe that these statements are true only if certain linguistic tokens exist. I find this claim no more convincing than the objection in its original form.

C. Proof

(i) Formalism

No discussion of the philosophy of mathematics would be complete without some discussion, however short, of proof. Nor could any discussion of proof be complete without remarks on formalism. In my case, the remarks serve only to point up the differences between my views and those of a formalist. Though there are different kinds of formalism, what I have to say about formalism is, by and large, true of all sorts of formalism, even recent semantic formalism.

The first matter of some importance concerns the epistemological views that were, at least in the beginning, associated with formalism. Hilbert himself stated one of these epistemological views when he said, "The goal of my theory is to establish once and for all the certitude of mathematical methods."[1] But it would seem clear from other remarks of Hilbert's that he wished not only to free mathematical _methods_ from all uncertainty but also to found the whole of mathematics on statements which are certain and indubitable. Thus we find Hilbert saying that the existence of "the paradoxes is intolerable." The paradoxes lead one to conclude that "mathematical thinking is defective." Yet mathematics, for Hilbert, is "the paragon of truth and certitude." Thus if mathimatics were riddled with paradoxes, we should not know where "to find truth and certitude."[2] The point of Hilbert's program was to found mathematics on such a basis that paradoxes would not arise "ever again."[3]

Thus Hilbert hoped to found mathematics on statements and methods which would insure that it would not even be possible for contradictions and absurdities to appear again in mathematics. Yet there are philosophers who deny that such hopes are legitimate. These philosophers argue that the program of providing all knowledge, or even a branch of it, with a certain and indubitable foundation is misconceived. They would, of course, allow that we are obligated to repair any breaches which appear in the wall of knowledge, but they would deny that we can take complete and sure precautions against them.[4] One reason given in support of their view is that an adequate understanding of a difficulty in some branch of knowledge may require concepts we do not presently have. We could hardly guard against difficulties which we are not yet capable of conceiving adequately.

Since I myself regard as chimerical any program of providing a foundation for knowledge, even elementary mathematical knowledge, I would not and, indeed, have not defended my reconstructions in chapter 4 on the grounds that they assure us of the certainty and indubitability of the statements of arithmetic. The same is true of the other reconstructions, even those of the theory of classes, found in chapter 6. That my reconstructions are correct in no way guarantees that we shall not sometime discover difficulties in what I have reconstructed; nor would it follow from _simply_ the existence of such difficulties that my reconstructions are incorrect. Since the appearance of difficulties, even contradictions, in a branch of knowledge is impossible to rule out completely, their appearance cannot be grounds for singling out some reconstruction as faulty unless the difficulties depend on some special feature of the reconstruction.

Not sharing Hilbert's epistemological aims, I have not been guided in my reconstructions by the epistemological considerations which led Hilbert to endow his formalist treatments of mathematics with certain characteristics. Of these characteristics I choose to discuss those that allow me to explain some important differences between my reconstruction of arithmetic and the formalist treatment of arithmetic.

Hilbert's epistemological goals were to be achieved by a program. The most important courses of action in this program were the development of formal systems and the employment of only absolutely certain, "finitary" methods in studying formal systems. The finitary methods treat of items of the formal system such as sequences of natural linguistic objects (some of which satisfy certain conditions and are called "formulas") and sequences of formulas (some of which satisfy certain conditions and are called "proofs"). A formal system is conceived as having a "syntax" that _inter alia_ specifies which sequences of natural linguistic objects are formulas and which sequences of formulas are proofs. These specifications are accomplished by giving definitions of "syntactical" predicates such as 'formula' and 'proof'.

What I shall call the "primary" characteristic of formal systems is that there must be an "effective" procedure associated with such syntactical predicates as 'formula' and 'proof'.[5] For example, there must be an "effective" procedure for deciding whether any sequence of natural linguistic objects of the formal system is a formula and an "effective" procedure for deciding whether any sequence of formulas of the formal system is a proof. For our purposes, a procedure is "effective" if and only if what to do at any step in the procedure is explicitly set out by directions and the procedure allows one to reach an answer to the question under consideration in a "finite" number of steps.

I now investigate some "secondary" characteristics of formal systems. These are some of the characteristics a formal system must have if there are to be effective procedures associated with any of its syntactical predicates. Since my later remarks do not require a complete account of syntactical predicates and effective procedures, I shall conduct my discussion by means of the example of the two predicates, 'formula' and 'proof'. I also restrict my attention to formal systems elaborate enough to deal with arithmetic.

The definition of 'formula' is an inductive definition, a kind of definition very familiar to readers of modern logic books.[6] One of the distinctive things about an inductive definition is that some of its clauses state ways in which the linguistic items being defined can be generated. I shall call these clauses "generating" clauses. Generating clauses are of two kinds. One kind ("independent" clauses) tell one how to generate linguistic items of the sort being defined from linguistic items of other sorts. The other kind ("dependent" clauses) tell one how to generate linguistic items of the sort being defined from items of the same sort.

The inductive definition of 'formula' has both kinds of generating clauses. Its dependent generating clauses state ways in which formulas are generated from other formulas. Its independent generating clauses state ways in which formulas can be generated from other sorts of linguistic items (e.g., predicates and singular terms).

The effective procedure associated with the predicate 'formula' depends on its being possible to determine effectively that, and how, a formula has been generated from another (other) formula(s) or from linguistic items of other sorts. But, more important for the present discussion, it must be possible to determine effectively that a linguistic item of the formal system is of one of these other sorts (e.g., a predicate, a singular term). Of course, the predicates for these other sorts of linguistic items may also be defined by an inductive definition which is like the inductive definition of 'formula'. In the end, however, one must come to syntactical predicates that have inductive definitions with a sort of clause the definition of 'formula' lacks or to syntactical predicates which are defined by lists. (An example of a syntactical predicate usually defined by a list is the predicate 'logical constant'.) The sort of clause that the definition of 'formula' lacks is what I shall call a "direct" clause.

Direct clauses list linguistic items of the formal system and say that these items are of the sort being defined. Thus, in either case, the syntactical predicates we reach in the end are defined with the aid of lists of linguistic items. Moreover, the lists must be given in such a way that one can effectively determine whether a linguistic item of the formal system is in the list.

The necessity for such lists can also be seen in the defitition of 'proof'. The crucial list in this case is the list of formulas which are said to be "axioms." The list of axioms of arithmetic is not "finite," but it is nonetheless stated in such a way that one can determine effectively whether or not a formula of the formal system is an axiom of arithmetic. If this were not the case, it would be impossible to determine effectively whether a sequence of formulas is a proof.

So one secondary characteristic of formal systems is that they contain lists of items of the formal system on which the definitions of certain syntactical predicates depend and which are such that one can effectively decide whether an item of the formal system is in the list.

Another secondary characteristic of formal systems is that it follows from the demand for effective procedures that all formulas and all proofs must be "finite" sequences. The reason for this is clear. If a sequence of items of the formal system were not "finite," the procedure for checking whether this sequence is of a certain syntactical sort could not end in a "finite" number of steps. Each of the elements of the sequence has to be checked and, of course, the "nonfinitely" many items of a "nonfinite" sequence cannot all be checked in a "finite" number of steps.

Turning to the differences between my reconstruction of arithmetic and formal systems of arithmetic I begin with some reflections on my account of statements. Statements, as I explained in chapter 2, are characterized by their function.

We need not go into detail again: the important point is that my characterization of statements is not in terms of the ways in which they can be generated from basic linguistic items. Moreover, I give no lists of basic linguistic items. Thus my notion of statement is not inductive and, more important, has no effective procedures tied to it.

At any given time, it may be possible to list the basic items that go into statements and the ways in which statements are put together from the basic items and from each other. However, any predicate defined, in imitation of inductive definitions in formal systems, from such a list of basic items and a list of means of generation would be only materially (extensionally) equivalent at that time to the predicate 'statement'. Statements, as I characterize them, are not determined by any lists of present items and means of generation. And it is not by accident that this is so.

While I have not argued directly about this matter, it is one of the underlying views of my position that inductive definitions, though acceptable and undoubtedly useful for certain purposes, are not adequate for understanding linguistic predicates. A comparable situation, it seems to me, is the inadequacy of explaining what an automobile is by giving a list of the present basic parts of automobiles and explaining the present ways in which these parts are put together. Definition by list seems to me no better. The telephone directory does not give a definition of being a subscriber to the services of a telephone company. An adequate account of statements and other linguistic items must be a functional account (in a broad sense of this term.)

The attack in the previous paragraphs should not be confused with an attack on certain truths about statements which are indeed preserved on my view. For example, on my view, there are truths about what kinds of linguistic items are the basic linguistic components of statements. But such truths cannot be used to imitate the independent generating clauses of the inductive definition of 'formula', since the kinds of linguistic items they mention (e.g., singular terms) are not characterized effectively any more than statements are. On my account, there is no effective procedure for deciding whether a linguistic item is a basic component of statements (e.g., whether it is a singular term).

Another confusion to be avoided stems from the incorrect assimilation of 'there is an effective procedure for deciding . . .' to 'there are a limited number of considerations which must be taken into account to decide . . .'. No doubt at any given time we have reasons to confine our deliberations on most questions (mathematical or otherwise) to a rather "limited number of considerations." However, it does not follow from this concession that at any given time we have effective procedures for deciding most questions. Indeed, we do not (and, I believe, cannot) have effective procedures for deciding most questions. This misassimilation is very dangerous in that it gradually leads us to forget how special and distinctive effective procedures are.

Another consequence of my account of statements is that it is in no way obvious that statements need be "finite" sequences of tokens. It may be true that all statements are. But this fact, if it is a fact, does not follow from my characterization of statements.

What has been said about the predicate 'statement' is also true of 'statement of arithmetic'. I admit that it is possible to define a predicate which is, at a given time, materially equivalent to 'statement of arithmetic'. One might even have reasonable confidence that this material equivalence would obtain for the foreseeable future. But, on my view, one could not prove that this is so any more than one could prove that automobiles will in the foreseeable future be put together in certain ways from certain parts. Further, no arguments which are supposed to be about statements of arithmetic and yet depend essentially on this material equivalence can lead to a conclusion about all statements of arithmetic; they can lead only to a conclusion about those statements of arithmetic which are generated in certain ways from certain lists of basic arithmetical terms at a certain time.

Another point is that there is no simple characterization of statements of arithmetic on my view. The reason for this is clear: my reconstructions are set within a complicated linguistic background involving quotation, special general terms, inferences, truth, and so on. Of the variety of statements which can be constructed within this linguistic setting, some can be singled out and called "statements of arithmetic." But exactly which ones are singled out depends very greatly on what one's interests are. In a philosophical discussion, it might well be quite important to include as statements of arithmetic numerical quantifier statements, the statements which reconstruct statements with 'the number of', and the statements which reconstruct statements with 'the NUMBER of'. But if one has an eye on books on number theory, one would certainly wish to cut down on the statements that qualify as statements of arithmetic. Thus one might decide that statements of arithmetic are either ML general statements about numerical quantifier statements or MML general statements about the DSTs which figure in the ML statements about numerical quantifier statements (along with molecular statements containing either of these sorts of statements). Notice also that these separations of statements of arithmetic from other statements are not such as to provide one with an effective procedure for deciding whether some statement is a statement of arithmetic.

It is not at all distressing to me that there is no easy

or simple characterization of the predicate 'statement of arithmetic'. One of the advantages of my reconstruction of arithmetic is that it places statements of arithmetic in a context in which their affinity to other statements, which would not usually be considered arithmetical, is reasonably clear. But the price of this advantage is that there are many possible separations of statements of arithmetic from other statements. A formal system of arithmetic can have a very straightforward distinction between what the formal system defines as statements of arithmetic and other statements, but only at the expense, from my point of view, of not adequately explaining the predicate 'statement of arithmetic'.

The situation becomes even more complicated when we turn our attention to proofs. As we have seen, the formalist definition of 'proof' utilizes a list of axioms for which there is an effective procedure to determine whether a formula is an axiom. Without this secondary characteristic in the case of axioms, there would be no effective procedure associated with the predicate 'proof'.

First, notice that if I had a list of axioms (say, my reconstruction of Peano's axioms), the list would be a list of statements. Thus since there is no effective procedure for determining that something is a statement, there is no effective procedure for determining that something is an axiom. Furthermore, my recent remarks about the definition of 'statement of arithmetic' make it clear that even if one assumed that one had a list of statements, one would not be able to determine effectively, relative to this assumption, that it was a list of statements <u>of</u> <u>arithmetic</u>. (I shall not bother to make anything of it, but it is true that the same points about effectiveness hold for inferences as well.)

Second, there is no reason on my account of arithmetic to think that any list of statements of arithmetic (e.g., my reconstruction of Peano's axioms) are going to be satisfactory as axioms of arithmetic. What is implied in calling statements of arithmetic axioms of arithmetic is that no statement of arithmetic which is not an axiom has a proof which has premises other than the axioms. Put another way, statements of arithmetic are satisfactory as axioms of arithmetic only if all proofs of statements of arithmetic (apart from the axioms themselves) have no other premises than the statements of arithmetic which have been chosen to be axioms. Not only is there no reason on my view to think that any list of axioms is satisfactory, there is some reason to think that no list of axioms is satisfactory. In any case, I surely have no reason to think that I should offer a definition of 'proof of arithmetic' which depends on a list of axioms.

Before I discuss the reasons for thinking that no list of statements of arithmetic is satisfactory as axioms of arithmetic, there are several points to clarify.

First, the points I shall be discussing have nothing to do with the fact that the truths of arithmetic vary with the definition of 'statement of arithmetic'. I shall suppose that, with our eyes on books on number theory, we have defined 'statement of arithmetic' in a way which fits our intuitive judgments exactly.

Second, I wish it to be clear that I am not going to discuss a trivial way in which any statements of arithmetic chosen to be axioms of arithmetic fail to be the premises of mathematically interesting proofs of some truths of arithmetic. The mathematically interesting proofs of some of the axioms themselves (such as the proofs I gave of my reconstruction of Peano's axioms) do not have the axioms as the only premises. But this is a trivial matter, since what we wish axioms of arithmetic to do is to be the sole premises in the proofs of other truths of arithmetic.

With these two points clarified, I turn to the reasons for thinking that no list of statements of arithmetic is satisfactory as axioms of arithmetic.

First, there is the very general consideration already alluded to: the linguistic setting of my reconstruction of arithmetic is very encompassing. Moreover, certain truths of arithmetic, viz., my reconstructions of Peano's axioms, have proofs which require the mobilization of truths and concepts from this linguistic setting, and these are not truths and concepts strictly of arithmetic. It is certainly not obvious that there are no other truths of arithmetic whose proof (or, proofs) will not require uneliminably premises which are from this linguistic setting and which are not even statements of arithmetic. Of course, it is not obvious that there are such truths of arithmetic, either. But I am not trying to prove that all lists are unsatisfactory, but only that my reconstruction of arithmetic provides no reason for supposing that any list is satisfactory and that there is _some_ reason for thinking that all lists are unsatisfactory.

One suggestion I wish to reject is that the list could consist of my reconstructions of Peano's axioms with any truths of arithmetic whose proof(s) require(s) (uneliminably) statements which are not among the reconstructions of Peano's axioms. Though the statements chosen in this way would be satisfactory as axioms of arithmetic, this suggestion fails in that it does not give a list of statements of arithmetic. My point is not that the suggestion does not give us a list which has an effective procedure associated with it. It is that to be _given a list_, to _have a list_, of statements of arithmetic as axioms of arithmetic is to be in a position to say, "These and only these statements of arithmetic are the premises of all proofs of other statements of arithmetic." Any listing of statements of arithmetic which would put us in the position to make this claim would be a listing which, on my view, we would have no reason to believe exhaustive of the statements mentioned in the suggestion. After all, if we had some reason for thinking that some list exhausted the statements spoken of by the suggestion, then we would have some reason for thinking that this list of statements of arithmetic would be satisfactory as axioms of arithmetic. But, of course, this is just the problem the suggestion was intended to avoid.

The second consideration which gives one pause about the satisfactoriness of any list of axioms of arithmetic is that very plausible candidates, viz., my reconstructions of Peano's axioms, are demonstrably not satisfactory. This consideration can be supported by two different arguments. The first argument is, on my view, important, though it would probably not carry much weight with a formalist.

A review of the proof of the principle of "infinite" induction in 4B(vi) would convince anyone that this principle cannot be proven from my reconstructions of Peano's axioms alone. But, for me, this principle is a statement of arithmetic and, in light of the arguments in 4B(vi), a truth of arithmetic. Thus, it follows that the list of statements of arithmetic which are the reconstructions of Peano's axioms are not satisfactory as axioms of arithmetic. Having to discard such an intuitively appealing candidate as the list of statements which are the reconstructions of Peano's axioms must, it seems to me, give one doubts about the possibility of finding any satisfactory list.

This argument does not impress a formalist very much, since the principle of "infinite" induction could not be a rule of inference for a formal system of arithmetic. A rule of inference, for a formalist, must have an effective procedure associated with it, an effective procedure for determining that an inference is an instance of the type of inference permitted by the rule. For a formal system of arithmetic the adoption of a rule of inference without this effective procedure would result in there being no effective procedure for determining whether a sequence of formulas is a proof of the formal system. The principle of "infinite" induction requires "infinitely" many premises and has no effective procedure associated with it. Consequently, the fact that the principle of "infinite" induction does not follow from my reconstructions of Peano's axioms does not impress the formalist: what would impress him is a true formula of a formal system of arithmetic which cannot be proven from his formalization of Peano's axioms. The second argument speaks to this concern.

Before turning to the second argument, I should like to summarize my claims about my reconstruction of arithmetic. The primary and secondary characteristics of formal systems are not possessed by my reconstruction of arithmetic. This fact makes it quite clear that my reconstruction of arithmetic is not a formal system. In particular, there is no effective procedure associated with my predicate 'proof of arithmetic'. More important there is no reason, and indeed some reason not, to define 'proof of arithmetic' with the help of a list of axioms of arithmetic. What definition of 'proof of arithmetic' I shall use is discussed at the end of this subsection and in the next subsection.

The second argument makes use of the best known theorems about the formal system of arithmetic: Gödel's incompleteness theorems. These theorems bring up numerous issues I shall not even try to deal with. Moreover, the complication of the proofs of these theorems is so great that I must suppose that the reader is familiar with at least the main outline of the proofs. I shall restrict myself to a few preliminary remarks about Gödel's theorems, make some minimal observations about the relationship of Gödel's theorems to my reconstruction of arithmetic, and finally show how the theorems help me to prove that my reconstructions of Peano's axioms are not satisfactory as axioms of arithmetic.

Gödel's incompleteness theorems are about formal systems of arithmetic. Of all the conditions which must obtain if the theorems are to be proven, one is that formal systems of arithmetic have what I called the "primary" characteristic of formal systems. In particular, it is essential that the syntactical predicate 'proof' have an effective procedure associated with it.[7] Another condition is that there be some means of assessing the truth-value of formulas of the formal system. These means are provided by what is usually called the "semantics" of the formal system (as opposed to its "syntax," which has been the main topic of discussion in this subsection thus far). The semantics of a formal system of arithmetic can be handled along the lines indicated in my discussion of semantic formalism in 3A. But, for our purposes in this subsection, it is only necessary to remember that the semantics of a formal system of arithmetic provides means whereby the truth-value of formulas of the formal system may be assessed.

To emphasize the importance of the conditions just discussed, my formulation of the incompleteness theorem which is pertinent to the present discussion incorporates these conditions. What I shall henceforth simply call "Gödel's theorem" is: given that any formal system of arithmetic has the primary characteristic of formal systems and thus, in particular, that in any such system there is an effective procedure for determining whether a sequence of formulas of the system is a proof, then

> if the system is consistent, then there is a formula of the system (call it a "Gödelian formula")

> which cannot be proven in the system (and thus is not a theorem of the system) and which is assessed as true by the semantics of the system.

Since the semantics usually provided for a formal system of arithmetic involves the intuitively understood system of arithmetic, it is generally agreed that the consequent of the theorem can be shortened to

> if the system is consistent, then there is a formula of the system which is not a theorem of the system, but is a truth of arithmetic.

Formal systems of arithmetic are, therefore, said to be "incomplete" because not all truths of arithmetic are theorems of the formal systems.

The basic point about the relationship of Gödel's theorem and my reconstruction of arithmetic is that the necessary conditions for the proof of the theorem do not obtain for my reconstruction. First, the primary characteristic of formal systems is not a characteristic of my reconstruction of arithmetic. Second, though I am content to avail myself of _a_ distinction between "syntax" and "semantics," it is not that distinction which is found in formalist literature. Though my reconstruction of arithmetic is set within a philosophy of language which makes use of many different sorts of statements involving truth, none of these statements is used to provide a "semantics," in the formalist's sense, for my reconstruction.

Despite the lack of direct connection between Gödel's theorem and my reconstruction of arithmetic, a link can be forged. To explain this link, I must point out several features of Gödel's theorem and its proof.

Under the usual semantics of a formal system of arithmetic, a Gödelian formula says (roughly) of itself that it has no proof in the formal system (i.e., is not a theorem of the system). Gödel produces such a formula in the proof of his theorem. Moreover, he produces it in such a fashion that there can be no doubt that this formula is a formula of the formal system of arithmetic. It is this combination--being a formula of the formal system of arithmetic and yet saying, under the usual semantics of the formal system, something about syntactical relations in the formal system--which must be achieved by a Gödelian formula. The key to securing this combination is showing how the formal system of arithmetic can provide its own syntax. This "arithmetization" of syntax involves producing arithmetical predicates which correspond (in a special way) to such syntactical predicates as 'formula' and 'proof'.

Given what I have said about those characteristics my reconstruction of arithmetic lacks, it is not possible that Gödel's procedures for constructing Gödelian formulas be literally reproduced in my reconstruction of arithmetic. Yet an imitation of these procedures can be reproduced. First, we match linguistic items of my reconstruction with linguistic objects of a formal system of arithmetic. This matching selects a proper part of the linguistic items of my reconstruction. This selection includes a list of statements to be used as axioms. With these selected items we imitate both the usual formalist definitions of 'formula' and 'proof' and the procedures by which Gödel "arithmetizes" syntax. Finally, then, we produce a "Gödelian statement" which is both a statement of arithmetic and says (roughly) of itself that it has no proof in that sense of 'proof' defined in the imitation of Gödel procedures. Thus the Gödelian statement says (roughly) of itself that it has no proof _on the basis of the list of statements selected by matching my reconstruction with a formal system of arithmetic_. The Gödelian statement says that it itself is not a theorem of that _part_ of my reconstruction of arithmetic which has been picked out by matching with a formal system of arithmetic.

Of course, the Gödelian statement has no such proof and therefore is also a true statement of arithmetic. This can be shown in either of two ways. The first requires that an imitation of Gödel's argument about his formula be given. This can be done. The second way commences with the observation that if the Gödelian statement had the sort of proof that is in question, this proof, because of the matching of a formal system and a part of my reconstruction, would match a proof of a Gödelian formula in the formal system. But we know from Gödel's theorem that there is no such proof in the formal system.

Moreover, a corollary to Gödel's theorem is that no formal system of arithmetic which increases its list of axioms by appending a Gödelian formula escapes incompleteness. This corollary is also obtainable for the part of my reconstruction of arithmetic selected by matching with the formal system.

How does Gödel's theorem, or, rather, the imitation of it for a part of my reconstruction of arithmetic, support my claim that there is some reason to think that no list of statements of arithmetic is satisfactory as axioms of arithmetic? My imitation of Gödel's theorem shows that for certain sorts of lists of statements of arithmetic, viz., those lists selected by a matching with a formal system of arithmetic, there are true statements of arithmetic which have no proof on the basis of such a list. Thus any definition of 'proof of arithmetic' which utilized such a list could _not_ include any proof of a Gödelian statement. But, on my reconstruction, a Gödelian statement _does have a proof_ and, moreover, a proof _of arithmetic_. Thus all those lists of statements which are selected by matching with a formal system of arithmetic are demonstrably _not_ satisfactory as axioms of arithmetic.

The argument to show that a Gödelian statement has a proof of arithmetic depends on another part of Gödel's proof: his argument for the truth of the Gödelian formula. This argument, too, I can imitate. But my imitation of this argument is within my reconstruction of arithmetic and thus turns out to be an argument of arithmetic. (A complete defense of this claim would require too much exposition of Gödel's proof to be feasible here.) It is true that I must include the principle of "infinite" induction as a statement of arithmetic in order to defend my claim about the proofs of Gödelian statements. But I am willing to do this in any case. In addition, I must set out my definition of 'proof of arithmetic'. It is to this matter that I now turn.

Since I have not accepted the formalist distinction between syntax and semantics, my definition of 'proof of arithmetic' is not restricted to concepts that a formalist would count as syntactical. Moreover, my definition does not rely on a list of axioms. One consideration that stands out, for me, is that proofs, in our ordinary way of talking, assure us of the truth of the statement which is proved. I wish to preserve this connection between having a proof and being true. I shall now offer a definition of 'proof of arithmetic' that is _of the sort_ to which one is led by the considerations of this subsection. It is not the definition for which I finally settle, but it is sufficient for this stage of my discussion. The definition is: a proof of arithmetic is a sequence of statements of arithmetic each of which is true or may be inferred from another (other) statement(s) of the sequence by an acceptable rule of inference. A necessary condition for the acceptability of a rule of inference is that no instance of the inference the rule permits has true premises and a false conclusion. Thus, proofs of arithmetic are simply special sequences of true statements of arithmetic.

An upshot of this arrangement is that the formalist distinction between the syntactical predicate 'theorem of arithmetic' and the semantical predicate 'truth of arithmetic' is not present in my account. One definition of 'theorem of arithmetic' is that a theorem of arithmetic is a statement of arithmetic which has a proof of arithmetic. On this definition all theorems of arithmetic are truths of arithmetic (but not all truths of arithmetic are theorems of arithmetic, since some truths of arithmetic have proofs which are not proofs of arithmetic). What is analogous in my view to the formalist distinction between 'theorem of arithmetic' and 'truth of arithmetic' is the difference, discussed earlier, between 'theorem of arithmetic' and 'theorem of arithmetic proven on the basis of this list of statements of arithmetic'.

My characterization of deductions from hypotheses leaves out the condition that the hypotheses are true. This analogously to proven statements, there are "deduced" statements. All proven statements are, on this account, deduced statements. The next subsection handles some of the consequences of distinguishing between deductions from hypotheses and proofs, as I do.

I conclude with a line of thought that returns us to the earlier discussions of the subsection. It may seem to the reader that another imitation of Gödel's proof can be put together in my reconstruction. This imitation would not rely on a notion of proof of arithmetic that depends on a list of axioms, but rather on that notion of proof of arithmetic which I have just explained. The new Gödelian statements of this imitation would show that my reconstruction of arithmetic is incomplete, just as formal systems of arithmetic are.

But this line of thought overlooks the absolutely crucial role the primary, and secondary, characteristics of formal systems have in Gödel's proof. A crucial step in Gödel's proof is showing that a Gödelian formula which, under the usual semantics, speaks _about_ the formal system of arithmetic is a formula _of_ that formal system of arithmetic. This feat can be accomplished _only_ by producing arithmetical predicates in the formal system which correspond (in a special way) to the syntactical predicates of the syntax of the formal system. But this in turn is possible only because the syntactical predicates in question have effective procedures associated with them--that is to say, only because the formal system of arithmetic has the primary and secondary characteristics of formal systems.

My reconstruction of arithmetic lacks, as I have insisted, both the primary and secondary characteristics of formal systems. Consequently, a statement which says of itself that it does not have a proof of arithmetic is a statement _about_ arithmetic, but there is no reason to think that it is a statement _of_ arithmetic.

The previous imitation of Gödel's proof worked because of the matching with a formal system of arithmetic. This matching allowed us to imitate the features of a formal system of arithmetic, including the list of axioms which is essential to the formalist definition of 'proof'. This matching did not, of course, endow my reconstruction of arithmetic with the primary and secondary characteristics of formal systems. But it did make it possible to imitate the workings of a formal system in _part_ of my reconstruction by returning via the matching to the formal system and then judging the workings of that part of my reconstruction by the workings of the formal system.

Finally, it is important to notice that the statement which says of itself that it has no proof of arithmetic does not lead to any "paradox." Assume that this statement is false. It follows from this assumption that it does have a proof of arithmetic. Hence it is a theorem of arithmetic and thus a truth of arithmetic and thus true. Hence there is a contradiction. Therefore the statement is true. So it has no proof of arithmetic. Hence it is not a theorem of arithmetic and thus not a statement of arithmetic which may be inferred from (a) true statement(s) of arithmetic by acceptable rules of inference. So this statement is a true statement about arithmetic (and, of course, also about itself). It is just one of many, many statements that do not have proofs of arithmetic. It _can_ be a statement of arithmetic, since there are true statements of arithmetic which do not have proofs of arithmetic. But the failure of the imitation of Gödel's proof in this case removes a possible reason for thinking that it _is_ a statement of arithmetic, and I see no other reason to include it as a statement of arithmetic.

(ii) More on Proof and Deduction

I begin this subsection with two different treatments of proofs and deductions. Then, in the light of these treatments, I give an account of the notion of sameness of proof and of deduction. Finally, I consider some of the consequences of these treatments and discuss some of the differences between my treatments and more usual treatments of proof and deduction.

Both my treatments of proofs depend on a statement matrix. By containing the term 'true', this statement matrix reflects my intention, expressed in the previous subsection, to characterize proofs in such a way that the statement proven is true. In this regard, it is important to remember that a necessary condition of being an acceptable rule of inference is preserving truth. The statement matrix is formulated with the help of the predicate matrix

F statement.

This predicate matrix is an abbreviation for the predicate matrix

> statement which is F.

No restriction is placed on which predicates are instances of this predicate matrix. In some cases, the instances involve disjunctive predicates containing identity; an example is:

> statement which is identical to the statement S or to the statement T.

The statement matrix is:

(11)[i] every F statement either is a true statement or may be inferred from other true F statements by an acceptable rule of inference and

[ii] C, which is not an F statement, may be inferred from F statements by an acceptable rule of inference.

For convenience, I have understood the phrase 'other F statements' as 'another F statement or other F statements' and the phrase 'F statements' as 'an F statement or F statements'. An equivalent condition which brings out some of what is packed into (11) is:

(11.1) every F statement either is a true statement or may be inferred from F statements by an acceptable rule of inference and

some F statement is a true statement and

(G)(if G statements are F statements and not all F statements are G statements, then some G statement either is a true statement or may be inferred by an acceptable rule of inference from other F statements at least one of which is not G) and

C, which is not an F statement, may be inferred from F statements by an acceptable rule of inference.

Speaking loosely, (11) is a condition which if satisfied by certain statements, ones that are F and another statement, C, insures that the F statements are a proof of the statement C. Further, notice that an instance of (11) is true only if a variety of other statements are true: e.g., that this F statement is true, that this F statement may be inferred from that F statement and that one, that C may be inferred from these F statements, and so on. Thus, (11) is like a condition for certain persons' being a particular family (e.g., a family of John Smith). An instance of a general condition for being a family is true only if a great variety of other statements about certain persons are true (e.g., that John is married to Mary, that Mary and John are the progenitors of George, and so on).

I shall abbreviate (11) to

... F, C ...

and I shall abbreviate the statement matrix

(12)[i] (11)[i] and

[ii] some statement, which is not an F statement, may be inferred from F statements by an acceptable rule of inference

to ... F ....

A condition like (11), but concerning proofs of arithmetic is:

(13)[i] every F statement of arithmetic either is a true statement of arithmetic or may be inferred from other true F statements of arithmetic by an acceptable rule of inference and

[ii] C, which is not an F statement, but is a statement of arithmetic, may be inferred from F statements of arithmetic by an acceptable rule of inference.

My first treatment of proofs is an imitation of the usual class-theoretic definition of 'proof'. This class-theoretic definition of 'proof' makes a proof a (certain sort of) class of sentences. In my reconstruction of class theory, to be given in chapter 6, I can produce a faithful version of this definition. But even without that reconstruction it is possible now to produce an imitation of the class-theoretic definition which will suffice for the present discussion. In fact, on my view, the faithful version of the class-theoretic definition has nothing much to recommend it over the one I shall give in this subsection.

Let us ask what a philosopher who has no qualms about properties and the like and no predilection for classes would say about proofs if he used the class-theoretic definition of 'proof' as a model for his own. Details aside, he would surely say that a proof is a (certain sort of) property of propositions. This claim would be what corresponds in his view to the class-theoretician's claim that a proof is a class of sentences. On the one view, propositions exemplify proofs; on the other, sentences are members of proofs.

Talk of statements exemplifying proofs and of proofs being properties I reconstruct along the lines set down in chapters 2 and 4. First, I need predicates. Understanding 'C' as a singular term, I abbreviate the statement matrix

(14) X is an F statement and ... F, C ...

to (14.1) pr-F, C(X)

and the statement matrix

(15) (E F)(X is an F statement and ... F, C ...)

to (15.1) pr-C(X)

and the statement matrix

(16) (E F)(X is an F statement and ... F ...)

to (16.1) pr(X).

The connections among (14.1), (15.1), and (16.1) are as follows:

pr-C(X) if and only if (E F)(pr-F,C(X)),

pr(X) if and only if (E F)(E Y)(pr-F,Y(X)),

and pr(X) if and only if (E Y)(pr-Y(X)).

Now the usual sorts of reconstructions are available. _Niceties aside_, the statement matrix

that THREE is prime exemplifies (pr-F,C)-ness

is reconstructed as

the :pr-F,C: is true of the :the :THREE is prime::,

i.e., the :pr-F,C(the :THREE is prime:): is true.

There may, of course, be many true instances of these statement matrices. With 'C' still understood as a singular term, the statement

that THREE is prime exemplifies (pr-C)-ness

is reconstructed as

the :pr-C: is true of the :the :THREE is prime::,

i.e., the :pr-C(the :THREE is prime:): is true

and the statement

that THREE is prime exemplifies pr-ness,

as the :pr: is true of the :the :THREE is prime::,

i.e., the :pr(the :THREE is prime:): is true.

The double quotation in

the :the :THREE is prime::

is necessary. The context '... exemplifies ___' is reconstructed in a way which quotes the term for the item which is said to exemplify something; for example,

Socrates exemplifies wisdom

is reconstructed (once again, details aside) as

the :wise: is true of the :Socrates:.

But, the singular term

that THREE is prime

is already reconstructed with quotation as

the :THREE is prime:.

The statement (where we take 'F' to be a predicate, not a variable)

(pr-F,C)-ness is a property

is reconstructed as

the :pr-F,C: is a predicate;

the statement

(pr-C)-ness is a property,

as the :pr-C: is a predicate;

and the statement

pr-ness is a property,

as the :pr: is a predicate.

Once again refinements have been omitted. Since proofs are a kind of property, there are statements like the ones which have just been reconstructed that contain the predicate

is a property which is a proof.

In order to reconstruct statements with the above predicate, it is necessary to give a general metalinguistic description of the instances of (14), a general metalinguistic description of E-quantified relational predicates like (15), and a metalinguistic description of the E-quantified conjunctive predicate (16). Once these descriptions are set down, it is possible to set out statements which say that a predicate is of a particular metalinguistic sort. For brevity, I shall say that there are many different "proof" predicates, those which are instances of

pr-F,C,

those which are instances of

pr-C,

and the predicate

pr

(where, in this case, both 'F' and 'C' are taken to be variables).

What has been done for proofs can also be done for deductions. The basic condition is:

(17)[i] every F statement either is a statement or may be inferred from other F statements by an acceptable rule of inference and

[ii] C, which is not an F statement, may be inferred from F statements by an acceptable rule of inference.

By following the path made in the case of proofs, we obtain

(18) ded-F,C(X),

(19) ded-C(X),

and (20) ded(X).

With these predicates the sorts of reconstructions just illustrated for proofs can be accomplished for deductions.

But, in addition to the talk of proofs as predicates, there is a way of characterizing statements as proofs. This second treatment of proofs is suggested by my earlier remarks about families and condition (11). We do speak about individuals "collectively" in a wide variety of contexts. Many philosophers are, perhaps, inclined to reconstruct such talk by the aid of class-theory. I, however, am inclined to believe that some (and, perhaps, all) "collective" predication can be understood without what I would call class-theory.

Consider

(21) John, Mary, and George are a family.

Statement (21) does not, of course, imply that

John is a family and Mary is a family and George is a family.

Notice also that "conjunctive" singular terms are not the only singular terms that can appear with the phrase 'are a family'; for example, consider

(21.1) all the persons on the couch are a family,

(21.2) those persons who are before you are a family,

and (21.3) the persons in the corner are a family.

I shall take as my standardized statement matrix

(22) the F persons are a family.

Of course, one instance of (22) is

(22.1) the persons who are identical to John or to Mary or to George are a family.

It seems to me that a reasonably good account of (22) can be given by a statement matrix which is, in structure, analogous to (11). In the case of (22), more than one matrix is plausible, since there are "nuclear" families, "extended" families, families solely by consanguinity, families by marriage and consanguinity, and so on. All these matrices, however, have the same basic features. The one I choose illustrates my points well enough. The first matrix I offer is for

the F persons are a family of P,

not for (22):

(23) every F person either is identical to P or is married to P or is a progeny of two F persons

(where we understand that 'is a progeny of' is asymmetrical). The matrix that pertains to (22) is:

(24) (Ex)(every F person either is identical to x or is married to x or is a progeny of two F persons).

One virtue of (23) and (24) is that their instances follow from statements about relations among persons. Thus suppose

John is married to Mary.
George is a progeny of John and Mary.

Taking 'person who is identical to John or to Mary or to George' for 'F person' and 'John' for 'P', an instance of (23) follows from the above two statements and an instance of (24) follows from that instance of (23). It seems to me that it is just this sort of inferential relationship between statements which captures what is at the heart of "collective" predication. Thus if (24) is taken as a sufficient condition for the truth of (22), statements like (21) (or, in its standardized form, (22.1)) are true if a variety of other statements which state relations of persons are true.

I am not, however, claiming that any condition like (24) _is_ suitable _by_ _itself_ as a definition (22), though I think that it _might_ be suitable with some commentary. Whatever definition is suitable for (22), I do think that it should be possible to show, on the basis of that definition, that (24) (with, perhaps, some commentary) is a necessary and sufficient condition for the truth of (22). I shall henceforth assume that this relationship between (22) and (24) does hold.

The example of families sets the strategy for my second treatment of proofs and deductions. The matrix which corresponds to (23) is the case of

(25) the F statements are a proof of C

is (11). The matrix which corresponds to (24) in the case of

(26) the F statements are a proof

is (12). The matrix for

(25.1) the F statements are a proof of arithmetic of C

is (13), and the matrix for

(26.1) the F statements are a proof of arithmetic

is to (13) as (12) is to (11).

A similar situation obtains for

(27) the F statements are a deduction of C

and (28) the F statements are a deduction

with respect to (17). With the matrices for (27) and (28), it is possible to construct matrices for

(27.1) the F statements are a deduction of arithmetic of C

and (28.1) the F statements are a deduction of arithmetic.

Matrices for statements related to (25) and (26) can be obtained in obvious ways from (11) and (12). Thus the matrix for

(29) C has a proof

is (29.1) (E F)(the F statements are a proof of C);

for (30) C is provable from the G statements,

(30.1) (E F)(every G statement is an F statement and the F statements are a proof of C);

for (31) X is in a proof of C,

(31.1) (E F)(X is an F statement and the F statements are a proof of C);

and for (32) X is in a proof,

(32.1) (E F)(X is an F statement and the F statements are a proof).

Similar statements are also available for deductions.

Notice that everything which is "in a proof" is a statement. This truth corresponds to a truth in my first treatment of proofs: viz., that "proof" predicates are true of statements. This point of contact between my treatments is valuable in two ways. First, in my subsequent discussion of the consequences of my treatments of proofs and deductions, it is not necessary to take up the two treatments separately. My points can be read to fit either treatment. Second, the question of the "sameness" of proofs and deductions is most easily approached from this point of contact between the two treatments.

5C(ii)

Many different relations of sameness for proofs and deductions might be constructed. My aim is to characterize one that is reasonably strict. The first step to this characterization is to weed out a few matters that might cause confusion. My remarks are restricted, for convenience, to proofs and deductions of mathematics.

Practicing mathematicians sometimes employ what is for me a rather loose notion of sameness of proof and deduction. Thus were one to pick up two mathematics books which both claim to have so-and-so's proof, one might well find that what is in the one book is substantially different from what is in the other book, though it is supposed to be the same proof in both. There might be several differences between the books, but not all of these differences will count for a difference in proofs under my account of sameness of proofs and deductions

First, at least one of the books may contain only a "sketch" of a proof. Sketches of a proof "leave out steps" or omit to mention what is obvious on slight reflection (e.g., that a certain truth is necessary in order to obtain some line of the proof). Of course, agreement about how to "fill in" a sketch of a proof or a deduction requires agreement on acceptable rules of inference. Where two mathematicians disagree about which rules of inference are acceptable, they may disagree about which "steps" have been "left out" or even whether any "steps" have been "left out." My account of sameness of proof and deduction is applicable solely to proofs and deductions, not to terse versions or sketches of proofs. Thus differences between sketches of proofs or deductions do not necessarily count as differences between proofs or deductions.

Second, the material in one book might differ from that in another book because certain subsidiary truths called "lemmas" are independent and the lemmas are proven in different order. My account of sameness of proof and deduction does not allow that such differences in arrangement are sufficient to produce different proofs or deductions. Moreover, the labelling of some statement which has to be proven in order to prove another statement a lemma is to be disregarded in determining sameness of proof or deduction.

My first treatment of proofs and deductions begins with a view modeled on the class-theoretic account of proofs and deductions and thus takes proofs and deductions as properties. It might seem that the obvious relation of sameness to consider is identity. Given my reconstructions of properties the identity in this case would be the identity of predicates (e.g., the identity of the :pr-C: and the :pr-D:, or of the :ded-C: and the :ded-D:). But, for a variety of reasons (some of which become clear in the next section), the identity of predicates is too strong to be of any interest as sameness for proofs and deductions.

Reflection on my second, "collective" treatment of proofs and deductions suggests a weaker relation of sameness. I revert to my example of families. The conditions under which

(33) the F persons are the same family as the G persons

is true are

[i] that for every F person, some G person is identical to that F person and for every G person, some F person is identical to that G person

and, intuitively speaking,

[ii] that an F person stands in a familial relation to other F persons if and only if the G person who is identical to that F person stands in that familial relation to the G

persons who are identical to the other F persons and vice versa.

Given a sufficiently strong characterization of identity for persons, condition [ii] may be redundant. But even if it is redundant, there is no harm done in including it. The point of condition [ii] is easily brought out by example: if

John is identical to the person on the couch nearest the bookcase

and Mary is identical to the person on the couch with a drink

and John is married to Mary,

then John and Mary and George are the same family as the persons on the couch,

only if

the person on the couch nearest the bookcase is married to the person on the couch with the drink.

An account analogous to that of (33) can be given for

(34) the F statements are the same proof as the G statements.

The account of (34) is built into the account of

(35) the F statements are the same deduction as the G statements.

I state the conditions for (35) in more detail than I did those for (33). As a preliminary, I state the condition for the statement matrix

the Hs (which are F) are identical to the Is (which are G).

The condition is:

(x)(if x is an H (which is F), then (Ey)(y is an I (which is G) and x is identical to y)) and (x)(if x is an I (which is G), then (Ey)(y is an H (which is F) and x is identical to y)).

The conditions for (35) are:

(36)[i] (E X)(the F statements are a deduction of X and the G statements are a deduction of X)

and [ii] the F statements are identical to the G statements

and [iii] (X)(Y)(if X is an F statement and Y is the G statement identical to X and X may be inferred by an acceptable rule of inference from other F statements, then Y may be inferred by that acceptable rule of inference from other G statements and the F statements from which X may be inferred by that acceptable rule of inference are identical to the G statements from which Y may be inferred by that acceptable rule of inference).

The matrix (34) has the conditions

(37) the F statements are a proof

and the G statements are a proof

and (36).

The appropriate "sameness" relation is easily defined for "deduction" and "proof" predicates by using (36). There are, of course, several different sorts of such predicates. I deal with the basic sort; the others can be handled by minor modifications in the conditions I present. To avoid having to introduce new metalinguistic variables, I give an instance of the definition for two "deduction" predicates. I suppose, for this case, that 'F' and 'G' are predicates and that 'C' and 'D' are singular terms. The definition of

(38) same ded(the :ded-F,C:, the :ded-G,D:)

is (39)[i] the statement of which the statements that the :ded-F,C: is true of are a deduction is identical to the statement of which the statements that the :ded-G,D: is true of are a deduction

and [ii] the statements that the :ded-F,C: is true of are identical to the statements that the :ded-G,D: is true of

and [iii] (X)(Y)(if X is a statement that the :ded-F,C: is true of and Y is the statement that the :ded-G,D: is true of and that is identical to X and X may be inferred by an acceptable rule of inference from other statements that the :ded-F,C: is true of, then Y may be inferred by that acceptable rule of inference from other statements that the :ded-G,D: is true of and the statements from which X may be inferred by that acceptable rule of inference are identical to the statements from which Y may be inferred by that acceptable rule of inference).

Notice, first, that, in cases like (38), condition (39)[i] is equivalent to

C is identical to D.

Second, (39) applies without change to "proof" predicates like the :pr-F,C:. This is so because the statements of which the :pr-F,C: is true are also a deduction. Third, my two treatments of proof and deduction obviously agree on sameness of proof and deduction. There would be no such agreement if, instead of 'same ded' as the sameness relation for "proof" and "deduction" predicates, I used identity. This claim will be made clearer in the next section. Fourth, in the next section I supply what is missing in (36) and (39): viz., an account of the identity of statements. With this account is a treatment of the identity of predicates and other linguistic items.

I turn now to a discussion of some of the consequences of my treatments of proofs and deductions.

First, my treatments make distinctions which are not commonly expressed in the terminology I use. Nevertheless, for every distinction among arguments commonly made in modern logic books, there is a corresponding distinction in my accounts of proof and deduction. Proofs correspond to what in a logic book would be called "sound" arguments; deductions, to "valid" arguments; nondeductions, to "invalid" arguments.

A few examples will help to make these and other distinctions clearer:

(40) THREE is prime and TWO is even
hence, THREE is prime

is a proof (of arithmetic), but

(40.1) FOUR is prime and TWO is even
hence, FOUR is prime

is a deduction (of arithmetic) but not a proof (of arithmetic). It is true that from the point of view of "first-order" logic, both (40) and (40.1) are of the "form"

(41) P and Q
hence, P.

Correspondingly, on my view, it is true that (40) and (40.1) are permitted by the same rule of inference.

Moreover, further distinctions can be made within my terminology. For example, since proofs of statement logic require truths of statement logic, (40) is not a proof of statement logic though it is a proof of arithmetic and, of course, a proof. Whether (40) and (40.1) are to count as deductions of statement logic as well as deductions of arithmetic (and, of course, as deductions) depends on decisions not yet made. One could decide to count deductions with only statement matrices of the statement logic as deductions of statement logic. Thus, (41) would be a deduction of statement logic, but (40) and (40.1) would not be deductions of statement logic. Or, one could decide to make a different sort of distinction by counting every deduction that required only acceptable rules of statement logic as a deduction of statement logic. In that case, (40) and (40.1) would both be deductions of statement logic. No important issues, it seems to me, depend on elaborating such distinctions.

Given that for every distinction among arguments which is found in a modern logic book there is a corresponding distinction within my account, I can see no objection to my arranging the separation of proofs and deductions as I have. I have given my reasons for preferring my arrangements to more common ones in this subsection and the previous subsection. Most of these reasons pertain primarily to proofs of mathematics and, in particular, to proofs of arithmetic, but there is no reason not to make my total account of proof and deduction consonant with my account of proofs and deductions of arithmetic.

As (40) and (40.1) make clear, my treatments of proof and deduction allow, as do the more usual treatments, "unsatisfying" proofs and deductions. Among the sorts of unsatisfying proofs and deductions are ones, like (40) and (40.1), which are "trivial." Besides unsatisfying proofs and deductions, there are "inelegant" proofs and deductions. Two common forms of inelegance are having unused statements and having used but unnecessary statements. Both my treatments of proof and deduction and the more usual treatments allow inelegant proofs and deductions. (Of course, on my treatment of proof, any statements in a proof which are unused or unnecessary must still be true statements.)

There are various additional restrictions that can be placed on proofs and deductions to rule out unsatisfying and inelegant ones. For example, the standards for acceptable rules of inference can exclude some of the rules that are found in classical predicate logic. Another possible restriction is that the conclusion of a proof or deduction can be allowed to appear nowhere in the proof or deduction (save in certain special cases perhaps). However, since these issues are not the source of objections to my treatments of proof and deduction, I see no reason to pursue them further.

My final topic of this subsection are those proofs which depend on deductions. The example I take is _reductio ad absurdum_ proofs. A _reductio ad absurdum_ proof contains, like any other proof, only true statements. But the true statements of _reductio ad absurdum_ proof include a statement that from certain true statements along with another statement, A, a contradiction is deducible. From this true statement about a deduction, it follows that at least one of the statements which lead to the contradiction is false. Since all the other statements, except A, are true, it follows that A must be false. Given the usual principles of truth for negation, it follows that the negation of A is true.

Thus, on my account, a _reductio ad absurdum_ proof speaks about a deduction. Nothing prevents me from symbolically illustrating such a proof in a manner similar to that which is found in many modern logic books. But such ways of illustrating a *reductio ad absurdum* proof should not blind us to the fact that the proof must contain a statement which is about a deduction and therefore that the proof is, in one way, more complicated than many other proofs. Moreover, the conclusion reached in the *reductio ad absurdum* proof is not reached by inferences from those true statements which with the statement, A, lead to a contradiction. It is reached by inferences from a true statement about these statements and their place in a deduction, and this requires the application of principles of truth and falsity, particularly those relating to negation. It seems to me that a distinctive virtue of my treatment of *reductio ad absurdum* proofs is that it shows that principles of truth and falsity are necessary to the steps in such a proof. However, further elaboration of this topic is beyond the scope of this book.

D. The Identity of Statements, Predicates, and Numerical Quantifiers

The discussion of this subsection continues that of 3C, though it ignores some of the questions broached in that section. For example, the question, discussed in 3C, of the relation of reconstructions to what they reconstruct is an important one, but it is not of paramount relevance to the topic of the identity of the linguistic items of, say, my reconstruction of arithmetic. I shall assume that the linguistic items under consideration in this subsection are in some reconstruction (usually, my reconstruction of arithmetic).

The most important point about the account of the identity of linguistic items is implicit in the discussion of 3C: the identity of linguistic items is like any other identity. Thus, loosely speaking, a linguistic item is identical to another if and only if neither of them lacks a property the other has.

Consider a simple example:

(42) the :square a:

and (43) the :trilateral a:.

What properties might (42) and (43) have? They have, among others, properties which are formulated in rules of inference. Consider the rules

(44) (INDCON)(the (:has sides: INDCON) may be inferred from the (:square: INDCON))

and (45) (INDCON)(the (:has sides: INDCON) may be inferred from the (:trilateral: INDCON)).

Given that (44) and (45) are acceptable, it is a property of both (42) and (43) that the :has sides a: may be inferred from each of them. Further, consider the acceptable rule

(46) (INDCON)(the (:is four-sided: INDCON) may be inferred from the (:square: INDCON))

and the unacceptable rule

(47) (INDCON)(the (:is four-sided: INDCON) may be inferred from the (:trilateral: INDCON)).

Thus it is a property of the :square a: that the :is four-sided a: may be inferred from it, but the :trilateral a: lacks this property. Hence (42) and (43) are not identical.

A more complete account of such cases requires a characterization of identity. The characterization of identity I give makes it a defined logical constant. The definition is one that is quite familiar:

(48) $x = y$

is defined by

(49) (F)(Fx if and only if Fy).

I do not intend to argue for the wisdom of adopting this definition. I do wish to point out again that according to the views of quantification explained in chapter 3, the quantification in (49) does not make (49) a metalinguistic statement and it does not bequeath commitment to abstract entities.

Given identity as defined above, it is clear that

(50) the :square a: = the :trilateral a:

is false, i.e., that

(51) (F)(F(the :square a:) if and only if F(the :trilateral a:))

is false. It follows from

the :is four-sided a: may be inferred from the :square a:

and not(the :is four-sided a: may be inferred from the :trilateral a:)

that (E F)(F(the :square a:) and not(F(the :trilateral a:))).

The conclusion that (50) is false could also be reached by using statements concerning the truth of (42) and (43); for example,

the :square a: is true only if the :is four-sided a: is true

and not(the :trilateral a: is true only if the :is four-sided a: is true).

One warning is necessary at this point: my account of the identity of statements does not settle epistemological questions. I leave completely aside, as I have throughout the book, questions of how one comes to know rules of inference and all related questions. Thus how we know what we do about (46) and (47), and so how we know that (51) is false, are matters I have not attempted and shall not attempt to discuss. Such topics require far too much investigation to be taken up in this book.

There are, of course, more complicated cases of statement identity and nonidentity, examples of which were given in 3C. It is a claim of the account in 3C that some statements which were provably equivalent (and thus materially equivalent) are not identical. The primary example in 3C is that of the statements

(52) the :a is triangular:

and (53) the :a is trilateral:.

More important examples are easily given. The statement that A is a set of formulas of the classical first-order predicate logic and is consistent is provably equivalent to the statement that A is a set of formulas of classical first-order predicate logic and is simultaneously satisfiable. It is very unlikely that anyone would wish to argue that these statements are identical.

If, on my view, there are to be different, i.e., nonidentical, statements which are provably equivalent, I must show how my account of the identity of statements handles such cases. The point to be remembered from 3C is that (52) and (53) cannot be shown to be different in the simple way in which (42) and (43) are. The rules of inference which are the reconstructions of

triangularity entails trilaterality

and trilaterality entails triangularity

insure that, to put it loosely, (52) and (53) can "stand in for" each other in any inference. Thus we must consider certain less obvious properties of (52) and (53) and of similarly equivalent statements.

Within each reconstruction, there are two distinctions which are germane to this problem. One distinction is that between primitive and derived rules of inference and, correspondingly, between primitive and derivative inferences. In a reconstruction, the primitive rules of inference are those which are accepted as rules of the reconstruction, but not on the basis of other rules of the reconstruction. For present purposes, it is most convenient to take the primitive rules of the reconstruction as <u>the</u> rules of the reconstruction.

The other distinction depends on my account of definitions in 3C. In 3C, I suggested that definitions are rules of inference which permit one to infer an equivalence solely from an equivalence which is a truth of logic. Definitions are, on this account, primitive rules of inference. So the second distinction is that between rules of inference which are definitions and those which are not.

In 3C, the identity of (52) and (53) was considered within various reconstructions. For example, I discussed one reconstruction in which both predicates, 'triangular' and 'trilateral', are undefined. In this reconstruction, there is a rule which permits one to infer

the :a is a three-angled:

from (52), but no rule permits one to infer this statement from (53). Thus, with respect to this reconstruction, (52) and (53) are not identical.

What happens in a reconstruction in which 'triangular' and 'trilateral' are defined? In section 3C, I adopted a familiar position on this question: the identity or nonidentity of linguistic items which are defined or which, like (52) and (53), contain linguistic items which are defined depends on the definitions given. I wish to discuss this sort of dependence in more detail since it is important to the case of defined linguistic items in my reconstruction of arithmetic. For this purpose I abandon my present examples and begin the discussion of defined linguistic items anew with the simplest sorts of cases.

I take a simple example of defined predicates and, for the sake of completeness in this case, I state the definitions in unabbreviated form. Let us assume that some reconstruction has the rule

(54) (INDCON)(the ((:bricle:) INDCON (:if and only if:)(:brown:) INDCON (:and:)(:circle:) INDCON) may be inferred from the ((:brown:) INDCON (:and:)(:circle:) INDCON (:if and only if:) (:brown:) INDCON (:and:)(:circle:) INDCON))

and the rule

(55) (INDCON)(the ((:orbicle:) INDCON (:if and only if:)(:brown:) INDCON (:or:)(:circle:) INDCON) may be inferred from the ((:brown:) INDCON (:or:)(:circle:) INDCON (:if and only if:) (:brown:) INDCON (:or:)(:circle:) INDCON)).

As I would usually put it,

x is a bricle

is defined by

x is brown and x is a circle,

and x is an orbicle

is defined by

x is brown or x is a circle.

Accordingly, then, the question whether

(56) the :a is a bricle:

and (57) the :a is an orbicle:

are different statements should depend on (54) and (55) and the statements

(58) the :a is brown and a is a circle:

and (59) the :a is brown or a is a circle:.

I shall assume that the reconstruction which has (54) and (55) also has rules which correspond to what are usually called "introduction" and "elimination" rules for statement connectives. So, the reconstruction has the rule

(60) (STATA)(STATB)(the STATA may be inferred from the (STATA :and: STATB)).

So statements which are conjunctions are such that, from them, a statement of the conjunction may be inferred. Disjunctions, of course, lack such a property. In the case of (58) and (59),

the :a is brown: may be inferred from the :a is brown and a is a circle:,

but not(the :a is brown: may be inferred from the :a is brown or a is a circle:).

Hence, the conjunction (58) and the disjunction (59) are different statements despite the fact that the statements of the conjunction and the disjunction are identical.

The question of the identity of (56) and (57) can now be handled. Consider

(61) (E STATA)(the STAT is definitionally equivalent to the STATA and the :a is brown: may be inferred from the STATA).

The matrix (61) is satisfied by (56), but not by (57). Thus (56) and (57) are not identical.

With such cases in mind, we can see that statements which

are definitionally equivalent to different statements are themselves different. This claim goes some way to unpacking the implication of what I called the "familiar" view that the identity of linguistic items with defined terms "depends on the definitions given." But even more can be done. There are many statements which show that the logical connectives, the :or: and the :and:, are not identical. An example of such a statement is (60). Moreover, since conjunctions and disjunctions are not, in general, materially equivalent, other examples are general statements concerning the truth of conjunctions and of disjunctions:

(STATA)(STATB)(if not(the STATA is true), then not(the (STATA :and: STATB)) is true)

and (STATA)(STATB)(if the STATA is true, then the (STATA :or: STATB) is true.

Given that the claim that the :or: is not identical to the :and: is backed up by the sorts of general statements just discussed, we can then say that statements which are definitionally equivalent to statements with different connectives are different.

Similarly, in the case of the :bricle: and the :orbicle:, the differences extend to all statements containing :bricle:s and :orbicle:s. For example, any statement with only a :bricle: and an individual constant is definitionally equivalent to a conjunction, and from this conjunction a statement with that individual constant and a :brown: may be inferred. The same thing is not true for the term ':orbicle:'. So, we can say that the predicates, the :bricle: and the :orbicle:, are not identical. (The same conclusion can also be reached by invoking principles which take account of the fact that the definitions of these predicates contain different logical connectives.)

What has been illustrated for connectives and predicates may also be done for the ordinary quantifiers. Like the :and: and the :or: and like the :bricle: and the :orbicle:, the universal quantifier and the E-quantifier are not materially equivalent. Thus it is not difficult to find general statements, either rules of inference or statements concerning the truth of quantified statements, which show that the universal quantifier and the E-quantifier are not identical.

Another case similar to the above ones is that of numerical quantifiers. First, consider the following numerical quantifier statements:

(62) the :there be one horse:

and (63) the :there be two horses:.

Since every numerical quantifier is defined by an NQD-matrix, (62) and (63) are, respectively, definitionally equivalent to

(62.1) (Ex)(horse x and (z)(if horse z, then z = x))

and (63.1) (Ey)(Ex)(horse y and horse x and not(x = y) and (z)(if horse z, then z = x or z = y)).

Since I am assuming that my reconstruction has "introduction" and "elimination" rules for logical terms, it follows from (63.1), but not from (62.1), that

(63.2) (Ey)(Ex)(horse y and horse x and not(x = y)).

Therefore the matrix

(64) (E STATA)(the STAT is definitionally equivalent to the STATA and the :(Ey)(Ex)(horse y and horse x and not(x = y)): may be inferred from the STATA)

is satisfied by only one (viz., (63)) of (62) and (63). Thus (62) and (63) are not identical.

Moreover, the sort of difference illustrated in the case of (62) and (63) is backed up by general statements about all the statements in which the :there be one: and the :there be two: appear. So, as in the cases of the connectives, the :and: and the :or:, and the ordinary quantifiers, I conclude that the numerical quantifiers, the :there be one: and the :there be two:, are not identical.

This conclusion can also be reached by invoking the principle that if the definientia of the :there be one: and the :there be two: are different, then these numerical quantifiers are different. In the definiens of the :there be one:, there is one E-quantifier, whereas it is not the case that in the definiens of the :there be two:, there is one E-quantifier. It is true that this difference is stated with a numerical quantifier; this situation could be avoided by using the definiens of this numerical quantifier (or, by using 'at most one'). But, even if this situation were not avoidable, I would find no problem in it any more than I find a problem in the fact that differences between certain logical connectives are stated by means of some of these connectives.

Next I turn to more complicated cases of the nonidentity of linguistic items. The first of these concerns complex statements that are not only materially equivalent but also demonstrably equivalent. Consider

(65) the :a is brown and a is a circle:

and (66) the :not(not(a is brown) or not(a is a circle)):.

Let us again suppose that (65) and (66) are in a reconstruction which contains a system of logic in which conjunction, disjunction, and negation are undefined and in which there are, for each of these connectives, a rule of "introduction" and a rule of "elimination." In such a system the equivalence of (65) and (66) can be demonstrated. Therefore we know that what may be inferred from the one may be inferred from the other and that what the one may be inferred from the other may be inferred from. Despite these facts, there are many properties which distinguish (65) and (66). For example, the :a is brown: may be inferred by a (primitive) rule of the logic from (65) but not from (66); (65), but not (66), may be inferred by a (primitive) rule from the :a is brown: and the :a is a circle:.

In addition, (65) contains the :and: but not the :not:, whereas the opposite is true of (66). These differences between (65) and (66) reflect the fact that, intuitively speaking, statements which are "built up" from simpler statements may be "built up" differently even though they are demonstrably equivalent.

A consequence of my remarks on (65) and (66) is that a statement which is an instance of

x is a bricle,

defined by

x is brown and x is a circle,

and a statement which is an instance of

x is a nerbicle,

defined by

not(not(x is brown) or not(x is a circle)),

are not identical. Moreover, since this difference between these statements is a general one, the :bricle: is not identical to the :nerbicle:. These consequences are an apt illustration of how severe a condition identity is. Of course, nothing prevents us from introducing a weaker equivalence relation of "sameness" for statements and other linguistic items. For example, we could allow that statements are the "same" if their equivalence is demonstrable solely by a rule which is a definition, or by a rule which is a definition or rules which are rules of "first-order" logic. By the latter criterion, (65) and (66) are the "same" statement and the :bricle: is the "same" predicate as the :nerbicle:.

A similar sort of case arises for numerical quantifiers. (I confine my remarks to the ML level; the MML level works out similarly.) This case involves numerical quantifier statements and other items which are, in a sense, demonstrably equivalent. For example, in chapter 4 it is shown that

4B(iii)(47) the :there be eight: mbif the :there be five: and the :there be three: and
the :there be five and there be three: mbif the :there be eight:

and

4B(iii)(49) the :there be eight: mimp the :there be five: and the :there be three: and
the :there be five and there be three: mimp the :there be eight:.

Both 4B(iii)(47) and 4B(iii)(49) are abbreviations for conjunctions of quantified conditional statements. They and their fellows formulate conditional "equivalence" or "sameness" relations for numerical quantifier statements and conjunctions of numerical quantifier statements and for numerical quantifiers, additive quantifiers, and multiplicative quantifiers. The case of additive quantifiers is easily illustrated by invoking the definition of additive quantifiers and rewriting 4B(iii)(47) and 4B(iii)(49) with SGTs true of additive quantifiers:

the :eight: mbif the :five && three: and the

:five && three: mbif the :eight:

and the :eight: mimp the :five && three: and the :five && three: mimp the :eight:.

Despite these "sameness" relations, it is false that

the :eight: is identical to the :five && three:.

The rules of my reconstruction that are definitions permit an inference from any statement with the :eight: to an E-quantified statement, whereas these rules permit an inference from any statement with an additive quantifier to a statement with a conjunctive quantifier and thence to a statement which is a conjunction of numerical quantifier statements. This conjunction of numerical quantifier statements differs from the numerical quantifier statement much as (66) differs from (65). (Similar points can be made about the multiplicative conjunctions one reaches from statements with multiplicative quantifiers.)

Let me restate these points in unreconstructed arithmetical terminology. Under my reconstruction, the "equality" in

4B(iii)(40) FIVE plus THREE equals EIGHT

is an equivalence relation, but it is not identity. (A similar statement holds for 'EQUALS' on the MML level.) Thus on my view there is no unique number to which both

(67) FIVE plus THREE

and (68) SEVEN plus ONE

are, under my reconstruction, identical. Neither of them is identical to

EIGHT.

Of course, it is possible, on my reconstruction, to make sense out of the claim that

> there is a unique natural number to which both (67) and (68) are equal.

The truth of this claim is insured by singling out certain "privileged" DSTs, viz., those DSTs for quantifiers defined by finite NQD-matrices. This characterization excludes conjunctive, additive, and multiplicative quantifiers and leaves only bumerical quantifiers themselves. Therefore, (67) and (68) are equal to one and only one number and that number is reconstructed by a privileged DST, viz., the number EIGHT which is reconstructed (details aside) as the numerical quantifier, the :there be eight:.

Chapter 6: Further Reconstruction

A. Numerals, Numerical Words, and Counting

(i) Introduction

Like the other sections of this chapter, section A enlarges the reconstruction of chapter 4. The main topic of this section is numerals, their relation to the numerical expressions in chapter 4, and their functions in contexts related to those discussed in chapter 4. In all of chapter 4, I assiduously avoided employing the numerals

(1) 0, 1, 2, 3, 4, 5, 6, 7, 8, 9

and the numerals for natural numbers greater than or equal to ten. (I shall always include '0' in the list of numerals, for, without it, it is impossible to have the usual positional construction of numerals for numbers greater than or equal to ten.) Now, however, I shall consider the place of numerals in the scheme I have been adumbrating, thereby tying together some of the issues raised in chapter 1 with the work of the succeeding chapters.

My basic claim about numerals can be stated succinctly: numerals have many different functions in our language. Some of these functions are conceptual functions; others of them are not, though they are in complicated ways connected with conceptual functions. Though I shall limit my discussion to those functions which are relevant to what I have said about natural numbers, I do not suggest that I have treated all the functions of numerals.

(ii) Some Conceptual Functions of Numerals

It is not difficult to explain a family of conceptual functions of numerals. These are indicated sufficiently by the claim that, on a given occasion, the token

(2) 3 + 5 = 8.

may be any one of the following statements:

4B(ii)(8) (H)(I)(E J)(if no H be an I, then if there be five H and there be three I, then there be eight J) and
(J)(E H)(E I)(if no H be an I, then if there be eight J, then there be five H and there be three I)

or

4B(iii)(47) the :there be eight: mbif the :there be five: and the :there be three: and
the :there be five and there be three: mbif the :there be eight:

or the statement 4C(v)(136) or any of the other statements which appear in the metalinguistic hierarchy that goes on from 4C(v)(136). Correspondingly,

(3) pr(3)

could be either the statement which reconstructs

(4) prime(THREE)

or the statement which reconstructs

(5) PRIME(<u>THREE</u>)

or any of the other appropriate metalinguistic statements in the hierarchy commencing with (5).

Thus, numerals have a variety of related functions in connection with my reconstruction of arithmetic. They function as the DSTs which reconstruct terms for number universals and as the DSTs which reconstruct the terms for number individuals. They also have at least one other function which is conceptual. This function is their role in tokens like (2) when (2) is understood to be the statement 4A(ii)(8). In this function they are numerical quantifiers of any tense whatsoever. (Similar remarks could be made about the functions of numerals in such tokens as '3 x 5 = 15'.)

The reasonableness of numerals having this family of functions (and thus the reasonableness of the resulting simplification in the embodiment of different statements of my reconstruction of arithmetic) lies in the account given in chapter 5. That is, it lies in the way in which 4A(ii)(8), 4B(iii)(47), and 4C(v)(136) are related to each other and to the definitions of numerical quantifiers. It is these relations which are dealt with in detail in chapter 4.

In order to forestall one objection, let us consider a different sort of simplification which is effected in the computational procedures by which we produce truths like (2) by the use of a positional notation for the numerals for numbers greater than 9. In the positional notation the numeral for each number greater than 9 is a sequence that is derived from the numerals for the coefficients in the series

$$(6)\quad a_1 10^0 + a_2 10^1 + a_3 10^2 + a_4 10^3 + \ldots a_n 10^{n-1}.$$

It can be proven that any number can be written in terms of this series when the coefficients $a_1, a_2, a_3, \ldots, a_n$ are numbers between 0 and 9. Hence by taking the coefficients and writing them in a string in the order opposite to which they appear in (6),

$$(7)\quad a_n \ldots a_4 a_3 a_2 a_1,$$

we produce a numeral that stands for exactly one number. We can lay down simple procedures whereby we can obtain other truths like (2) which involve numbers at least one of which is greater than 9. These procedures make use of the facts I have just stated about (6) and (7) and the truths we know pertaining to the addition of numbers smaller than or equal to 9. Similar computational procedures can be devised for the other operations.

The justifications for using such computational procedures are proofs about the series (6), the sequence (7), and the characterizations of the operations in question. These proofs are rather complicated and there is no point in giving them.[1] Someone might, however, think it objectionable, first, to claim that numerals play distinct, though connected, roles which are explained by a philosophical account of some complication and, second, to add insult to injury by claiming that the reasonableness of this phenomenon is based on this elaborate philosophical account. Such persons should note that the computational procedures we learn as children also require complicated justifications that we neither received nor would have understood. (Nor, I am sure, were my teachers in any more enlightened position.) The average person may well have a good enough grasp of the principles of computation to justify certain of his arithmetical activity by reference to the nature of the case and these principles. Nonetheless, any questions about the reasonableness of the general procedures he uses will manifest nothing but, perhaps, his belief that there is a justification for these procedures. As I understand this example, it is one of many that show that there is a distinction between what is accepted as a sufficient understanding in ordinary circumstances and what sort of understanding can be attained by philosophical reflection. Such a difference does not provide grounds for any objection to philosophical accounts of ordinary concepts or to my account of arithmetic.

(iii) Nonconceptual Functions of Numerals

In contrast to those conceptual functions of numerals just discussed, there are functions of numerals which are not conceptual. Numerals could have these latter functions without having the roles discussed in the previous subsection. The main example of a nonconceptual function of numerals will be developed by elaborating that view of counting which, in chapter 1, section B, I called the "nominalist's view." Along the way I shall develop subsidiary issues which are of interest in themselves.

As far as possible I intend to avoid issues about counting that belong to epistemology or the philosophy of mind. The cases I treat will be straightforward cases of counting (not such unusual things as: I just counted the horsemen of the Apocalypse. There are four.). The sort of case of counting I wish to consider is one in which a person is in a position to observe the entities he is counting. Thus we can suppose that Jones is looking at a row of books on a table and tokens

(8) 1, 2, 3, 4, 5.

Roughly speaking, the nominalist's view of what Jones is doing in saying (8) is that Jones is assigning one and only one of the tokens in (8) to each book on the table. If Jones has done this correctly, he has effected a 1-1 correspondence between the numeral tokens and the books on the table. Given that he is confident that he has tokened five numeral tokens, he can then conclude that there are five books on the table. So that there is no confusion, let me restate one of my main points from chapter 1: even on the nominalist's view of counting, numerical quantifiers are essential to counting. Indeed, as we can see in the above case, numerical quantifiers figure essentially in counting in two ways.

The first way, of which I did not speak in chapter 1, arises in connection with the establishing of a 1-1 correspondence between two collections of entities. In order for Jones to arrive at knowledge of "how many" by counting, he must know that he has established the 1-1 correspondence correctly. But in Jones's case, knowing that this has been done correctly is knowing that for every member of the initial segment of the numerals which Jones produced <u>there is one</u> member of the collection of books on the table to which the numeral has been assigned and that for every book on the table <u>there is one</u> member of an initial segment of the numerals to which Jones has assigned the book. (In such cases as "counting by twos" and "counting from one hundred," the formulation of the two "that" clauses has to be altered in obvious ways.)

It does not matter for the present purposes how Jones comes to know that he has correctly placed the books on the table and an initial segment of the numerals in 1-1 correspondence. Most often one's confidence about this rests on knowledge about the reliability of one's past attempts and knowledge that in this particular case the usual precautions have been taken (e.g., that the books have been assigned numerals according to a procedure, say, that of beginning with the book farthest to one's left and nearest to one). What does matter for my present point is that what Jones knows when he knows that he has effected the 1-1 correspondence correctly requires that he understand the numerical quantifier, the :there be one:. (More accurately, he must understand the numerical quantifier, the :there be one:, or the definiens of the :there be one:. All the points of this subsection for which it is necessary can, without damage, be restated in this more accurate fashion.)

The second way, which I did mention in chapter 1, can also be described so that it has a connection with performing part of the activity of counting correctly, viz., that part which has to do with producing an initial segment of the numerals. However, it is simpler to put it as I did in chapter 1: Jones must know how many numeral tokens he has produced.

He can draw no conclusion about how many books there are from the fact that the books on the table and the numerals he has produced are equinumerous. That is, from the fact that there are as many books on the table as there are numeral tokens which Jones has produced, nothing follows about how many books there are. But, of course, from the premise stating the equinumerosity and a premise that there were five numeral tokens produced by Jones, it follows that there are five books on the table. Once again, how Jones comes to have this knowledge is unimportant. What is important is that Jones has to understand numerical quantifiers in order to gain knowledge of "how many" by counting, even on the nominalist's view of counting.

With these points in mind, we can proceed to the main claim of the subsection: the function of numerals in counting, as the nominalist explains counting, is a nonconceptual function. The most straightforward explanation of this claim is through the elaboration of a point made in chapter 1: that on the nominalist's view of counting, any serially ordered natural linguistic objects could replace the numerals in counting. The example given in chapter 1 was the serially ordered strings of letters of our alphabet. Let us return to this example.

Consider our English alphabet where, in the present context, by 'our alphabet' I mean the twenty-six kinds of natural linguistic objects (i.e., letters) that are the physical parts in our language of the physically complex natural linguistic objects that are produced in writings. The following is a list of instances of the first ten kinds:

(9) a, b, c, d, e, f, g, h, i, j.

These natural linguistic objects are displayed in their usual order. We learn, by rote, to produce instances of these letters in the order illustrated in (9) (along with sixteen more).

Clearly, this order or a different one could have been established by fiat; of course, the order illustrated in (9) developed by a complex historical process. What should be noted is that the cultural transmission of this order depends on nothing more than learning, by rote, to produce instances of certain kinds of linguistic objects one after the other. Any natural symbol kinds with distinguishable instances would be capable of such an ordering.

Given that we know the ordering of the ten letters illustrated in (9), we can proceed to order strings of two or more letters by a simple rule: In putting any two strings of these letters in order, you must compare them from left to right. Beginning in this way you must determine the "first letter" in each string; this letter is the first letter in a string that is not of the kind which is illustrated by the first letter in (9). Then if one of the two strings has more letters to the right of this "first letter" than the other, this string comes after the other in the order we are establishing, i.e., is "larger." If each of the two strings has as many letters as the other to the right of this "first letter," then you must note whether the "first letter" in one of the strings comes after the "first letter" in the other in the order in (9). If so, then the string with the "larger" "first letter" is "larger." If there are as many letters in one string as in the others and the "first letters" are of the same natural kind, then you must proceed to the next letter to the right in each string. In this case, the previous part of the rule applies again. Thus

aagbdfi

is "larger than"

aaachgb,

which is "larger than"

bied.

The serially ordered kinds of objects,

1B(7) b, c, d, e, f, g, h, i, j, ..., ba, bb, bc, ..., ca, cb, cc, ..., baa, bab, ...,

are isomorphic to the numerals. And in fact the usual ordering for numerals could be achieved by simply using

(10) 0, 1, 2, 3, 4, 5, 6, 7, 8, 9

in place of (9). Indeed, any distinguishable sequence of kinds of natural linguistic objects will do, e.g.,

(11) zero, one, two, three, four, five, six, seven, eight, nine

or (12) there be no, there be one, there be two, ..., there be nine.

The important point is that all that is necessary to produce the serial order of the last paragraph is that there be a basic list of kinds of distinguishable natural linguistic objects that are arranged in a serial order. The ordering is built on no special properties of the objects such as height or weight. _Nor need any of the kinds of natural objects figure in a rule-governed activity wherein their instances are produced in embodiments of certain linguistic kinds, in particular, numerical quantifiers_. Therefore, a serial order among the ten kinds of numerals and strings made from these basic kinds _could_ be made, even though the numerals did not have any conceptual function. And this order would be isomorphic to the order the numerals do have in virtue of the conceptual functions discussed in the last subsection.

My present claims should not be confused with another claim that is, on my reconstruction of natural numbers, false:

namely, that such orderings as we have been discussing are completely independent of natural numbers. This is _not true_, for no one could understand the ordering unless he understood numerical quantifiers and kinds. One need only look at the description of the basic list and the explanation of the rules for the ordering of strings to realize that the fundamental notions pertaining to natural numbers are present in them.

However, the limited scope of this point should not be allowed to obscure its importance. If one ignores it, one may come to argue as follows: what is _really_ essential to being a natural number is what is _common_ to all uses of numerals. And the only thing that is common to them _all_ is that the numerals have a serial order like the one described for strings of letters. Then it is a great temptation to accept some sort of view that treats the natural numbers as "just any one" of the isomorphic ordered collections of strings of objects. Such a view was mentioned in chapter 1, in the midst of a discussion of nominalism, though the argument I have sketched in this paragraph could as easily be employed by an intuitionist.)

However, my aim is to forestall such arguments by explaining how some functions of numerals are not even connected, except by convenience or historical accident, with their function as embodiments of numerical quantifiers and of DSTs which reconstruct terms for natural numbers. One example of these former functions of numerals is the one discussed in connection with the nominalist's view of counting; other examples are the appearance of numerals in:

(13) addresses, telephone numbers, model numbers, postal codes, serial numbers, indexing (as with superscripts and subscripts).

All these uses of numerals could, in principle, be done by the ordered system of strings of letters.

Of course, numerals were picked for the above tasks because they did come in the sort of ordered system needed for the job. If I may call all the jobs done in the list (13) "indexing," then we can say that the only requirement for indexing is that one have kinds of natural linguistic objects that are serially ordered. Numerals do have the necessary order. Moreover, they would have the required order even if they were not used in counting, for anything which has those functions discussed in the previous subsection *must* have a serial order. Consequently, it is simply a mistake to think that what is common to *all* uses of *numerals*, i.e., serial order, is what is at bottom essential to being a natural number. *Rather it is in their being connected, in a special way, with what is essential to natural numbers that numerals are insured of being serially ordered whether or not they are used in counting and indexing. What is essential to natural numbers* is what is laid out in chapter 4; serial order among numerals comes as a necessary concomitant of being an embodiment of the types of linguistic entities discussed in chapter 4.

(iv) *Counting and a Conceptual Function of Numerals*

Though, on my view, there is nothing objectionable about the nominalist's view of counting when it is appropriately elaborated, other plausible reconstructions of cases of counting do exist. The one I wish to take up in this subsection accords to numerals a conceptual function and does this by making the closest of all possible connections between numerals and numerical quantifiers.

So let us return to Jones, who, looking at the books on the table, has tokened

(8) 1, 2, 3, 4, 5.

On the view of this subsection, what Jones has said is

simply a gramatical ellipsis for

(14) 1 book; 2 books; 3 books; 4 books; 5 books.

The second move is to understand (14) as

(15) there is one book; there are two books; there are three books; there are four books; there are five books.

Thus counting, on the view of this subsection, is, in part, making numerical quantifier statements about entities of some kind. Thus, the numerals in (14) are numerical quantifiers.

However, our task is not quite done, for the statements in (15) must be supplemented with additional clauses. In the ordinary sorts of cases of counting which I am considering in this section, each of the objects to be counted is in a unique spatial relation to the person who is counting. For example, in Jones's case, some book is farthest to his left and nearest to him. Indeed we can reasonably expect that anyone who is counting is following some procedure in counting the books, for such procedures are designed to help insure that for each book exactly one numerical quantifier statement is made. (Once again obvious adjustments must be made for such things as "counting by twos.") Without the reasonable precaution of a procedure to insure the satisfaction of this condition, neither the person who is counting nor his audience can have good reason to believe that the person who is counting will come to have knowledge by counting. Jones, for example, might count the books from left to right or he might put the books in a row as he counted them. In any case, each book has a relational property derived from its relation to Jones which distinguishes it from every other book on the table. Let us symbolize these properties by using the letter 'P' written in various styles, the style being determined by having a letter from 1B(7) affixed to it; thus we have 'Pb', 'Pc', 'Pd', etc.

Finally, then, (15) becomes in its finished form

(16) there is one book which is Pb; there are two books which are Pb or Pc; there are three books which are Pb or Pc or Pd; there are four books which are Pb or Pc or Pd or Pe; there are five books which are Pb or Pc or Pd or Pe or Pf.

Therefore, on my reconstruction of such cases of counting as Jones's, counting is the making of numerical quantifier statements with suppressed phrases modifying the kind terms. The numerals tokened in such cases of counting are present tense numerical quantifiers.

Notice that counting the books, even on this reconstruction, indexes them. Counting does require that one "go through" the books on the table, and, as one does this, each book will be assigned a numeral, if (8) or (14) is what is tokened. If (15) or (16) is what is tokened, then each book is assigned a numerical quantifier token which, in English, involves the production of a natural linguistic object such as the natural linguistic objects in the following serially ordered string of natural linguistic objects:

there is one, there are two, there are three, etc.

(The numerical quantifier tokens which involve the production of such natural linguistic objects I shall call "TA" tokens.)

Thus even on the view of counting explained in this subsection, numerals have an indexing function in counting that could easily be served by any serially ordered kinds of natural linguistic objects. But, in addition, the numerals are embodiments of present tense numerical quantifiers. That is, numerals have a conceptual function in these cases which is not to be equated with their indexing function.

As a final word about the functions of numerals, it

should be noted that sometimes they are used to replace numerical words,

one, two, three, four, five, etc.,

in TA tokens. Thus we might find (in writing since such differences are not marked in speech)

there is 1, there are 2, there are 3, there are 4, there are 5, etc.

(I shall extend my terminology and also call the numerical quantifier tokens which involve the production of such natural linguistic objects "TA" tokens.)

Numerals are no more names for anything in their function in TA tokens than they are in their function as indexes or as present-tense numerical quantifiers. The role of both numerical words and numerals in TA tokens is to articulate the numerical quantifier in a numerical quantifier statement in a particular manner, and that manner is the embodiment of the fact that different types of numerical quantifiers are unpacked differently into the more usual quantifiers.

Thus consider

(17) there be three

and (18) there be 3.

A statement in which either (17) or (18) appears is connected definitionally with an E-quantified statement of a special sort--an instance of an NQD-matrix in which there are three E-elements (the K-elements, I-elements, and NI-elements are determined by the E-elements).

A general characterization of numerical words and numerals in TA tokens can be given. This characterization is modeled on the characterization of logical words like connectives and quantifiers. A TA token contains the numerical word 'one' (the numeral '1') if and only if

> (19) a statement containing this TA token is definitionally equivalent to an instance of the NQD-matrix in which there is one E-element.

Every statement that differs from the statement (19) only in the numerical quantifier which appears in it characterizes a numerical word and numeral in a TA token. The order of numerical words and numerals is parasitic on that of numerical quantifiers.

The numerical words which appear in exact quantifiers, i.e.,

> (20) Ex 1, Ex 2, Ex 3, Ex 4, etc.,

serve the same function as the numerical words and numerals in TA tokens.

B. Numerousness and Object-Language Logic

(i) Object-Language Numerical Connectives

The account, at the end of the last subsection, of numerical words and numerals in TA tokens provides the materials for clearing up several outstanding problems. The one discussed in this subsection concerns what I shall now call "numerical connectives" (see 4A(ii)).

What must be kept clearly in mind from the account of the last subsection is that the parts of TA tokens which are numerical words or numerals do play roles in the language. They contribute essentially to the inferences in which the statements in which they appear participate. The roles they play are, in a sense, very subsidiary roles, since they contribute to statements in that they are significant parts of tokens that play the role of numerical quantifiers. Given these conditions and my account of quantification in 3A, it is possible to introduce variables for those significant parts of numerical quantifiers that are numerical words or numerals. Thus we have

(21) there be n

or (22) Ex n.

Let me emphasize that these variables are <u>not</u> proxies for singular terms or names; nor are the variables themselves anything like "ambiguous names."

Now notice that numerical words and numerals in TA tokens are "logical" terms in the sense that they have to do with the determinate structure of statements and statement matrices. Indeed, as I pointed out in the last subsection, their characterizations are modeled on those for logical terms (in a narrower sense of 'logical'). In fact, the really important terms in their characterizations are numerical quantifiers. Thus what I have, in effect, done in (21) and (22) is introduce a variable for "logical" terms. Once one starts down this path there seems to be no reason to stop.

So, instead of making use of variables for numerical words and numerals in TA tokens, I shall employ variables for numerical quantifiers themselves. The variables will be 'nq' and all its stylistic variants, the style being a matter of adding a letter from the serially ordered string of letters to 'nq'.

With these resources we can give an account of the numerical connectives:

... fewer than ..., ... as many as ..., ... more than....

Consider the matrices

4A(ii)(7.1) there be Hs more than there be Ks,

4A(ii)(7.2) there be Hs as many as there be Ks

and

4A(ii)(7.3) there be Hs fewer than there be Ks.

The matrix 4A(ii)(7.2) becomes

(23) (E nq)(nq H and nq K).

The matrix 4A(ii)(7.3) is a little more complicated:

(24) (E nq)(E J)(E I)(no I be a J and something be an I and
(x)(Kx if and only if (I or J)x) and
nq H and nq J).

Matrix 4A(ii)(7.1) can be handled as 4A(ii)(7.3) is or defined in terms of the other two connectives. Many more complicated statements involving these connectives can be accommodated by the above account.

However, the above account is in no way incompatible with an account which is my imitation of a much more common way of handling numerical connectives. This technique makes use of the notion of a 1-1 correspondence. Using 'R' as a variable for relation tokens, I shall abbreviate the minimal condition which must be satisfied in order that a relation be a 1-1 correspondence, i.e.,

(x)(y)(z)(if (Rxz and Ryz) or (Rzx and Rzy), then x = y)

to (25) ---R---.

With (25) in hand, we can take 4A(ii)(7.2) to be

(26) (E R)((---R---) and (x)(if Hx, then (Ey)(Ky and Rxy)) and (y)(if Ky, then (Ex)(Hx and Ryx))).

And 4A(ii)(7.3) would become

(27) (E R)((---R---) and (x)(if Hx, then (Ey)(Ky and Rxy)) and not((y)(if Ky, then (Ex)(Hx and Ryx)))).

We could, if we thought it necessary, include in either (26) or (27) the phrase 'there be Ks'.

Though this second technique utilizes quantification with relation variables, given my account of variables and quantification it does not _in and by itself_ involve commitment to abstract entities, nor does it mean that (26) and (27) are metalinguistic. Quantification with predicate variables is as much part of the object-language as quantification with singular term variables.

Let us suppose that we are faced with a case in which Jones makes some statement in which one of the numerical connectives appears essentially. Which of the two accounts should be used? While I think that perhaps an extended discussion could produce a fairly definite answer to this question, for our purpose the answer surely must be that it all depends on the exact circumstances. For example, suppose Jones knows that there be four cows and that there be four horses and that it is on this ground Jones says

(28) there be cows as many as there be horses.

In this case it would perhaps be most natural to analyze (28) by the first technique. On the other hand, if Jones had in some way effected a correlation between the cows and horses, then it would be most natural to represent him as making some claim involving the correlation. Of course in the first case it is reasonable to suppose that Jones would agree, if asked, that some sort of correlation could be arranged between the cows and horses, but given the grounds on which he makes his claim, there is little reason to analyze his remark so that he is saying something concerning a correlation.

With further investigation, we would probably be able to set out some general remarks for adjudicating such cases. But all that is important for my purposes is that there are adequate object-language means of accounting for statements with numerical connectives. And this surely has been shown. It is true, though, that I do lean toward the account which does not use the correlation. The reasons for this inclination are complicated. One reason is that, in general, it seems dubious that there is always an appropriate relation between equinumerous collections (e.g., four cows and the horsemen of the Apocalypse). It is true, however, that in the case of spatio-temporal objects we are guaranteed a unique 1-1 spatial relation between equinumerous collections. In addition, my proclivity for the first account is strengthened by its fitting appropriately with what I discuss in the next subsection.

Moreover, the first account also permits me to give further statements which correspond, in a natural way, to metalinguistic statements in my reconstruction. The sort of correspondence I have in mind was illustrated in A(ii) when I claimed that

(2) $3 + 5 = 8$

could be either the statement

4A(ii)(8) (H)(I)(E J)(if no H be an I, then if there be five H and there be three I, then there be eight J) and
(J)(E H)(E I)(if no H be an I, then if there be eight J, then there be five H and there be three I)

or the statement

4B(iii)(47) the :there be eight: mbif the :there be five: and the :there be three: and the :there be five and there be three: mbif the :there be eight:

or the statement 4C(v)(136) and so on. I also said that

(3) pr(3)

could be either the statement which reconstructs

(4) prime(THREE)

or the statement which reconstructs

(5) PRIME(THREE)

and so on. Notice that I gave no statement which corresponds to the reconstruction of (4) as 4A(iii)(8) corresponds to 4B(iii)(47). Now, however, I can give such a statement.

I consider a simpler example than (3), viz.,

(29) gr(5, 3),

and restrict my attention to the appropriate statement on the ML level. This statement is:

4B(iii)(41) FIVE is greater than THREE.

Statement 4B(iii)(41) is definitionally equivalent to

(30) (E L)(THREE plus L equals FIVE).

The ML statement which reconstructs (30) is (in its abbreviated form):

(31) (E NUMQUANT)(the :there be five: mbif the :there be three: and the NUMQUANT) and (E NUMQUANT)(the (NUMQUANT :and there be three:) mbif the :there be five:).

The statement which corresponds to (31) as 4A(ii)(8) corresponds to 4B(iii)(47) is related to 4A(ii)(8) as (31) is related to 4B(iii)(47); it is:

(32) (H)(I)(E J)(E nq)(if no H be an I, then if there be three H and nq I, then there be five J) and
(J)(E H)(E I)(E nq)(if no H be an I, then if there be five J, then there be three H and nq I).

A similar, though much more complicated, statement could be produced in the case of (3). In fact, for every metalinguistic statement which is the reconstruction of a statement about the sum or product of natural numbers there is a statement which corresponds to it as (32) does to (31).

As a final remark on this subject, I note that this last claim is not that there is an object-language statement corresponding to every metalinguistic statement which is the reconstruction of an arithmetical statement. For example, the statement

4B(iv)(55) ONE is a natural number

is the arithmetical statement which can be reconstructed as

4B(iv)(55.1) (KINDPREDCON)(the (:there be one: KINDPREDCON) is a numerical quantifier statement).

But there is no object-language statement corresponding to 4B(iv)(55) for the simple reason that it is a classificatory statement and does not speak of the sum or product of natural numbers. All statements which are or which contain such classificatory statements fail to have corresponding object-language statements. The reason that classificatory statements fail to have corresponding object-language statements can be explained from the perspective of my reconstruction: classificatory statements do not, as the other ML statements of my reconstruction do, speak directly about the inferential connections of numerical quantifier statements. It is only these inferential connections between statements which can be mirrored naturally in the object-language.

(ii) Multiplication Again

The use of quantification with the variable 'nq', properly understood, provides the key to finishing the account of multiplication begun in 4B(v). This subsection commences, therefore, with a discussion of some issues concerning the employment of the variable 'nq'. Then while giving a short review of what was done in 4B(v), I present a more elaborate account of multiplicative numerical words and, from this, move to the reconstruction of statements involving multiplication.

As a preliminary, I remind the reader of features of my account of definition. More often than not, I state definitions as follows:

I define

(33) there be two Ks

as (34) (Ey)(Ex)(Ky and Kx and not(x = y) and (z)(if Kz, then x = z or y = z)).

This manner of stating definitions is an acceptable and convenient shorthand. Definitions are, on my account, rules which, speaking generally, permit the inference of "if and only if"s from other "if and only if"s (see 3C and especially 5D). The examples of definitions I have given are all such that they justify, among other "if and only if"s, a universally quantified one. For example, in the above case, the universally quantified equivalence is:

(35) (K)(there be two Ks if and only if (Ey)(Ex) (Ky and Kx and not(x = y) and (z)(if Kz,

then x = z or y = z)).

I shall assume, for present purposes, that definitions must be formulated so that equivalences like (35) can be demonstrated with the help of the definition.

Another feature of my account of definitions is that I do not hesitate to state them with, as it were, "built in" restrictions. Thus in the case of the definitions of numerical quantifiers, their definientia, finite NQD-matrices, contain a free variable for kind predicates, not for any predicates whatsoever. Such a variable is 'K' in (34). It is important to notice that such restrictions do not make the definitions of numerical quantifiers "conditional definitions" in the usual sense of this phrase. It is not as if numerical quantifier statements are definitionally equivalent to instances of NQD-matrices only under certain conditions. What is the case is that

there be two triangulars

is not a numerical quantifier statement since numerical quantifier statements must have a kind term, not just any predicate. Thus though numerical quantifier statements and, of course, NQD-matrices have a strong restriction on them, numerical quantifier statements are unconditionally equivalent to instances of NQD-matrices.

With this in mind, I turn to a consideration of the variable 'nq'. Consider

(36) nq horse.

One instance of (36) is:

(33.1) there be two horses

which is definitionally equivalent to

(34.1) (Ey)(Ex)(horse x and horse y and not(x = y)

and (z)(if horse z, then x = z or y = z))

Since, in principle, we could always do without defined terms, it does seem reasonable to think that we should have some matrix which relates to (36) as (34.1) relates to (33.1). Put another way, we might ask: What would we have in place of (36) if we did without numerical quantifier statements and contented ourselves with instances of NQD-matrices? What is it which contains the predicate 'horse' and of which (34.1) is an instance?

The answers to these questions are found in reflecting on (33.1) and (34.1) from the vantage of (33) and (34). What the instances of (33) share is the numerical quantifier, the :there be two:. (Indeed, by my account of variables in 3A(iii), matrices are a device for "showing" just this, rather than "saying" it.) Similarly, what all the instances of (34) share is something a little more complicated, something for which we do not as yet have a term. An instance of it is everything in (34.1) but the tokens of the predicate 'horse'. I shall say that this thing is a "context." In this case, the context is a context for a kind term, and it is a logical context because I count all the terms except the kind term in (34.1) as logical terms. This context is described in describing the NQD-matrix which is the definiens of the :there be two:. Moreover, every description of a finite NQD-matrix describes a context for a kind term. For convenience, I shall call these "finite NQD-matrix contexts."

On my account of variables, there is no objection to introducing a variable for these contexts. We know a great deal about these contexts, indeed as much as we know about numerical quantifiers. Ignoring the technical details, I shall write the matrix which has a variable for a finite NQD-matrix context and which corresponds to (36) as

(37) ...(horse).

The contexts for which '...' is a variable are finite NQD-matix contexts and must not be thought of as predicates. They are no more predicates than numerical quantifiers are.

These points are the basis for the elaboration of my account of multiplication. I shall present a brief review of the pertinent material in 4B(v), adding new points where it is convenient.

The primary tasks of 4B(v) were to find reconstructions of

4B(v)(60) TWO times THREE equals SIX

and

4B(v)(72) N times M equals L.

My attempt to reconstruct 4B(v)(60) began with an investigation, not of the rule which would be the reconstruction of it, but of the object-language quantified statement which would correspond to this rule. In order to have such quantified statements which are distinctly "multiplicative," I defined "multiplicative numerical words" by means of "multiplicative conjunctions": For example,

4B(v)(66.1) two(there be three)(H, I)

is defined by

4B(v)(66) there be three H and there be three I.

By means of 4B(v)(66.1), I set out the quantified statement 4B(v)(67), the conjunction of

4B(v)(67.1) (H)(I)(E J)(if no H be an I, then if two(there be three)(H, I), then there be six J)

and

4B(v)(67.2) (J)(E H)(E I)(if no H be an I, then if there

be six I, then two(there be three)(H, I)).

The first clarification of the account of 4B(v) is in the definition of multiplicative numerical words. Multiplicative conjunctions are conjunctions of numerical quantifier statements all of which have the same numerical quantifier. Further, the predicate of any of these numerical quantifier statements is disjoint from the predicate of any other of these numerical quantifier statements; that is, a predicate from one conjunct and a predicate from another conjunct must satisfy the condition

(38) no H be an I.

Thus, given what we know about human beings, the predicates 'creature with kidneys' and 'creature with lungs' could not both be predicates in a multiplicative conjunction. To mark in my symbolism that multiplicative conjunctions are rather special conjunctions, I shall write them with 'andM', instead of simply 'and'.

Since multiplicative numerical words are defined by multiplicative conjunction matrices, the multiplicative quantifiers which contain the multiplicative numerical words are restricted to kind predicates which are disjoint. For example, 4B(v)(66.1) will be defined in such a way that the instances of it must contain disjoint predicates.

As a matter of convenience in 4B(v), I simply carried the kind variables of the multiplicative conjunction matrix into the symbolism for statement matrices with multiplicative quantifiers. However, for technical reasons, it is easier to switch to the disjunction of the kind variables. For example, instead of 4B(v)(66.1), we shall have

(39) two(there be three)(H or I).

(See 4B(ii) about disjunctive predicates and numerical quantifier statements.)

The matrices which are the definientia for multiplicative numerical words are all easily described with help of numerical quantifiers. The definiens of the multiplicative numerical word 'one' is a statement matrix which has the variable 'nq' and a kind variable. The definiens of the multiplicative numerical word 'two' is a multiplicative conjunction matrix in which there are two conjuncts and each conjunct has the variable 'nq' and a kind variable different from the kind variable of any other conjunct. In general, the definiens of a multiplicative numerical word succeeds another definiens of a multiplicative numerical word if and only if in the former definiens there is one more conjunct than in the latter definiens.

I shall give some examples of these definitions in their more convenient shorthand form; along with a definition I shall also give the equivalence that the definition helps to justify. I begin with the multiplicative numerical word 'one'. I define

(40) one(nq)(H)

as nq H,

(41) two(nq)(H or I)

as nq H andM nq I,

(42) three(nq)(H or I or J)

as nq H andM nq I andM nq J,

and so on. The equivalences justified by the help of these definitions are, respectively,

(H)(nq)(one(nq)H if and only if nq H),
(H)(I)(nq)(two(nq)(H or I) if and only if nq H andM nq I),
(H)(I)(J)(nq)(three(nq)(H or I or J) if and only

if nq H andM nq I andM nq J),

and so on.

Given the above characterization of multiplicative numerical words, there is no objection, on my view, to introducing a variable for multiplicative numerical words. The variable is 'mnw' (and the usual stylistic variants). But the introduction of this variable leads to a difficulty. The difficulty was illustrated in 4B(v) with respect to the rule which was to be the reconstruction of 4B(v)(72). I shall not review that illustration of the difficulty, as the present illustration of it is clear. Consider

(43) mnw(nq).

Matrix (43) is a matrix for multiplicative quantifiers and as such causes no trouble. But it is not possible to form a statement matrix with (43) by combining it with a kind variable; for example,

(43.1) mnw(nq)(H).

Many instances of (43.1) do not have the appropriate kind of predicate.

Moreover, if we look at the multiplicative conjunction contexts which must go with the variable 'mnw', we find that they are contexts for numerical quantifiers, that the predicates of a multiplicative conjunction are in the multiplicative conjunction context, and that there are more predicates in some contexts than others. On the model of (37), I write the matrix with the variable for such contexts as

(44) ---M(nq).

The 'M' is just to remind us that the variable is for contexts all of which are described in describing multiplicative conjunctions.

Thus instead of (43.1), I offer the statement matrix

(45) mnw(nq)(dkp),

where 'dkp' is a variable for disjunctive kind predicates, each kind predicate of which is disjoint from the others in the disjunction. Furthermore, in the matrix (45), these variables function under another restriction: something is an instance of (45) only if in its disjunctive predicate there are as many disjuncts as there are conjuncts in the multiplicative conjunction which defines its multiplicative numerical word. It is not implausible, it seems to me, to consider (45) as having only two variables, 'nq' and a complex variable. Much the same would have occurred in the case of (34.1) and (37) had I decided to form a context, not just for a kind predicate, but also for the logical terms which are common to every finite NQD-matrix. A partial example of this is:

... and (z)(if ***, then ___ (horse).

The context variables, '...', '***', and '___' cannot function without restriction and thus are better viewed as one complex variable.

The same sort of moves take place on the ML level. Previously, the (primary) reconstruction of 4B(v)(60) was 4B(v)(68), the conjunction of

4B(v)(68.1) (KINDPREDCONA)(KINDPREDCONB)(E KINDPREDCON) (given the KINDPREDCONA disj the KINDPREDCONB, the (:there be six: KINDPREDCON) may be inferred from the (:two(there be three): (KINDPREDCONA, KINDPREDCONB)))

and

4B(v)(68.2) (KINDPREDCON)(E KINDPREDCONA)(E KINDPREDCONB) (given the KINDPREDCONA disj the KINDPREDCONB, the (:two(there be three): (KINDPREDCONA,

KINDPREDCONB)) may be inferred from the (:there be six: KINDPREDCON)).

Two changes must now be made. First, the DST matrix

the (:two(there be three): (KINDPREDCONA, KINDPREDCONB))

becomes

the (:two(there be three): (KINDPREDCONA :or: KINDPREDCONB)).

Second, an analog of the restriction on the predicates in multiplicative quantifier statements is needed: the ML variables which are for SGTs true of kind predicates and which appear in DST matrices with SGTs true of multiplicative quantifiers are restricted to SGTs which are true of kind predicates each of which is disjoint from every other. Given this restriction, the conditions in 4B(v)(68) are no longer necessary. The new (primary) reconstruction of 4B(v)(60) is (46), the conjunction of

(46.1) (KINDPREDCONA)(KINDPREDCONB)(E KINDPREDCON) (the (:there be six: KINDPREDCON) may be inferred from the (:two(there be three): (KINDPREDCONA :or: KINDPREDCONB)))

and (46.2) (KINDPREDCON)(E KINDPREDCONA)(E KINDPREDCONB) (the (:two(there be three): (KINDPREDCONA :or: KINDPREDCONB)) may be inferred from the (:there be six: KINDPREDCON)).

Moreover, corresponding to the quantified statement

(H)(I)(two(there be three)(H or I) if and only if there be three H andM there be three I)

is the rule

(KINDPREDCONA)(KINDPREDCONB)(the (:there be three: KINDPREDCONA :andM there be three: KINDPREDCONB) may be inferred from the (:two(there be three): (KINDPREDCONA :or: KINDPREDCONB)) and the (:two(there be three): KINDPREDCONA :or: KINDPRED-CONB)) may be inferred from the (:there be three: KINDPREDCONA :andM there be three: KINDPREDCONB)).

The reconstruction of

two times M equals L

is easily obtained from (46). The DSTs

the (:there be six: KINDPREDCON)

and the (:two(there be three): KINDPREDCONA :or: KINDPREDCONB))

which appear in (46) have their places taken in the reconstruction of the above matrix by, respectively,

the (NUMQUANT KINDPREDCON)

and the (:two:(NUMQUANTA)(KINDPREDCONA :or: KINDPRED-CONB)).

To reconstruct 4B(v)(72) one faces the same sort of problem faced in the case of (44) and (45). (In subsection 4B(v), it was this case of the general difficulty which was discussed.) So, once again, I set out a matrix with variables which function under a restriction. The two variables are 'MULTNUMWORD' and 'DISJKINDPREDCON' (with stylistic variants). The matrix is:

(47) the (MULTNUMWORD(NUMQUANT)(DISJKINDPREDCON)).

The restriction is that, in an instance of (47), the SGT true of disjunctive kind predicates must be true of disjunctive predicates in which there are as many predicates as there are conjuncts in the multiplicative conjunction which is the definiens of the multiplicative numerical word that the SGT which is true of multiplicative numerical words (and which is in the instance) is true of. With these provisos, the (primary) reconstruction of 4B(v)(72) is (48), the conjunction of

(48.1) (DISJKINDPREDCON)(E KINDPREDCON)(the (NUMQUANT KINDPREDCON) may be inferred from the (MULTNUMWORD(NUMQUANTA)(DISJKINDPREDCON)))

and (48.2) (KINDPREDCON)(E DISJKINDPREDCON)(the (MULTNUMWORD(NUMQUANTA)(DISJKINDPREDCON)) may be inferred from the (NUMQUANT KINDPREDCON)).

With the reconstruction of 4B(v)(72) in hand, I am now in a position to give the (primary) reconstructions of

4C(vi)(138) <u>TWO</u> TIMES <u>THREE</u> EQUALS <u>SIX</u>

and

4C(vi)(139) <u>N</u> TIMES <u>M</u> EQUALS <u>L</u>.

These reconstructions are, as might be expected, very much like their approximations in 4C(vi).

One preliminary matter is the abbreviation of (48) to the conjunction of

the NUMQUANT mbif the (MULTNUMWORD(NUMQUANTA)(DISJKINDPREDCON))

and the (MULTNUMWORD(NUMQUANTA)(DISJKINDPREDCON)) mbif the NUMQUANT.

Second, to complement the MML variables '<u>ML!MNW!SGT</u>' and '<u>ML!NQ!SGT</u>', I need the MML variable '<u>ML!DKP!SGTMAT</u>'. This last variable is for such MML SGTs as

:(KINDPREDCONA :or: KINDPREDCONB):,

which is true of ML matrices for SGTs true of disjunctive

kind predicates.

The reconstruction of 4C(vi)(138) is:

(49) (E ML!NQ!SGTA)(E ML!NQ!SGTB)(E ML!MNW!SGT) (E ML!DKP!SGTMAT)(the :the (:there be six: KN): contains the ML!NQ!SGTA and the :the (:two(there be three): (KNA :or: KNB)): contains the ML!NQ!SGTB and the :the (:two(there be three): (KNA :or: KNB)): contains the ML!MNW!SGT and the ML!DKP!SGTMAT and the ((:the:) ML!NQ!SGTA (:mbif the:) ML!MNW!SGT(ML!NQ!SGTB)(ML!DKP!SGTMAT)) is true and the ((:the:) ML!MNW!SGT(ML!NQ!SGTB) (ML!DKP!SGTMAT)(:mbif the:) ML!NQ!SGTA) is true).

Notice that no additional restrictions, ones for MML variables, need to be stated for (49). The ML restrictions carry over because (49), in a sense, incorporates the abbreviation of (48) and involves only E-quantification.

The reconstruction of 4C(vi)(139) is obtained from (49) by replacing the MML SGTs

:the (:there be six: KN):

and :the (:two(there be three): (KNA :or: KNB)):

by MML variables. A fine point concerns the MML variable which replaces the latter of these two SGTs. It is an MML variable, not only for this latter SGT, but also for any MML SGT true of ML DSTs which contain both ML SGTs true of multiplicative quantifiers and ML SGT matrices whose instances are ML SGTs true of disjunctive kind predicates (no matter how many ML variables the SGT matrices have).

C. Classes

(i) The Reconstruction

The need to provide a Sellarsian reconstruction of class theory arises from several sources. A rather minor one is the use to which classes of a special sort are usually put in the construction of the integers and the rationals from the natural numbers. But though I shall be able to reproduce the usual construction of these special classes called "ordered pairs," I shall not, as it will turn out, need or want to use them in the construction of the integers and rationals. A more important need is to demonstrate the ability of the Sellarsian machinery to produce a reconstruction of a theory as important as the theory of classes. More important yet is the fact that classes are usually thought of as a kind of abstract entity and thus are in need of Sellarsian reconstruction. Lastly, there can of course be no doubt that it is possible to produce systems of classes with the same mathematical structure as the system of natural numbers. It is a confirmation of the power of the Sellarsian scheme that such classes can be easily reproduced in the theory of classes which is constructible by Sellarsian methods.

I shall not bother with intuitive motivation for the steps in the Sellarsian construction of class theory.[2] The reader who has come this far in the book is familiar with my reasons for proceeding as I do. My comments will be limited to those special problems which arise solely in the context of the reconstruction of classes.

In the object-language, classes appear only as predicates. Thus I introduce

(50) /K/x

as (51) x is a K

or, in mimicry of a common definition found in books on class theory, as

(52) (E H)(x is an H and (y)(y is an H if and only if y is a K))

(where suitable provisions for preventing unwanted variable binding are made). Remember that the appearance of quantification with predicate variables in (52) in no way removes (52) from the object-language nor does it bequeath commitment to abstract entities.

The predicates introduced in (50) I shall call "monadic class predicates." It is possible, regardless of whether (51) or (52) is the definiens of (50), to define "union," "intersection," "inclusion," and "complement" for class predicates. All the resources needed for these definitions are to be found in predicate logic; one needs only disjunction, conjunction, an "if . . . , then . . ." connective, negation, and the universal quantifier.

Of course, there is no "membership relation," since class predicates are predicates and not singular terms and thus cannot flank a relation token. There is the miscalled "relation of predication," and we could introduce a sign for this.

Socrates mem /man/

would be equivalent by definition to

Socrates is a man.

But 'mem' is not a relation any more than 'is a' is a relation. Were either one a relation, it would require two singular terms. However, the predicate '/man/' is not a singular term (see 2D). In order to avoid confusion, I shall not employ the symbol 'mem'.

What has been accomplished for monadic predicates can be done for relation tokens, i.e., for polyadic predicates. Dyadic class predicates, triadic class predicates, and so on, symbolized

(53) /R/xy,

(54) /R/xyz,

and so on, can be introduced by definientia which are derived from (51) or (52) by making the obvious changes.

One of the main principles of the theory of classes is the so-called principle of extensionality: classes which have the same members, i.e., which are "coextensive," are the same class. With class predicates, this principle is trivially preserved by taking as "sameness" not identity but that "equivalence relation" in the object-language which is formulated by an "if and only if" statement connective and the universal quantifier. Since there is no membership relation for class predicates, "being coextensive" and "being the same class as" are expressed by the same condition:

(55) (x)(/K/x if and only if /H/x).

It can easily be shown, whether (50) has (51) or (52) as its definiens, that (55) may be deduced from

(x)(Kx if and only if Hx)

and vice versa.

The metalinguistic part of the reconstruction begins in the manner painstakingly discussed in chapter 4. Therefore, assuming that the reader will refresh his or her memory by reviewing parts of chapter 4 when necessary, I commence the construction on the ML level.

First, we form those Sellarsian general terms which are true of class predicates. Thus, for example, we have

(56) :/trilateral plane figure/:

and (57) :/triangular plane figure/:.

We need, of course, not only these SGTs but the ML variables which accompany them. We thus obtain

(58) :/trilateral plane figure/: INDCON

and (59) :/triangular plane figure/: INDCON.

The ML variable for SGTs true of class predicates is 'CLASS-PREDCON' (with the usual stylistic variants).

With these resources, we can produce statements:

(60) (INDCON)(all (:/trilateral plane figure/: INDCON)s are class predicate statements),

i.e., (61) (INDCON)(the (:/trilateral plane figure/: INDCON) is a class predicate statement)

and (62) (INDCON)(all (:/man/: INDCON)s are class predicate statements),

i.e., (63) (INDCON)(the (:/man/: INDCON) is a class predicate statement).

Assuming that the expression 'kind', in one of its roles, forms singular terms for classes, then one might take (61) and (63) as reconstructions of, respectively,

(64) trilateral-plane-figurekind is a class

and (65) mankind is a class.

Like exemplification, membership is reconstructed by means of the phrase 'is true of'. Thus, using the DSTs introduced above, I reconstruct

(66) Socrates is a member of mankind

as (67) the :/man/: is true of the :Socrates:.

And by the same steps which were set out in detail in chapter 4, (67) becomes, in the end

all :/man/ Socrates:s are true.

Thus on this reconstruction the only feature that distinguishes 'is a member of' from 'exemplifies' is that 'is a member of' will appear only with singular terms for classes.

Henceforth, I drop the variable 'INDCON' from most of my examples. The resulting simplification does not affect the points I make.

The principle of extensionality can be preserved on the present reconstruction by characterizing an equivalence relation for the DSTs which reconstruct singular terms for classes and taking this equivalence relation for "identity" between classes. This equivalence relation is only trivially different from the reconstruction of 'is coextensive with'; it is material equivalence between predicates:

(68) the PREDCONA meq the PREDCONB

is defined as

(69) (INDCON)(the (PREDCONA INDCON) is true if and only if the (PREDCONB INDCON) is true).

An example of a material equivalence with SGTs for class predicates is

(70) the :/triangular plane figure/: meq the :/trilateral plane figure/:.

Given the principles pertaining to truth, (70) follows from

(71) (x)(x is a triangular plane figure if and only if x is a trilateral plane figure)

and (71) follows from (70).

Correspondingly,

(72) triangular-plane-figurekind is coextensive with trilateral-plane-figurekind

is reconstructed as

(73) (INDCON)(the :/triangular plane figure/: is true of the INDCON if and only if the :/trilateral plane figure/: is true of the INDCON).

Statement (73) also follows from (71) and vice versa.

For convenience, I abbreviate

triangular plane figure

to triangpf

and trilateral plane figure

to trilatpf.

Thus in place of

the :/triangular plane figure/:

and the :/trilateral plane figure/:,

we have

the :/triangpf/:

and the :/trilatpf/:.

The question of the identity of class predicates like the :/triangpf/: and the :/trilatpf/: is decided by the doctrine of section 5D: such predicates (within the reconstructions I have considered) are not identical. Of course, the nonidentity of these class predicates must be shown through their definitions. But, given my discussion of the predicates, the :triangular: and the :trilateral:, this task is not difficult. So, class predicates, like other predicates, are not necessarily identical if they are materially equivalent (or even demonstrably equivalent).

Notice also that the ML SGTs for class predicates are, in general, not even equivalent. For example, it is not true that

(74) (x)(x is a :/triangpf/: if and only if x is a :/trilatpf/:)

even though (71) is true. In fact, not only is (74) false, it is true that

not((Ex)(x is a :/triangpf/: and x is a :/trilatpf/:)).

Though I do not think that there is anything objectionable in what I have done so far, it is possible to do even more by imitating on the ML level the definition of (50) by (52). This ML imitation allows us to define what I shall call "ML class predicates." I shall write these ML predicates with the same slanting lines I used in (50). Thus

(75) /:/triangpf/:/x

is defined by

(76) (E CLASSPREDCON)(x is a CLASSPREDCON and the CLASSPREDCON meq the :/triangpf/:)

and (77) /:/trilatpf/:/x

by (78) (E CLASSPREDCON)(x is a CLASSPREDCON and the CLASSPREDCON meq the :/trilatpf/:).

In general,

(79) /CLASSPREDCON/x

is defined by

(80) (E CLASSPREDCONA)(x is a CLASSPREDCONA and the CLASSPREDCONA meq the CLASSPREDCON).

It is important to notice that (80) is not a faithful imitation of (52) because it does not utilize 'if and only if' directly, though it does utilize a related equivalence relation.

The first important point about the ML class predicates

(81) /:/triangpf/:/

and (82) /:/trilatpf/:/

is that

(83) all :/triangpf/:s are /:/triangpf/:/s

and (84) all :/trilatpf/:s are /:/trilatpf/:/s

are true. I illustrate the argument for the case of (83). Clearly it is true that

the :/triangpf/: meq the :/triangpf/:.

By the definition of (75), it follows from the conjunction of this material equivalence with the hypothesis that something is a :/triangpf/: that it is a /:/triangpf/:/. Thus we conclude by the usual rules of logic that (83) is true.

Second, I noted before that (70) follows from (71). Thus given (71), it follows that

(85) all :/trilatpf/:s are /:/triangpf/:/s

and (86) all :/triangpf/:s are /:/trilatpf/:/s.

The argument for (85) begins with the observation that given (71), (70) is true. From the conjunction of (70) with the hypothesis that something is a :/trilatpf/:, it follows that it is a /:/triangpf/:/. And thus we conclude that (85) is true.

Given (71), it follows from (85) that

(87) the :/trilatpf/: is a /:/triangpf/:/.

Moreover, for every SGT for which

(88) the CLASSPREDCON meq the :/triangpf/:

is true,

(89) all CLASSPREDCONs are /:/triangpf/:/s

and (90) the CLASSPREDCON is a /:/triangpf/:/

are also true. Of course, an instance of (88), e.g., (70), is true if and only if a corresponding "if and only if" statement, e.g., (71), is true. Similar remarks hold for the ML predicate '/:/trilatpf/:/'.

The preceding paragraph shows us that any predicate which is materially equivalent to the :/triangpf/: is a /:/triangpf/:/. But given the definition of (81), it is clear that if a predicate is a /:/triangpf/:/, then it is materially equivalent to the :/triangpf/:. Combining these two statements, we have

(91) (CLASSPREDCON)(the CLASSPREDCON is a /:/triangpf/:/ if and only if the CLASSPREDCON meq the :/triangpf/:).

A similar truth holds for (82).

Moreover, because of (70), every SGT for which (90) is true is an SGT for which

(92) the CLASSPREDCON is a /:/trilatpf/:/

is also true and vice versa. Therefore

(93) (CLASSPREDCON)(the CLASSPREDCON is a /:/triangpf/:/ if and only if the CLASSPREDCON is a /:/trilatpf/:/)

and (93.1) (CLASSPREDCON)(all CLASSPREDCONs are /:/triangpf/:/s if and only if all CLASSPREDCONs are /:/trilatpf/:/s).

Given (70) and the definientia of (75) and (77), it follows easily that

(94) (x)(/:/triangpf/:/x if and only if /:/trilatpf/:/x).

This conclusion can also be obtained by an argument which includes (93.1). So, given (93) and (94), we know that anything which is a /:/triangpf/:/ is a /:/trilatpf/:/ and vice versa. Thus, unlike the SGTs,

(56) :/triangpf/:

and (57) :/trilatpf/:,

for which we know that (74) is false, the ML class predicates, (81) and (82), are equivalent (and hence also materially equivalent).

But the most interesting question remains: Is it true that

(95) the /:/triangpf/:/ is identical to the /:/trilatpf/:/?

I begin the investigation of this question by explaining what it is _not_.

It is _not_ a question about either the _ML class predicates_ (81) and (82) or the _ML DSTs_ constructed with these predicates. The question whether the predicate (81) is identical to the predicate (82) can be stated on the _MML_ level: Is

the :/:/triangpf/:/: identical to the :/:/trilatpf/:/:?

Notice the double quotation. The question involving (95) is not about the ML predicates (81) and (82), as the above question is. As a parallel case, consider the two statements:

the :triangular: is identical to the :trilateral:

and the ::triangular:: is identical to the ::trilateral::.

On other occasions I have used the first of these statements as an example. Statement (95) is like the first of these statements, not like the second.

I notice, in passing, that the answer to the question about ML predicates (81) and (82) is that they are not identical. The definitions of these predicates are different, viz., (56) and (57).

Despite what one might be led to think by the preceding paragraph, the answer to the question about (95) is affirmative on the assumption that (71) is true.

On my definition of identity in 5D, (95) is equivalent to

(96) (F)(F(the /:/triangpf/:/) if and only if F(the /:/trilatpf/:/)).

The statement matrices

(97) F(the /:/triangpf/:/),

i.e., the /:/triangpf/:/ is F,

and (98) F(the /:/trilatpf/:/),

i.e., the /:/trilatpf/:/ is F,

are equivalent by definition to, respectively,

(97.1) all /:/triangpf/:/s are F

and (98.1) all /:/trilatpf/:/s are F.

Now let us consider some consequences of (97.1) and (98.1) and other statements which have been proven. We know from (93) and (94) that something is a /:/triangpf/:/ if and only if it is /:/trilatpf/:/. We also know that (83) and (85) are true. Any predicate for which (97.1) is true must be a predicate for which

(99) the :/triangpf/: is F,

i.e., all :/triangpf/:s are F,

and (100) the :/trilatpf/: is F,

i.e., all :/trilatpf/:s are F,

are true. The same thing is true of predicates for which (98.1) is true. Therefore, in the case of the /:/triangpf/:/, anything which is true of it must not be something which would distinguish :/triangpf/:s and :/trilatpf/:s, for then only one of (99) and (100) would be true. A similar remark holds for the /:/trilatpf/:/.

Now notice not only that (56) and (57) appear in the definientia of, respectively, (81) and (82), but that these definientia are exactly the same except for (56) and (57). Of course, there are predicates for which (99) is true (false) and (100) false (true). But these differences cannot be transferred, by the definientia (76) and (78), from :/triangpf/:s and :/trilatpf/:s to /:/triangpf/:/s and /:/trilatpf/:/s. No such transference is possible since, in every case, neither (97) nor (98) can be true unless both (99) and (100) are true. What has just been argued for the predicates, the :/triangpf/: and the :/trilatpf/:s, holds for any of the materially equivalent predicates that (81) and (82) are true of. Therefore given (71), (95) is true.

The upshot of this is that we have found some ML predicates for which

(101) the PREDCONA meq the PREDCONB if and only if the PREDCONA is identical to the PREDCONB

is true. For example,

(101.1) the /:/triangpf/:/ meq the /:/trilatpf/:/ if and only if the /:/triangpf/:/ is identical to the /:/trilatpf/:/

is true.

In light of (101.1), I take as the reconstruction of (64)

(102) (INDCON)(the (/:/triangpf/:/ INDCON) is

a class predicate statement),

and as the reconstruction of (65)

(103) (INDCON)(the (/:/man/:/ INDCON) is a class predicate statement).

The reconstruction of exemplification is altered only to the extent of replacing the SGTs previously used in this reconstruction by ML class predicates.

The topic of the "union," "intersection," and "complement" of classes in the ML part of my reconstruction calls forth a host of issues many of which are very complicated. I shall illustrate some of the main considerations in the case of union.

In many treatments of class theory, the union of classes is defined with the help of membership and disjunction. I shall not follow this model. But I shall preserve, in some form or other, the "principle of union": something is a member of the union of a class with another class if and only if it is a member of one class or it is a member of the other class.

I begin with class predicates. The first question to answer is: Which predicate is the union of two class predicates? First I define

(104) x is a man or trilatpf

by (105) x is a man or x is a trilatpf.

Then with (104), I define

(106) /man or trilatpf/x

by (51) or (52). By either definition it is true that

(106.1) (x)(/man or trilatpf/x if and only if x is a man or trilatpf).

By (51) or (52), we can define the class predicates

(107) /man/

and (108) /trilatpf/.

By either definition, it is true that

(107.1) (x)(/man/x if and only if x is a man)

and (108.1) (x)(/trilatpf/x if and only if x is a trilatpf).

Then the statement

(109) (x)(/man or trilatpf/x if and only if /man/x or /trilatpf/x)

follows from the definitional equivalence of (104) and (105) and the equivalences (106.1), (107.1), and (108.1).

I shall say that the class predicate

(110) /man or trilatpf/

is the union of the class predicates (107) and (108). The principle of union is preserved as (109).

Notice that I have chosen (110) over another possible candidate for the predicate which is the union of (107) and (108), namely,

(111) /man/ or /trilatpf/.

We obtain this predicate through the definition of

(112) (/man/ or /trilatpf/)x

by (113) /man/x or /trilatpf/x.

The predicate (111) is a candidate for the position of the union of (107) and (108) because it fits the intuitive idea that the union of two predicates should contain these two predicates. What is wrong with (111) from my point of view is that it is <u>not</u> a class predicate, though it is a disjunction of class predicates. That is, (111) is a disjunction of predicates which have the sort of definition which qualifies predicates as class predicates, but it itself does not have such a definition. This is reflected in my symbolism by the fact that (111) does not have an outermost brace of slanting lines. On the other hand, (110) *is* a class predicate, a "disjunctive class predicate." So (110) is included within the class predicate portion of my reconstruction of classes, but (111) is not.

It might seem that the truth of

(109.1) (x)(/man or trilatpf/x if and only if (/man/ or /trilatpf/)x

is a source of an objection to what I have just said. But this is not so. It is not part of my view that class predicates cannot be equivalent to predicates which are not class predicates. Statement (109.1) is just an equivalence involving two predicates, only one of which is a class predicate.

Now I turn to the ML level. Given my decision to take (110) as the class predicate which is the union of the class predicates, (107) and (108), it is natural to reconstruct

(114) mankind union trilatpfkind

by means of the SGT

(115) :/man or trilatpf/:.

This SGT is true of class predicates, whereas the SGT

(116) :/man/ or /trilatpf/:

is true of disjunctions of predicates both disjuncts of which are class predicates.

There are several points which should be made about

(117) the :/man or trilatpf/:

and (118) the :/man/ or /trilatpf/:.

It is false that

(119) the :/man or trilatpf/: is identical to the :/man/ or /trilatpf/:

and false that

(120) (x)(x is a :/man or trilatpf/: if and only if x is a :/man/ or /trilatpf/:).

But (119) is <u>not</u> about the identity of class predicates because, though the :/man or trilatpf/: is a class predicate, the :/man/ or /trilatpf/: is not.

Similarly the truth

(121) the :/man or trilatpf/: meq the :/man/ or /trilatpf/:

is <u>not</u> about two class predicates. The term 'meq' is defined for predicates generally. Thus (121) states the material equivalence of two predicates, but not two class predicates. This is not to say that truths like (121) cannot be helpful in dealing with class predicates. For example, one can use (121) to show

(122) (INDCON)(the :/man or trilatpf/: is true of the INDCON if and only if the :/man/: is true of the INDCON or the :/trilatpf/: is true of the INDCON).

By (121), any statement with a :/man or trilatpf/: combined with an individual constant is true if and only if a statement with a :/man/ or /trilatpf/: combined with that individual constant is true. But any statement of this latter sort is true if and only if a disjunction is true, viz., a disjunction one disjunct of which is that individual constant combined with a :/man/: and the other disjunct of which is that individual constant combined with a :/trilatpf/:. But any such disjunction is true if and only if one of its disjuncts is true or the other of its disjuncts is true and therefore if and only if a :/man/: is true of the individual constant or a :/trilatpf/: is true of the individual constant.

Now I introduce the ML class predicate defined with the help of the SGT ':/man or trilatpf/:'. Thus

(123) /:/man or trilatpf/:/x

is defined by

(124) (E CLASSPREDCON)(x is a CLASSPREDCON and the CLASSPREDCON meq the :/man or trilatpf/:).

Using the ML class predicate

(125) /:/man or trilatpf/:/,

I reconstruct (114) as

(126) the /:/man or trilatpf/:/.

Such definientia as (124) are restricted by the variable 'CLASSPREDCON'. Thus, for example, (124) does not follow from

x is a :/man/ or /trilatpf/: and the :/man/ or /trilatpf/: meq the :/man or trilatpf/:.

Therefore one cannot show that

(127) all :/man/ or /trilatpf/:s are /:/man or trilatpf/:/s,

i.e., (127.1) the :/man/ or /trilatpf/: is a /:/man or trilatpf/:/.

Of course there are truths like (127) and (127.1), but they involve SGTs true of class predicates.

In addition to (116), there are other ML predicates which do not figure in the reconstruction of singular terms for classes. For example, suppose we define

(128) x is a :/man/: or :/trilatpf/:

by (129) x is a :/man/: or x is a :/trilatpf/:

and then define

(130) /:/man/: or :/trilatpf/:/x

by (131) (E CLASSPREDCON)(x is a CLASSPREDCON and the CLASSPREDCON meq the (:/man/: or :/trilatpf/:)).

The DST

the /:/man/: or :/trilatpf/:/

is not in my reconstruction of abstract singular terms for classes, despite the fact that all :/man/: or :/trilatpf/:s and all /:/man/: or :/trilatpf/:/s are class predicates.

Returning to (126), I state the principle of union which is preserved for (126):

(132) (INDCON)(the /:/man or trilatpf/:/ is true of the INDCON if and only if the /:/man/:/ is true of the INDCON or the /:/trilatpf/:/ is true of the INDCON).

The argument for (132) is similar to others used in this section. I illustrate the major points by an example:

the /:/man/:/ is true of the :Socrates: or
the /:/trilatpf/:/ is true of the :Socrates:

if and only if

the :/man/: is true of the :Socrates: or
the :/trilatpf/: is true of the :Socrates:

if and only if

the :/man/ Socrates: is true or the :/trilatpf/ Socrates: is true if and only if

/man/ Socrates or /trilatpf/ Socrates

if and only if

/man or trilatpf/ Socrates.

The remainder of what is required can be obtained by repeating, in reverse order, the moves which led to the last statement above.

Let us halt for a moment and consider what has thus far been completed in the reconstruction of class theory. First, we have class predicates in both the object-language and ML. For these predicates class-theoretic notions of union, intersection, and so on can be introduced. There is no membership relation that accompanies class predicates. Second, there are ML DSTs constructed using ML class predicates. For these singular terms there is a "membership relation" constructed with the notion of truth. Thus

Socrates is a member of mankind

and Socrates is a member of featherless-bipedkind

are reconstructed, respectively, as

(E INDCON)(E CLASSPREDCON)(the (/:/man/:/ INDCON) is true of the (CLASSPREDCON :Socrates:)),

i.e., the (/:/man/:/ :Socrates:) is true

and (E INDCON)(E CLASSPREDCON)(the (/:/featherless biped/:/ INDCON) is true of the (CLASSPREDCON :Socrates:)),

i.e., the (/:/featherless biped/:/ :Socrates:) is true.

The reconstruction of classes as individuals follows the same pattern as that set down for the reconstruction of numbers as individuals. Moreover, the same dialectic concerning the "identity" of classes and the principle of extensionality could be worked through on the MML level. However, I shall assume that enough of the considerations have been discussed so that the possibility of reconstructing classes as individuals is clear.

Many technical questions might be broached in connection with the reconstruction of classes I have provided. They cannot of course be answered in full without considering all the levels of the reconstruction in detail, not just the ML level. But I shall consider some of these questions as well as can be with the resources at hand and leave a more complete discussion for some other time. One concerns Russell's paradox; another, the common definition of ordered pairs by means of classes of classes; a third, the sequences of classes which are the elements of systems which have the same structure as the system of natural numbers. The Russell paradox is handled in the next subsection.

Ordered pairs are handled by mimicking a common definition of ordered pairs as classes of classes. On this definition, the ordered pair of a and b is the class whose only members are the class whose only member is a and the class whose only members are a and b.

My reconstruction of such classes begins with the definitions:

(=a)x

for x = a

and (= a or b)x

for x = a or b,

which is in turn defined by

x = a or x = b.

From the above we obtain the class predicates:

/= a/

and /= a or b/.

I shall take

(= a)kind

as the class whose only member is a and

(= a or b)kind

as the class whose only members are a and b. As before, I define ML class predicates:

/:/= a/:/

and /:/= a or b/:/.

Then the DST

the /:/= a/:/

reconstructs the first of the singular terms above and the DST

the /:/= a or b/:/

reconstructs the second.

I now define

(= the /:/= a/:/ or the /:/= a or b/:/)x

in the same manner in which I defined '(= a or b)x'. Then we have the class predicate

/= the /:/= a/:/ or the /:/= a or b/://,

the SGT

:/= the /:/= a/:/ or the /:/= a or b/://:,

and the ML class predicate

/:/= the /:/= a/:/ or the /:/= a or b/://:/.

The singular term for Kuratowski's class,

(= (= a)kind or (= a or b)kind)kind,

is reconstructed as

the /:/= the /:/= a/:/ or the /:/= a or b/://:/.

I shall abbreviate such a DST to

(a, b).

Is it the case that

(133) (a, b) is identical to (c, d) if and only if a is identical to c and b is identical to d?

The answer is yes. The required proof follows the usual lines, because the DSTs '(a, b)' and '(c, d)' are constructed with ML class predicates, and we know that

(101) the PREDCONA meq the PREDCONB if and only if the PREDCONA is identical to the PREDCONB

is true for ML class predicates.

I give a general illustration of the most important steps in the proof. Consider the class predicates

/= A or B/

and /= C or D/

and the DSTs

the /:/= A or B/:/

and the /:/= C or D/:/.

It is clearly true that

(x)(/= A or B/x if and only if x = A or x = B)

and (x)(/= C or D/x if and only if x = C or x = D).

But if

A = C

and B = D,

then /= A or B/C,
/= A or B/D,
/= C or D/A,
and /= C or D/B.

Then it is easily shown that the /:/= A or B/:/ is true of something if and only if the /:/= C or D/:/ is true of the same thing. Therefore

the /:/= A or B/:/ meq the /:/= C or D/:/

and hence, by (101),

the /:/= A or B/:/ is identical to the /:/= C or D/:/.

Reasoning in reverse, from the identity just given, will get us to the conclusion that

A = C and B = D

or A = D and B = C.

But, with the additional premise that

the /:/= A/:/ is identical to the /:/= C/:/,

the second disjunct gives the conclusion

A = C and B = D.

Thus in either case we conclude that A = C and B = D.

Next, I expound briefly the matter of the familiar set-theoretic sequences of classes which can be used as the elements of a system which has the same mathematical structure as the system of natural numbers. The key to these set-theoretic constructions is the empty class. To reconstruct the empty class, I begin with identity. By means of identity, we define nonidentity:

not=(x, x)

for   not(=(x, x)).

Now I simply list linguistic items which are obtained in the usual way; the last linguistic item in this list reconstructs the singular term

(not identical to itself)kind.

The list is:

/not=/,
:/not=/:,
the :/not=/:,
/:/not=/:/,
and   the /:/not=/:/.

The statement

Socrates is a member of the empty class

is reconstructed (with all the necessary ML variables) as

(E CLASSPREDCON)(E INDCON)(the (/:/not=/:/ INDCON, INDCON) is true of the CLASSPREDCON :Socrates:)),

which leads to

the (/:/not=/:/ :Socrates:, :Socrates:) is true,

which is false since

/not=/(Socrates, Socrates)

is false. Thus, as we of course wished, the empty class on this reconstruction has no members.

With the empty class at our disposal, it is simple enough to develop sequences of classes. One sequence begins with the empty class and then next has the class whose sole member is the empty class. In general, the successor of a class, c, is just the class which has c as its sole member.

The class whose sole member is the empty class is reconstructed by starting with the predicate 'is identical to the empty class'. Then by the route illustrated above for the empty class itself, one moves to the DST which is true of only the empty class, viz.,

the /:/= the /:/not=/://:/.

This DST reconstructs the singular term for the class which has the empty class as its sole member. The same process repeated for this class produces the next in the sequence and so on.

The other sequence also begins with the empty class, but the successor of a class, c, is the class whose members are c and all the members of c. So the successor of the empty class is the class whose sole member is the empty class, and the successor of this class is the class whose members are the empty class and the class whose sole member is the empty class. Reconstructing the classes of this sequence requires only that we elaborate the predicates our process utilizes. Thus the third class in this sequence is reconstructed by beginning with the predicate 'is identical to the empty class or to the class whose sole member is the empty class'.

The production of _a version_ of the Frege-Russell sequence of classes is a little more complicated. The classes of this sequence are classes whose members are classes that are "equinumerous"; for example, if mankind and trilatpfkind are members of a class in this sequence, then it must be true that

(134) there are members of mankind as many as there are members of trilatpfkind.

In 6B(i), I gave two accounts of '... as many as ...'; either account will suffice for present purposes. The matrix

x is a member of mankind

has been reconstructed as

the /:/man/:/ is true of the INDCON.

In order to have an expression that reads as 'member of mankind' does in (134), I define

the INDCON is an E of the /:/man/:/

as the INDCON is an individual constant and the /:/man/:/ is true of the INDCON.

(Every instance of the first conjunct of this matrix is, given my account of the variable 'INDCON', true.) The reconstruction of (134) is:

(135) there are Es of the /:/man/:/ as many as there are Es of the /:/trilatpf/:/.

I shall abbreviate (135) to

(135.1) the /:/man/:/ ama the /:/trilatpf/:/.

Given 'ama', it is possible to give a reconstruction of the class which is, on the Frege-Russell view, the "cardinal number of a class"; for example, the cardinal number of mankind is the class of all classes "equinumerous" to mankind. This class of classes is reconstructed by the DST which ends the following list:

/ama the /:/man/://,
:/ama the /:/man/://:,
the :/ama the /:/man/://:,
/:/ama the /:/man/://:/,
and the /:/ama the /:/man/://:/.

With 'ama', all that are needed for my reconstruction of a Frege-Russell sequence of classes are predicates of each of which an exact quantifier statement is true. The first such predicate is 'not=' since it can be shown that

not((Ex)(not=(x, x))).

The first class of the Frege-Russell sequence is reconstructed by the DST which ends the following list:

/not=/,
the /:/not=/:/,
ama the /:/not=/:/,
/ama the /:/not=/://,
:/ama the /:/not=/://:,
the :/ama the /:/not=/://:,
/:/ama the /:/not=/://:/,

and (136) the /:/ama the /:/not=/://:/.

It is easily shown that

the /:/ama the /:/not=/://:/ is identical to

the /:/= the /:/not=/://:/.

The remaining predicates can be obtained in a variety of ways. For example, by letting 'O' be the abbreviation of (136), the next class is reconstructed by the DST which ends the following list:

/= O/,
the /:/= O/:/,
ama the /:/= O/:/,
/ama the /:/= O/://,
:/ama the /:/= O/://:,
the :/ama the /:/= O/://:,
/:/ama the /:/= O/://:/,

and the /:/ama the /:/= O/://:/.

Another way of obtaining the remaining predicates is to make use of the DSTs in the reconstruction of the other sequences of classes I have discussed. For my own part, I can, because of what I have shown about the identity of numerical quantifiers, use the predicates

/= the :there be one:/,
/= the :there be one: or the :there be two:/,
/= the :there be one: or the :there be two: or the

:there be three:/,

and so on.

(ii) <u>The Russell Paradox</u>

Intuitively put, Russell's paradox concerns that supposed class which has as members all those classes which satisfy the predicate 'is not a member of itself'. So given the nature of my reconstruction of classes, I must begin my investigation of this paradox by asking what can be said about predicates and Russell's paradox.[3]

The predicate needed for the paradox must contain the membership relation and this relation must be flanked by tokens of the same variable. But for predicates there is no membership relation, only predication, and no predicate, on my account of predicates in 2D, can be configured with a predicate. Thus

man man

is <u>not</u>, given that we understand both tokens as predicates, a statement, and therefore it involves no predication. Consequently, if we are to have a predicate of the sort needed for the paradox, it will be necessary to formulate it in a metalanguage with the help of my reconstruction of 'is a member of'.

I turn, therefore, to an investigation of the reconstruction of

(137) K-kind is a member of K-kind.

From (137), we can get

(138) not(K-kind is a member of K-kind).

Clearly, the classes which satisfy (138) (assuming this matrix is well formed) are all and only those which satisfy the predicate 'is not a member of itself' (assuming this predicate is well formed). Thus (137), if satisfactory as a statement matrix, does provide what is needed for the paradox.

I have reconstructed

(66) Socrates is a member of mankind

as (139) the /:/man/:/ is true of the :Socrates:.

Notice that the singular term for the individual which is said to be a member of a class is reconstructed by a term involving quotation, in particular, an ML DST. That is, the term 'is a member of', like the term 'exemplifies', brings quotation with it. However, singular terms, like 'mankind', which are the substituends of the variable 'K-kind', are reconstructed as ML DSTs in contexts which do not bring quotation with them. Therefore, the reconstruction of the following instance of (137),

(140) mankind is a member of mankind,

must be

(141) the /:/man/:/ is true of the :the /:/man/:/:.

But (141) becomes

(141.1) the (/:/man/:/ :the /:/man/:/:) is true,

i.e., (141.2) all (/:/man/:/ :the /:/man/:/:)s are true.

The SGT in (141.1) is

(142) /:/man/:/ :the /:/man/:/:.

This SGT is true of such statements as

(143) /man/(the /:/man/:/),

which is definitionally equivalent to

(143.1) the /:/man/:/ is a man.

Both (143) and (143.1) are indeed well formed; the SGT (142) is as well.

However, matrices of which (143.1) and (143) are instances are, respectively, such matrices as

x is a K

and /K/x

or the PREDCON is a K

and /K/(the PREDCON).

Correspondingly, a matrix of which (142) is an instance is

(144) PREDCON ML!PRED!DST.

The variable 'ML!PRED!DST' is an MML variable for MML SGTs which are true of ML DSTs which contain an ML class predicate true of class predicates. Such an MML SGT is

:the /:/man/:/:.

Finally, if we consider (141) and formulate matrices of which it is an instance, the result of our labors will be matrices, like (144), with two different free variables in them. For example, one of these matrices is

(145) the PREDCON is true of the ML!PRED!DST.

Though there are other matrices of which (141) is an instance, they all share the same feature: they have two free variables, not one. Thus if I were to introduce an operator which formed predicates from statement matrices by binding variables, it would not be possible to use only one operator token to bind both variables in (145).

What this investigation shows is that, according to my account of 'is a member of', (137) really has occurrences of two different variables rather than two occurrences of the same variable. Put in terms of the example (140), we can say that (140) does not contain two occurrences of the same singular term but rather occurrences of two different singular terms. Notice that this is not to say that either (137) or

(140) is not well formed. Both are well formed. In fact, (140) is false and some instances of (137) are false and some are true.

On the other hand, it may <u>seem</u> that my reconstruction does allow statements with 'is true of' which do have only one variable. Though these statements would not be the reconstructions of statements like (140), they might still be the means of producing a paradox like Russell's. However, this appearance is misleading. Statements which are instances of

the ... is true of the ---

reduce to statements which are instances of

(145) the (...---) is true.

There is a restriction, in my account, on (145): the ML predicates which appear in instances of (145) must be such that they satisfy

the (...---) is a statement.

This condition is never satisfied by the ML predicates which appear in statements which are instances of

the ... is true of the ....

For example, consider

the /:/man/:/ is true of the /:/man/:/

and the :man: is true of the :man:,

which reduce, respectively, to

the (/:/man/:/ /:/man/:/) is true

and the (:man: :man:) is true,

i.e., the :man man: is true.

It is certainly not true that

the (/:/man/:/ /:/man/:/) is a statement

or that

the :man man: is a statement.

In fact, '/:/man/:/ /:/man/:/' and ':man man:' are no more intelligible than 'man man'; in short, they are not, on my view, classifiable in any semantical category and are thus not, in a sense, well formed.

Similar remarks could be made about exemplification and the form of the Russell Paradox which treats of properties rather than classes. It should also be fairly clear that the Russell Paradox cannot be constructed on any higher metalinguistic level. Both membership and examplification preserve, throughout the metalinguistic levels, the features which were illustrated in the above discussion and which are crucial in blocking the Russell Paradox.

D. Ordered Pairs, Integers, and Rationals

In this subsection, my remarks on ordered pairs are limited to what is necessary for the task of constructing the integers and the rationals. Moreover, on the subject of integers and rationals I shall say no more than what is required for an account of the integers and rationals in terms of the natural numbers.

How can the machinery of ordered pairs be obtained? One alternative is to return to my account of ordered pairs in C(i); in that subsection, I showed that my reconstruction of classes is capable of handling ordered pairs as certain classes of classes. Or, I could take ordered pairs simply as natural numbers determined by a singular term matrix which has two variables and which, depending on which numeral is substituted for which variable, has as instances numerical expressions for different natural numbers (e.g., $x + (x + y)^2$).[4] Though both of these alternatives are open to me, I shall make use of neither.

The course I shall pursue is one that is not entirely unrelated to that of the second alternative, since it does share a striking feature of the course suggested in that alternative. Roughly speaking, the striking feature is that my account of "ordered pairs" does not really include ordered *pairs*. More specifically, my account characterizes statements which speak of, not *pairs* of natural numbers as contrasted with what they are pairs of, but rather natural numbers themselves. Of course, these statements speak of more than one natural number (at least some of them do), and order is very important to these statements. Nevertheless, the account does not include anything which could be called a "pair" and which is distinct from the natural numbers themselves.

I begin my account with some examples. We are all familiar with statements containing so-called definite descriptions; a satisfactory example would, I think, be

(146) the man in the corner is bald.

It is widely agreed that, roughly speaking, the definite description

the man in the corner

is a term which, given that (146) is true, contributes to making (146) about one and only one man who is in the corner and who is bald. But it seems to me that we often make statements with descriptive phrases which are not definite descriptions. Consider

(147) the horses which are in the south field are sold,

(148) the kinds of platonic solids the number of

whose vertices is evenly divisible by 3 are illustrated on the blackboard,

and (149) the older sisters of John are sitting on the couch.

It is true that one plausible understanding of (147), (148), and (149) makes them universally quantified statements; in certain cases this understanding would no doubt be the correct one. On the other hand, it seems very plausible to me that, in certain cases, the correct understanding of (147), (148), and (149) makes them examples of a general phenomenon of which (146) is the most widely discussed instance.

I shall call the descriptive phrases in (147), (148), and (149) "multiple descriptions." It also seems to me that multiple descriptions are of (at least) two sorts. The first sort, which I shall call "exact multiple descriptions," includes definite descriptions. The distinctive characteristic of exact multiple descriptions is most easily brought out by remembering that the presence of a definite description in a statement is made more manifest by a certain rewriting; for example, (146) is rewritten as

the one and only one man on the couch is bald.

We can easily imagine similar rewritings for (147), (148), and (149); for example, (148) becomes

the two and only two kinds of platonic solids the number of whose vertices is evenly divisible by 3 are illustrated on the blackboard.

In general, then, in addition to

(150) the one and only one H is F,

we have

(150.1) the two and only two H are F,

(150.2) the three and only three H are F,

and so on.

A careful account of exact multiple descriptions would require delving into the issues surrounding definite descriptions. Since the points I wish to make in this subsection can be made equally well no matter what account of multiple descriptions is adopted, I see no point in wrestling with these issues here and now. I shall make just one assumption about accounts of multiple descriptions: any such account makes the truth of statements with exact multiple descriptions depend in an intimate way on the truth of certain quantified statements. Thus, for example, in the case of (150), the quantified statement is

(151) there is one H and it is F.

Similarly, in the cases of (150.1), (150.2), and so on, the statements are, respectively,

(151.1) there are two H and they are F,

(151.2) there are three H and they are F,

and so on.

The other sort of multiple description is not "exact." For example, in some sorts of cases, it seems plausible that an accurate rewriting of (147) would be

> the at most three horses in the south field are sold.

I do not wish to argue about whether many statements could be accurately rewritten as I have just rewritten (147). What is important is that what I shall call "maximal multiple descriptions" do make sense.

There are quantified statements which are as intimately connected with the truth of

(152) the at most one H is F,

(152.1) the at most two H are F,

(152.2) the at most three H are F,

and so on as the (151)s are with the (150)s. These are, respectively,

(153) (Ex)(Hx and (z)(if Hz, then x = z) and Fx),

(153.1) (Ey)(Ex)(Hx and Hy and (z)(if Hz, then x = z or y = z) and F(x and y)),

(153.2) (Ew)(Ey)(Ex)(Hx and Hy and Hw and (z)(if Hz, then x = z or y = z or w = z) and F(x and y and w)),

and so on.

Several points should be noted. First, the (153)s are so formulated that an instance of them cannot be true unless there is at least one thing of the appropriate sort. Thus this condition preserves what seems to me to be one of the distinctive features of all statements containing descriptive phrases. Second, this formulation of the (153)s makes (153) equivalent to (151). Third, the manner in which the final conjunct of the (153)s is stated allows for collective predicates.

My strategy for this subsection can now be clarified. The maximal multiple description matrix

(154) the at most two H

is close to what I need for my construction of the integers and the rationals: the instances of (154) appear in statements which are about either one or two entities without being about <u>pairs</u> as distinct from the entities themselves. But what is yet lacking is order among the entities. Though it is not difficult to solve the problem about order, the solution requires that I extend the workings of maximal multiple descriptions to a sort of case not yet mentioned. So my next move is to explain how multiple descriptions come to involve order; then I discuss the extension of (154) to a case not yet treated; and finally I use the results to introduce the integers and the rationals.

Consider the matrices

(155) m and n are natural numbers and m = p and n = q and (Er)(m + r is the same as n)

and (155.1) m and n are natural numbers and m = 2 and n = 5 and (Er)(m + r is the same as n).

I have written these matrices in notation that can be interpreted on both the ML and the MML level of my reconstruction of arithmetic (see C(i)). For example, the phrase 'is the same as' is not identity, but either 'equals' or 'EQUALS'; '=' is identity. Thus my forthcoming treatment of integers and rationals introduces them simultaneously on both metalinguistic levels of my reconstruction of arithmetic.

The statements

(155.2) 2 and 5 are natural numbers and 2 = 2 and 5 = 5 and (Er)(2 + r is the same as 5)

and (155.3) 5 and 2 are natural numbers and 5 = 2 and 2 = 5 and (Er)(5 + r is the same as 2)

are both instances of (155.1); but (155.2) is true and (155.3) is not. (The identity statements in (155.3) are alone sufficient for the falsity of (155.3), but I have included the E-quantified matrix in (155.1) since it is the mathematical "equation" corresponding to this matrix which has traditionally been considered in introducing the integers.) Thus instances of (155.1) are capable of distinguishing between

2 and 5

and   5 and 2.

But what must now be explained is how this capability is to be put to use with multiple descriptions.

In English, there is no trouble in stating (155.1) so that it <u>seems</u> to contain a predicate which could appear in an instance of (154). Thus I can rewrite (155.1) as

(156) m and n are natural numbers such that m = 2 and n = 5 and (Er)(m + r is the same as n).

Then the description

(157) the at most two natural numbers such that m = 2 and n = 5 and (Er)(m + r is the same as n)

<u>seems</u> to be an instance of (154).

Though I do not think that there is anything wrong with (157), it is wrong to claim that (157) is an instance of (154). The obvious falsity of such a claim is seen in (153.1) which is the quantified statement matrix that is intimately connected with (152.1) which contains (154). Matrix (153.1) does not accomodate two-place predicates and that is what (155.1) contains. Therefore, in order to utilize (155.1) and its ilk, I must extend my account of maximal multiple descriptions to cases involving two-place predicates. (Though this extension is done only for two-place predicates, the points I shall make are applicable to other predicates as well.)

I need a more convenient notation in which to write two-place predicates. From the matrix

Rxy

I shall form the <u>predicate</u> (with appropriate restrictions about variable binding)

(158) (x, y; Rxy),

and from (158) I obtain the matrix

(159) (x, y; Rxy)(z, w).

Matrices (155.1) and (156) are instances of (159); and (157) is, despite its appearance, an instance of

(160) the at most two (x, y; Rxy).

What quantified statement is intimately connected with

(161) the at most two (x, y; Rxy) are G

as (153.1) is with (152.1)? Out of the various alternatives, I pick

(162) (Em)(En)((x, y; Rxy)(m, n) and (z)(w)(if (x, y; Rxy)(z, w), then m = z and n = w) and G(m and n)).

(On this choice it is not easy to decide whether to allow both the matrices 'the at most three (x, y; Rxy)' and 'the at most three (x, y, z; Rxyz)'; but whatever is decided about these matrices will not affect the present case.)

Very little more can be said about maximal multiple descriptions, or any sort of multiple description, without delving into the kinds of issues that have come up in treatments of definite descriptions. But I will take up two more matters briefly.

First, what quantified statement is connected with

(163) the at most two (x, y; Sxy) R the at most two (u, v; Tuv)?

I shall work up to the answer to this question by considering the same question for a simpler example involving one-place predicates:

(164) the at most two H R the at most two I.

As an instance of (164), consider

(164.1) the at most two sisters of John are behind the at most two brothers of Fred.

Suppose that a and b are the sisters of John and c and d are the brothers of Fred. Under this supposition, one would presumably wish to say that (164.1) is equivalent to

(164.2) a and b are behind c and d.

But (164.2) can be unpacked as either

a is behind c and b is behind d or a is behind d and c is behind b

(as in the case of two rows) or

a is behind c and d and b is behind c and d,

i.e., a is behind c and a is behind d and b is behind c and b is behind d

(as in the case of a single line). I shall call the first unpacking of (164.2) the "minimal unpacking" and the second, the "maximal unpacking." Neither unpacking seems to be in itself unacceptable; adopting one or the other will depend on the case.

For purposes of illustration, I shall adopt the minimal unpacking. Given this decision, the quantified statement connected with (164) is:

(Ey)(Ex)(Hx and Hy and (z)(if Hz, then x = z
or y = z) and
(Et)(Es)(Is and It and (w)(if Iw, then s = w
or t = w) and
x and y R s and t)),

where the last conjunct is unpacked minimally as

xRs and yRt or xRt and yRs.

Similarly, the quantified statement connected with (163) is:

(Em)(En)((x, y; Sxy)(m, n) and (z)(w)(if
(x, y; Sxy)(z, w), then m = z and n = w) and
(Es)(Et)((u, v; Tuv)(s, t) and (q)(r)(if
(u, v; Tuv)(q, r), then s = q and t = r) and
m and n R s and T)),

where once again the final conjunct is unpacked minimally.

The second matter concerns identity. Identity for multiple descriptions must be introduced and once again there are many choices. In cases where order is unimportant, the minimal unpacking of (163) and (164) provides one plausible model. Thus if the 'are' in the statement

a and b are the sisters of John

is taken to be identity, then under the assumption that there are at most two sisters of John, this statement could be unpacked as

(Ey)(Ex)(x is a sister of John and y is a sister
of John and x = a and y = b or x = b and y = a).

Without considerably more investigation it is not clear whether this treatment of identity is satisfactory in more complicated cases. I shall not pursue such an investigation since the issue of identity and multiple descriptions has very little bearing on the construction of the integers and the rationals. What is needed in those constructions are equivalence relations which, like 'is the same as', are not identity.

For my account of the integers,

(155) m and n are natural numbers and m = p and
n = q and (Er)(m + r is the same as n)

is only half, as it were, of what I need. The instances of the statement matrix

(m, n; m and n are natural numbers and m = p and

n = q and (Er)(m + r is the same as n))(s, t)

are true statements only if the condition

gr(q, p) or q is the same as p

is satisfied and thus only if the condition

gr(t, s) or t is the same as s

is satisfied. For example, it is true that

(Es)(Et)(m, n; m and n are natural numbers and m = 2 and n = 5 and (Er)(m + r is the same as n))(s, t)

and that

(Es)(Et)(m, n; m and n are natural numbers and m = 5 and n = 5 and (Er)(m + r is the same as n))(s, t)

but false that

(Es)(Et)(m, n; m and n are natural numbers and m = 5 and n = 2 and (Er)(m + r is the same as n))(s, t).

So, in addition, I need the matrix

(165) m and n are natural numbers and m = p and n = q and not(Er)(m + r is the same as n).

The instances of the statement matrix

(m, n; m and n are natural numbers and m = p and n = q and not(Er)(m + r is the same as n))(s, t)

are true statements only if the condition

gr(p, q)

is satisfied and thus only if the condition

gr(s, t)

is satisfied.

Thus my construction of the integers utilizes the instances of (160) which are obtained from the matrices

(166) the at most two (m, n; m and n are natural numbers and m = p and n = q and (Er)(m + r is the same as n))

and (167) the at most two (m, n; m and n are natural numbers and m = p and n = q and not(Er)(m + r is the same as n)).

At this point it is extremely convenient to introduce several abbreviations. I abbreviate the predicate matrix

(168) (m, n; m and n are natural numbers and m = p and n = q and (Er)(m + r is the same as n))

to (168.1) (m, n; Pos ... m = p and n = q ...)

and the predicate matrix

(169) (m, n; m and n are natural numbers and m = p and n = q and not(Er)(m + r is the same as n))

to (169.1) (m, n; Neg ... m = p and n = q ...).

Instances of (168) and (169) are abbreviated by instances of (168.1) and (169.1) respectively. I also introduce

(p, q)

as an abbreviation; it is (166) if

gr(q, p) or q is the same as p

and it is (167) if

gr(p, q).

For example,

(3, 5)

is the abbreviation of an instance of (166) and

(5, 3)

is an abbreviation of an instance of (167).

Notice that the E-quantified statement connected with

(170) (3, 5) are F

is (170.1) (Es)(Et)((m, n; Pos ... m = 3 and n = 5 ...) (s, t) and (z)(w)(if (m, n; Pos ... m = 3 and n = 5 ...)(z, w), then s = z and t = w) and F(s and t)).

But it is a truth of arithmetic that

(Es)(Et)((m, n; Pos ... m = 3 and n = 5 ...)(s, t) and (z)(w)(if (m, n; Pos ... m = 3 and n = 5 ...) (z, w), then s = z and t = w)).

A similar state of affairs holds for

(5, 3) are F.

In general, for any instance of

(p, q),

there is either a demonstrably true instance of

(Es)(Et)((m, n; Pos ... m = p and n = q ...)(s, t) and (z)(w)(if (m, n; Pos ... m = p and n = q ...)(z, w), then s = z and t = w)

or a demonstrably true instance of

(Es)(Et)((m, n; Neg ... m = p and n = q ...)(s, t) and (z)(w)(if (m, n; Neg ... m = p and n = q ...)(z, w), then s = z and t = w)).

I shall use this fact as a justification for dealing only with the final conjunct of the E-quantified statements which are connected with the statements containing instances of the matrix '(p, q)'.

I define

(171) (p, q) is an integer

as (171.1) (p, q) are natural numbers.

The final conjunct of the E-quantified statement associated with (171.1) is

s and t are natural numbers,

which is true if and only if

p and q are natural numbers.

And of course all the instances of this latter matrix are true.

I now define an equivalence relation for integers:

(172) (p, q) is the same I as (j, k)

is defined as

(172.1) (p, q) is an integer and (j, k) is an integer and p + k is the same as q + j.

This definition imitates one found in standard mathematical treatments of the construction of the integers.

The usual mathematical treatments of the integers differ from mine in that, very roughly speaking, they take what I call "integers" to be members of equivalence classes which, on the mathematical treatments, are the integers. There are several ways in which I can produce a reasonable imitation of this feature of the mathematical treatments. But nothing of any real interest is gained by doing all this work. Moreover, the equivalence relation of being the same I as allows me to prove theorems of roughly the same import as the ones usually proven about equivalence classes.

What remain to be dealt with are addition and multiplication for integers. The definition of the predicate 'I-sum' is:

(173) I-sum((p, q), (j, k), (u, v))

is defined as

(173.1) (p, q) is an integer and (j, k) is an integer and (u, v) is an integer and (u, v) is the same I as (p + j, q + k).

Thus it is true that

I-sum((2, 5), (3, 6), (2 + 3, 5 + 6))

and that

I-sum((2, 5), (3, 6), (0, 6)).

And of course it is also true that

(0, 6) is the same I as (2 + 3, 5 + 6).

Clearly integer addition can be proven unique under the equivalence relation being the same I as.

One reason for introducing the integers is that

(Er)(m + r is the same as n)

is false when

gr(m, n).

That this is not so for I-sum is easily illustrated. I define

I-gr((p, q), (j, k))

as (p, q) is an integer and (j, k) is an integer and gr(p + k, q + j).

With this definition of 'I-gr', there is a true instance of

I-sum((p, q), (u, v), (j, k))

even when

I-gr((p, q), (j, k)).

For example, even though

I-gr((2, 10), (3, 4)),

it is true that

I-sum((2, 10), (8, 1), (3, 4)).

The definition of multiplication also imitates the usual mathematical definition:

(174) I-product((p, q), (j, k), (u, v))

is defined as

(174.1) (p, q) is an integer and (j, k) is an integer and (u, v) is an integer and (u, v) is the same I as ((p x j) + (q x k), (p x k) + (q x j)).

With these definitions of addition and multiplication all the usual mathematical results concerning the integers are demonstrable.[5]

It is also no trouble to introduce the usual notation for integers. We know from chapter 4 that we can distinguish between natural numbers which involve addition and multiplication those which do not. For example, those expressions for number universals which are reconstructed by a numerical quantifier, rather than a conjunctive or multiplicative quantifier, do not contain 'plus' or 'times'. If we call such natural numbers "uncompounded," then we can characterize "representative" integers as follows:

(p, q) is a representative integer

is defined as

(p, q) is an integer and p = 0 and q is an uncompounded natural number or q = 0 and p is an uncompounded natural number.

Thus

(0, 0)

(1, 0)   (0, 1)

(2, 0)   (0, 2)

(3, 0)   (0, 3)

and so on are representative integers. Every integer is the same I as some representative integer. The expressions for these representative integers can be abbreviated, in the obvious way, by the usual notation:

0

-1   1

-2   2

-3   3

and so on.

The procedure for constructing the rational numbers from the natural numbers is exactly like the procedure we have followed in introducing the integers from the natural numbers. Of course, instead of using (168) and (169), we must use the dyadic predicates

(175) (m, n; m and n are natural numbers and m = p and n = q and (Er)(m x r is the same as n))

and (176) (m, n; m and n are natural numbers and m = p and n = q and not(Er)(m x r is the same as n)).

However, to introduce both the integers and the rationals from the natural numbers is to leave out the negative rational numbers. Two alternatives are available for rectifying this matter. One is to construct the rationals from the integers and the other is to construct the integers from the rationals. Each alternative requires only a few alterations in what I have already done. Since the detail of this work is well known, I shall not bother to pursue either of these alternatives.

Notes

Chapter 1

1. N. Goodman and W. V. O. Quine, "Steps Toward a Constructive Nominalism," _Journal of Symbolic Logic_ 12 (1947): 111.

2. Goodman and Quine (1947), p. 122.

3. Goodman and Quine (1947), p. 122.

4. Goodman and Quine (1947), pp. 105ff.

5. S. F. Barker, _The Philosophy of Mathematics_ (Englewood Cliffs, N. J.: Prentice-Hall, 1964), pp. 100-1.

6. Barker (1964), pp. 100-1.

7. P. Benacerraf, "What Numbers Could Not Be," _Philosophical Review_ 74 (1965): 49ff, 71; Barker (1964), pp. 99, 101; W. V. O. Quine, _Word and Object_ (Cambridge, Mass.: M.I.T. Press, 1960), p. 263. For further exposition of these matters, see sections A and B of J. Sicha, "Counting and the Natural Numbers," _Philosophy of Science_ 37 (1970).

8. Quine (1960), pp. 262ff.; F. Waisman, _Introduction to Mathematical Thinking_ (New York: Harper and Row, 1959), pp. 118ff., 237ff. In section C of Benacerraf (1965), Benacerraf accepts a definition of 'natural number' similar to the one implicit in the present paragraph but incorporating in it as an essential part what I have called N's view of counting.

9. See Sicha (1970) for further comments on the points in this section.

Notes

Chapter 2

1. One of the earliest of the papers in which Sellars argues for this thesis is "Concepts as Involving Laws and Inconceivable Without Them," *Philosophy of Science* 15 (1948). See also B. A. Aune, *Knowledge, Mind and Nature* (New York: Random House, 1967), chapters 2, 3, 4, and 8, passim.

2. W. Sellars, "Some Reflections on Language Games," *Philosophy of Science* 21 (1954); idem, *Science and Metaphysics* (London: Routledge and Kegan Paul, 1967), chapter 3 (hereafter cited as [1967A]); idem, "Language as Thought and as Communication," *Philosophy and Phenomenological Research* 29 (1969).

3. For a discussion of such rules, see Sellars (1967A), chapters 3 and 7, and Sellars (1969).

4. Sellars (1967A), p. 76.

5. Sellars, "Abstract Entities," *Review of Metaphysics* 16 (1963): 635 (hereafter cited as [1963B]).

6. Sellars (1963B), pp. 627ff., 638ff.

7. Sellars (1963B), pp. 627ff., 638ff.

8. Sellars (1963B), pp. 627-47, passim.

9. Sellars (1963B), p. 631.

10. Sellars (1963B), pp. 652, 658.

11. B. van Fraassen, *Formal Semantics and Logic* (New York: Macmillan Co., 1971); R. Thomason, *Symbolic Logic* (London: Collier-Macmillan, 1970); J. W. Robbin, *Mathematical Logic: A First Course* (New York: W. A. Benjamin, 1969); A. Church, *Introduction to Mathematical Logic* (Princeton: Princeton Uni-

versity Press, 1956).

12. L. Wittgenstein, *Tractatus Logico-Philosophicus*, trans. D. F. Pears and B. F. McGuinness (London: Routledge and Kegan Paul, 1961), p. 23.

13. W. Sellars, "Naming and Saying," *Philosophy of Science* 29 (1962): 8.

14. G. Ryle, Letters and Syllables in Plato," *Philosophical Review* 69 (1960): 436.

15. The double role of SGTs like ':triangular:' in speaking both of names as configured determinately and of determinate configurations of names is, on my view, to be understood on the model of terms like 'somersault', 'smile', and 'flow'. Talk of somersaults, smiles, and flows is derivative from talk of things which somersault, smile, and flow. Thus

the river has a strong flow

and the flow of the river is strong

are derived from

the river flows strongly.

Similarly, talk of bodily and facial configurations is, on my view, introduced from talk of people as configured determinately. The ins-and-outs of this topic are too elaborate to pursue here.

16. Sellars (1963B), pp. 658ff.

17. See note 15 above.

18. See note 15 above.

19. Sellars (1963B), pp. 667ff.

Chapter 3

1. I have said that my "attempt at a mild nominalism *may* yet fail" because quantifiers with predicate variables are not really needed in the reconstructions of the last chapter. The proof that such quantification is not necessary is trivial once we recall how metalinguistic predicate variables were introduced into the PMese metalanguage. The terms 'INDCON' and 'PREDCON' (and, though it was not mentioned at the time, 'STAT') were first introduced as highly generic, nonillustrating ML general terms. Terms like 'INDCONA', 'INDCONB', etc., and 'PREDCONA', 'PREDCONB', etc. (and we could add 'STATA', 'STATB', etc.), were introduced as terms for species of their respective genuses. Then in order to highlight important features of the reconstructions the genus-species relationship was forsaken for the variable-substituend relationship. However, this last move need not have been made. The terms 'INDCON' and 'PREDCON' could have remained general terms and quantification would have been restricted to individual variables; individual variables would appear in such statement matrices as 'x is an INDCON' and 'x is a PREDCON' and more complicated matrices (e.g., 'x is a (:triangular: INDCON)'). Then instead of

2E(6.6) (INDCON)(all (:triangular: INDCON)s are statements),

we would have simply

(6.7) all (:triangular: INDCON)s are statements.

Statement (6.7) is in perfect order since 'INDCON' is a nonillustrating SGT. Then, *with due care*, (6.7) can be unpacked in a manner which involves only individual variable quantification.

However, in 2E I gave several reasons for deciding to treat 'INDCON' and 'PREDCON' as ML predicate variables.

There are others, of which I shall mention one. Though it is reasonably clear how an unpacking of (6.7) would go, it is much more difficult, though not impossible, to unpack the reconstruction of 'triangularity entails trilaterality' along the same lines. The major source of difficulty is the term 'may'. Even a cursory discussion of the intricacies of practical discourse would lead far afield. Therefore, since the use of ML variables for SGTs has the advantages cited in 2E and since unpackings of statements containing practical terms await a treatment of practical discourse which cannot be given in this book, I shall continue to employ ML variables and predicate variable quantification.

Moreover, the eliminability of predicate variable quantification in the metalinguistic contexts of the preceding chapter does not extend to all the contexts of predicate variable quantification in this book.

2. Any good modern logic book (see the ones referred to in note 11 of chapter 2) contains the essentials of the objectual interpretation of quantification. Consequently, I have discussed the objectual interpretation in just sufficient detail to clarify points for my subsequent remarks which explain the relationship that the objection against my views in chapter 2 sees between quantification and ontological commitment. Similarly, my later discussion of the substitution interpretation of quantification includes only those points necessary for my discussion. For further information on the substitution interpretation, see J. Wallace, "On the Frame of Reference," _Synthese_ 22 (1970) and M. Dunn and N. Belnap, "The Substitution Interpretation of the Quantifiers," _Nous_ 2 (1968).

3. W. V. O. Quine, "Designation and Existence," _Journal of Philosophy_ 36 (1939): 708, where Quine's slogan "to be is to

be the value of a variable" might be construed as an expression of this simple view of commitment. See also idem, "On What There Is," in _From a Logical Point of View_, rev. ed. (Cambridge, Mass.: Harvard University Press, 1961; New York: Harper and Row, Harper Torchbooks, 1963), p. 13 (page reference to Harper Torchbook edition)(hereafter cited as [1961B]), and Quine (1960), p. 242.

4. Quine (1961B), pp. 13-14; idem, "Existence and Quantification," in _Ontological Relativity and Other Essays_ (New York: Columbia University Press, 1969), pp. 93-95.

5. W. V. O. Quine, "Logic and the Reification of Universals," in _From a Logical Point of View_, p. 103; idem, "Notes on the Theory of Reference," ibid., p. 131.

6. G. H. Harmon, "Review of _Philosophical Perspectives_," _Journal of Philosophy_ 66 (1969): 139; C. Parsons, "A Plea for Substitutional Quantification," _Journal of Philosophy_ 68 (1971): 232, n. 4; Wallace (1970), pp. 148-49, n. 10.

7. Wittgenstein (1961), p. 57.

8. Quine (1960), pp. 162ff., 242; idem, _Methods of Logic_, 3rd ed. (New York: Holt, Rinehart and Winston, 1972), pp. 111-14.

9. Quine (1960), pp. 162ff., 242; Quine (1972), pp. 112-13.

10. Quine (1939), p. 708; Quine (1960), pp. 135ff.; idem, _Mathematical Logic_, rev. ed. (Cambridge, Mass.: Harvard University Press, 1961), pp. 68-70; Quine (1961B), p. 13.

11. Quine (1939), p 708; Quine (1961A), pp. 34ff., 68; A. N. Whitehead and B. Russell, _Principia Mathematica_ (Cam-

bridge: At the University Press, 1910), 1: 4-5.

12. W. Kneale, "Is Existence a Predicate?" Aristotelian Society Supplement 15: part 2, contains a view with consequences similar to the consequences I have just ascribed to my view.

13. The affinity of these two ideas is clear in Quine (1939), pp. 707-8.

14. See note 3 of this chapter.

15. Quine (1960), p. 242.

16. W. Sellars, "Grammar and Existence: A Preface to Ontology," Mind 69 (1960): 502ff.

17. W. V. O. Quine, "A Logistical Approach to the Ontological **Problem," in The Ways of** Paradise and Other Essays (New York: Random House, 1966), p. 65.

18. Dunn and Belnap (1968), section 2.

19. W. Sellars, "Realism and the New Way of Words," Philosophy and Phenomenological Research 8 (1948): part 3.

20. Since this book is directed toward the philosophy of elementary mathematics, I give little attention to implication in general. Nevertheless, I believe that much of what I say about entailments pertains to implication generally. See W. Sellars, "Is there a Synthetic A Priori?" Philosophy of Science 20 (1953): 136 ff. and idem, "Counterfactuals, Dispositions and Causal Modalities," in Minnesota Studies in the Philosophy of Science, eds. H. Feigl, M. Scriven, and G. Maxwell (Minneapolis: University of Minnesota Press, 1958), 2: part 4.

Chapter 4

1. See, for example, Quine (1972), pp. 242ff.

Chapter 5

1. D. Hilbert, "On the Infinite," in *Philosophy of Mathematics*, eds. P. Benacerraf and H. Putnam (Englewood Cliffs, N. J.: Prentice-Hall, 1964), p. 135.

2. Hilbert (1964), p. 141.

3. Hilbert (1964), p. 150.

4. W. Sellars, *Science, Perception and Reality* (London: Routledge and Kegan Paul, 1963), chapters 1, 5, and 10; Aune (1967), passim, but particularly chapters 1, 2, 3, and 4.

5. In making this claim, I am following a common account (see, for example, Church [1956], section 07). On some other accounts, my discussion is restricted to one sort of formal system (see, for example, Curry [1951], pp. 14, 15; on his account my discussion is confined to "definite" formal systems). I do not wish to haggle about the term 'formal'. The real point is that the systems I characterize are the ones which are primarily relevant to the original formalist program and to Gödel's incompleteness theorems (on this last matter see, for example, Robbin [1969], p. 115, 116).

6. Church (1956); Thomason (1970); van Fraassen (1971).

Chapter 6

1. L. Henkin et al., *Retracing Elementary Mathematics* (New York: Macmillan Co., 1962), pp. 166ff.

Notes

2. The treatment of class theory from which my own originates is W. Sellars, "Classes as Abstract Entities and the Russell Paradox," *Review of Metaphysics* 17 (1963)(hereafter cited as [1963C]).

3. Again see Sellars (1963C).

4. For more discussion of such views of ordered pairs, see Quine (1960), pp. 259-60 and idem, "On Ordered Pairs," *Journal of Symbolic Logic* 10, no. 3 (September 1945).

5. S. Feferman, *The Number Systems: Foundations of Algebra and Analysis* (Reading, Mass.: Addison Wesley, 1964), pp. 113 ff.

Bibliography

Aune, B. A. 1967. _Knowledge, mind and nature_. New York: Random House.

Barker, S. F. 1964. _The philosophy of mathematics_. Englewood Cliffs, N. J.: Prentice-Hall.

Benacerraf, P. 1965. What numbers could not be. _Philosophical Review_ 74: 47-73.

Church, A. 1956. _Introduction to mathematical logic_. Princeton: Princeton University Press.

Curry, H. B. 1951. _Outlines of a formalist philosophy of mathematics_. Amsterdam: North Holland Publishing Co.

Dunn, M., and Belnap, N. 1968. The substitution interpretation of the quantifiers. _Nous_ 2: 177-85.

Feferman, S. 1964. _The number systems: foundations of algebra and analysis_. Reading, Mass.: Addison Wesley.

Goodman, N., and Quine, W. V. O. 1947. Steps toward a constructive nominalism. _Journal of Symbolic Logic_ 12: 105-22.

Harmon, G. H. 1969. Review of _Philosophical perspectives_. _Journal of Philosophy_ 66: 133-44.

Henkin, L.; Smith, W.; Varineau, V.; and Walsh, M. 1962. _Retracing elementary mathematics_. New York: Macmillan co.

Hilbert, D. 1964. On the infinite. In _Philosophy of mathematics_, eds. P. Benacerraf and H. Putnam. Englewood Cliffs, N. J.: Prentice-Hall.

Kneale, W. 1936. Is existence a predicate? _Aristotelian Society Supplement_ 15: 154-74.

Bibliography

Parsons, C. 1971. A plea for substitutional quantification. *Journal of Philosophy* 68: 231-37.

Quine, W. V. O. 1939. Designation and existence. *Journal of Philosophy* 36: 701-9.

________. 1945. On ordered pairs. *Journal of Symbolic Logic* 10: 95-96.

________. 1960. *Word and object*. Cambridge, Mass.: M. I. T. Press.

________. 1961A. *Mathematical logic*. Rev. ed. Cambridge, Mass.: Harvard University Press.

________. 1961B. On what there is.

________. 1961C. Logic and the reification of universals.

________. 1961D. Notes on the theory of reference. All three in *From a logical point of view*. Rev. ed. Cambridge, Mass.: Harvard University Press. (Page references to Harper Torchbook Edition, New York: Harper and Row, 1963).

________. 1966. A logistical approach to the ontological problem. In *The ways of paradox and other essays*. New York: Random House.

________. 1969. Existence and quantification. In *Ontological relativity and other essays*. New York: Columbia University Press.

________. 1972. *Methods of logic.* 3rd ed. New York: Holt, Rinehart and Winston.

Robbin, J. W. 1969. *Mathematical logic: a first course*. New York: W. A. Benjamin.

Ryle, G. 1960. Letters and syllables in Plato. *Philosophi-*

cal Review 69: 431-51.

Sellars, W. 1948A. Realism and the new way of words. Philosophy and Phenomenological Research 8: 601-34. Reprinted in Readings in philosophical analysis, eds. H. Feigl and W. Sellars. New York: Appleton-Century-Crofts, 1949.

________. 1948B. Concepts as involving laws and inconceivable without them. Philosophy of Science 15: 287-315.

________. 1953. Is there a synthetic a priori? Philosophy of Science 20: 121-38. Reprinted in revised form in Sellars (1963A).

________. 1954. Some reflections on language games. Philosophy of Science 21: 204-28. Reprinted in revised form in Sellars (1963A).

________. 1958. Counterfactuals, dispositions and causal modalities. In Minnesota Studies in the Philosophy of Science, eds. H. Feigle, M. Scriven, and G. Maxwell, 2: 225-308. Minneapolis: University of Minnesota Press.

________. 1960. Grammar and existence: a preface to ontology. Mind 69: 499-533.

________. 1962. Naming and saying. Philosophy of Science 29: 7-26. Reprinted in Sellars (1963A).

________. 1963A. Science, perception and reality. London: Routledge and Kegan Paul.

________. 1963B. Abstract entities. Review of Metaphysics 16: 627-71. Reprinted in Sellars (1967B).

________. 1963C. Classes as abstract entities and the Russell paradox. Review of Metaphysics 17: 67-90. Reprinted in Sellars (1967B).

________. 1967A. Science and metaphysics. London: Routledge and Kegan Paul.

________. 1967B. Philosophical perspectives. Springfield, Ill: Charles C. Thomas.

________. 1969. Language as thought and as communication. Philosophy and Phenomenological Research 29: 506-27.

Sicha, J. 1970. Counting and the natural numbers. Philosophy of Science 37: 405-16.

Thomason, R. 1970. Symbolic logic. London: Collier-Macmillan.

van Fraassen, B. 1971. Formal semantics and logic. New York: Macmillan Co.

Waismann, F. 1959. Introduction to mathematical thinking. New York: Harper and Row.

Wallace, J. 1970. On the frame of reference. Synthese 22: 117-50.

Whitehead, A. N., and Russell, B. 1910. Principia mathematica. Vol. 1. Cambridge: At the University Press.

Wittgenstein, L. 1961. Tractatus logico-philosophicus. Translated by D. F. Pears and B. F. McGuiness. London: Routledge and Kegan Paul.

Index of Abbreviations and Special Terms

Index of Names and Subjects

This index is designed to be used in conjunction with the table of contents. It is incomplete both in entries and in references. Any topic treated only in sections whose titles indicate that they contain a discussion of that topic has not been entered. By contrast, many references are to discussions in which the term for the topic does not appear and which are not directly on the topic. My aim has been to include any reference which, in my judgment, is to a discussion that would contribute to the reader's understanding of my views on a topic. The reader will, in many cases, be able to discover why a reference is included by consulting the table of contents.

The references are by chapter, section, or subsection, not by pages.

Index

Index

Index

Index

Index